Sherrie L. Gradin

Romancing Rhetorics

Social Expressivist Perspectives ON THE Teaching OF Writing

BOYNTON/COOK
HEINEMANN
Portsmouth, NH

Boynton/Cook Publishers, Inc.
A subsidiary of Reed Elsevier Inc.
361 Hanover Street, Portsmouth, NH   03801–3912
Offices and agents throughout the world

Editor: Peter R. Stillman
Production: J. B. Tranchemontagne
Cover design: Julie Hahn

Every effort has been made to contact the copyright holders and students for permission to reprint borrowed material. We regret any oversights that may have occurred and would be happy to rectify them in future printings of this work.

The author and publisher wish to thank those who have generously given permission to reprint borrowed material:

Page 12   Excerpts from "Rhetoric and Ideology in the Writing Class" by James Berlin in COLLEGE ENGLISH, September 1988. Copyright © 1988 by the National Council of Teachers of English. Reprinted by permission of the publisher.

Page 82   Excerpts from *The Making of Meaning: Metaphors, Models, and Maxims for Writing Teachers* by Ann Berthoff. Copyright © 1981 by Boynton/Cook Publishers, Inc., A subsidiary of Reed Elsevier Inc.

Page 96   Excerpts from *Education Today* by John Dewey. Copyright © 1940 by John Dewey. Reprinted by permission of The Putnam Publishing Group.

Page 141   Excerpts from *Women's Way of Knowing* by Mary Field Belenky et al. Copyright © 1986 by Basic Books, Inc. Reprinted by permission of Basic-Books, a division of HarperCollins Publishers, Inc.

Library of Congress Cataloging-in-Publication Data
Gradin, Sherrie L.
     Romancing rhetorics : social expressivist perspectives on the
teaching of writing / Sherrie L. Gradin.
         p. cm.
     Includes bibliographical references.
     ISBN 0–86709–349–8
     1. English language—Rhetoric—Study and teaching—Theory, etc.
2. English language—Rhetoric—Social aspects.   3. Pluralism (social
sciences)   4. Romanticism.   I. Title.
PE1404.G66 1995
808'.042'07—dc20   95–26169
                                                                            CIP

Printed in the United States of America on acid-free paper
99 98 97 96 95   VB   1 2 3 4 5 6 7 8 9

Contents

iii

Preface

Sherrie Gradin's *Romancing Rhetorics: Social Expressivist Perspectives on the Teaching of Writing* is a welcome, important, and timely contribution to composition studies. In fact, I wish this book had been around when I first came to Syracuse University in 1987, when the emerging hegemony among theoretical discourses in the field was discourse community theory.

In my first days at Syracuse, I participated in frequent, curricular discussions with the other writing teachers who were doing "romantic" versions of the required expository writing courses. My ten years of college teaching at three very different institutions led me to think, at the time, that there were certainly worse things teachers could be doing. As I saw it, the field's problems were still with teachers who saw the writing course as primarily the place to police errors or to present elite models of textual products that functioned to dismiss student writing, and often students, as essentially deficient. In my naïveté, I believed that any course that valued student experience, centered on dialogue, and focused on the process of moving from experience to a variety of written texts and contexts, was probably a progressive thing, given the rampant elitism at most universities and in many English departments, and the bad attitude too many of the literati forced to teach composition had toward it. And yet it was clear from the context that romantic courses were "bad," that we in the field had just recently bootstrapped ourselves beyond all that romantic nonsense, and that we were now in a post-process period in which we countered the over-individualistic excesses of the previous decade with the truth of the social construction of writing.

Professor Gradin's book questions that too—easy narrative which is prominent now, not simply at Syracuse University, but in the field at large. Professor Gradin, in fact, provides the first book length corrective to the hegemonic discourses which have ruled composition and rhetoric for a long while. Our field's overemphasis on "academic discourse" and "discourse communities," or on what I shall call "discourse community theory," regardless of the values of this theory when it was first introduced (and there were values), has made it the dogma it sought to transform. What began as a legitimate move toward the social and away from, not, it must be emphasized, romantic or expressivist process theory, but cognitive process theory like that popularized by Linda Flower and John Hayes, has, more than a decade later, turned into simplistic fiats that our students must "appropriate or be appropriated by" the disciplinary languages of academe.

By historicizing the expressivist traditions in composition and rhetoric, Gradin's book takes a courageous and intelligent stand in opposing these prevailing notions of writing and teaching. By tracking romantic theory through writers like Wordsworth, Coleridge, and Shelley, as well as Arnold, Mill, and Dewey, and by contextualizing their ideas on education and contrasting them with the schools of the time, Professor Gradin, by implication, asks us to set our theory of language and writing down next to our own teaching practice and to ask ourselves some hard questions. Are the classrooms of liberation rhetorics, for example, any different in kind from the classrooms of conservative elitists that I had so frequently encountered in my college teaching odyssey? Is teaching composition a matter of indoctrination, the only choice being whether that indoctrination be of the right or the left?

Professor Gradin's book, in effect, responds that things are more complicated than these sort of dichotomies, too often produced by our current theory, would lead us to believe. Gradin connects romantic theory with the work of contemporary compositionists like Ann E. Berthoff, Donald Murray, Peter Elbow, D. Gordon Rohman, and Ken Macrorie, and shows the logic of their theory and practice. Yet Gradin's argument is simultaneously very responsive to the counterarguments, and she generously and fairly devotes a considerable proportion of her text to fair summary of, and response to, critics of expressivist pedagogy. After all, it is *social* expressivisms that Gradin is reconsidering. She begins from the assumptions that the individual is not necessarily the opposite of the social, but that instead we are always already both individual and social. And, finally, Gradin's argument enacts what it says, practices what it preaches. Gradin integrates her scholarship with her experience in powerful ways. That alone is refreshing in a field where the publications seem to get farther and farther away from everyday life.

This is a very important book. I am happy that Boynton/Cook—Heinemann Publishers are once again leading the way by presenting the field with the chance to open this dialogue. Gradin's book is one of the few in composition that recognizes that to do theory, you have to historicize. To historicize is to place theory in its contexts, to reclaim not only the conceptual and categorical work that theory does, but to understand how history and culture produce, circulate, appropriate, consume, and dispose of theory. It also gives us the opportunity to look at our later uses of theory.

To show the need for Gradin's historicizing of theory let me elaborate at some length with one example. The moral of this little parable is that it is not sufficient to essentialize expressivisms and then critique and dismiss it, unless one is prepared to do the preliminary historical work. As near as I can tell, James Britton (1970), in his classic *Language and Learning,* was one of the first compositionists to use the keyword "expressive" in talking about language development. What is significant is that he borrowed the term from Edward Sapir, an anthropologist, who was making the point that language is far more than a simple device for shuttling information back and forth, that language is a means for a culture to construct its very self. How ironic that later scholars sometimes critique expressivisms for its supposed individualism and solipsism when the word started its career in our field as a borrowing from a social field, anthropology, and was a way for a compositionist to balance out an overemphasis on purely rationalistic views of language and culture.

I think James Britton was well aware of this, even in his later work when he and his research team matched Sapir's concept with Roman Jakobson's model of communication, shifting from a term that referred to language and culture, to a term that pointed at one element in the communication process, the addressor. Jakobson's model, after all, argued that no discourse was pure, that any single language event was made up of mixtures of all the possible discourse types, and what mattered was which one was the dominant in this hierarchy of mixtures, and how the discourse functioned in the specific context. The very idea that one could even theorize an expressive discourse alone and in isolation must seem bizarre given these facts. That there is or was a whole community of such believers who focused only or mostly on it, is a further leap. And finally, that expressivism, however defined, was the dominant force in college composition programs ever, is a claim for which there is very little evidence and which simply does not fit my experience teaching writing, whether in the public schools from 1973 or in several universities since 1978.

So we see theoretical drift in this example. What started as a way of talking about language in culture, is borrowed to discuss just one aspect of any language event, is then used in a description of what sorts (plural) of writing should be done, and then finally turns into an assertion about a community that may never have existed, let alone had determining power, in the first place. We see a shift from expressive culture, to the expressive function of language, to expressive discourse, to expressivists to expressivisms, a full blown philosophy, that we are all now "against." Each shift in use and in time, each moment in the unconscious process of theoretical drift, is a further reification. Enter my strange conversation at Syracuse in 1987.

But historicizing our theory in the way Professor Gradin does in this remarkable book, helps us to avoid this very sort of theoretical drift and in that process sharpens our critiques, making it possible in this instance to initiate a broader, too long deferred project of theorizing the composing self, of examining how and why writing and its teaching constructs subjectivities and collectivities, and how the writing self, and our stories of the self, are potential sites of resistance. It helps us to examine how, in short, the personal is political, as the women's movement and gay and lesbian liberation movements, among others, long ago taught us.

Curiously, as I have been writing this preface to Professor Gradin's fine book, I have been accompanied by—I cannot get them out of my head as hard as I try—a series of songs I hardly know that have been floating through my consciousness. "Isn't It Romantic?" and "I'll Take Romance." Images of Fred Astaire and Ginger Rogers dancing up a storm to some Cole Porter ditty. I toyed with the idea of ending this preface with the assertion that, given some of the alternatives I see at this moment in the field of composition studies, I'd take romance, but that is not entirely accurate, and it certainly would get a quick response from the left critics. They might scold that this is precisely the point, that this romantic expressivist discourse supports an ideology of the self-made person that is essential to the reproduction of capital, that romantic rhetoric plays a role in maintaining the status quo by reproducing a certain subjectivity. To which my visceral response is, "oh get a life!" I'm just humming a tune for crying out loud. But, my more considered response is that it is certainly true that certain notions of creativity and genius and the struggling artist, perhaps exemplified by a movie like *Dead Poet's Society* can reproduce a certain subjectivity, but that this is not the inevitable result. Notice that, even with this movie example, it is no small thing that the viewer is not simply appropriating romantic discourse, but is situating himself or herself in a ruling class, male, heterosexist (all boys boarding school) subject position. It is the intersection of such positions that can reproduce a ruling subjectivity.

Yet if twenty years of postmodern language theory has taught us little else, it should have taught us that discourse and texts *depend*, that they are not a singular, reified, foundationalist essence, that they mean what they do, that an identical text does different things at different times. In my view, Professor Gradin's *Romancing Rhetorics* fulfills our field's increasing need to question a new dogmatism, and democratically functions at this time and place in a liberating way by critically, carefully, and fairly examining what too often are casual dismissals, if not bashings, of the work, the social struggles, and the lives of people to whom we still owe much. There is no work more political—or pedagogical.

James Thomas Zebroski

Acknowledgments

While it is not possible for me to thank everyone who had a hand in making this book a reality, I must acknowledge at least those whose support and critical insight ensured its completion. I would like to thank my mother, Sara Wiker, for reading the manuscript. I would also like to thank Brenda Robertson for taking time from her own graduate studies and teaching to offer suggestions. Peter Elbow offered continuous support in his belief that my ideas were worth pursuing. Behind the scenes, but always only a frantic phone call away, were Pat Sullivan, Bonnie Sunstein, Cindy Gannett, and Donna Qualley. Pat, Bonnie, Cindy, and Donna supplied the kind of constant support that few of us are lucky enough to experience.

The thorough and critical reviews of my manuscript by James Zebroski, Duncan Carter, and Elizabeth Chiseri-Strater were invaluable. Elizabeth has been especially supportive. Linda Anderson of Portland State University has offered important editorial advice and insight. Doug Robinson has been a true champion. For two years he stood beside me when things got rough. He encouraged me, believed in me, and read and reread without complaint. I cannot imagine having embarked on this project without his unflagging support. Joanne Tranchemontagne has been an insightful and patient production editor. Finally, I would like to thank Peter Stillman. He has been a kind, prompt, and highly professional editor.

Parts of Chapter Seven appear in *CEA Critic*.

Introduction

Only recently have compositionists begun to call into question the negative appraisals of expressivism. Finally, at the 1991 Conference on Composition and Communication in Boston and the 1992 Conference on Composition and Communication in Cincinnati, the reappraisals of expressivism from the advocates' position began showing up on the program in larger numbers than in previous years. In Cincinnati, at roundtable discussions and panels like the one entitled "Reconsidering Expressivist Rhetoric and Pedagogy," we began to question the ways in which anti-expressivists distort and misname what expressivism is and can be. I am pleased that we are finally beginning to make this move. In the years that I have been working on this project, I have felt alone—a maverick of sorts. My work and desires to reclaim expressivism have been ridiculed, scorned, and dismissed as "retrograde," "old hat," "obviously uninformed by more important social theories and feminist thought."

Reclaiming and establishing an intellectual tradition for expressivism are not retrograde, and my work is informed by social theories. My feminist perspective governs this entire project, my teaching and scholarship, and my everyday life in and out of the academy. It is the feminist in me that finds value in the expressivist concern for voice, emotive processes, and lived experience. I would argue that reclaiming expressivism is anything but retrograde because it has always been a sounder pedagogical and theoretical approach to the teaching of writing than postmodern/poststructural critics have granted.

The resurgence of positive talk surrounding expressivism is alarming to some in the field. Ross Winterowd is disturbed enough to once again take up intellectual arms against this "upstart" of expressivist talk ("I. A. Richards and Romantic Composition"). Anti-expressivists have begun to talk in terms of an expressivist "backlash." I prefer to see my attempt to historicize, and the move by my colleagues and me to reclaim expressivism, as a "reimaging" or "rereading." To view it in traditional terms, the return of interest in expressivism is one part of a dialectic: thesis (expressivism), antithesis (social-epistemicism), synthesis (a new thesis arising from a blending of thesis and antithesis). To reimage requires that we stop the reflex reactions against expressivism in order that we might

xiii

rediscover and reimplement what is valuable about it. To do so may also put a crimp in our tendencies to tidily place things in strict categorical terms; it may make agonistic intellectual debate less effectual and dialogue and theory sharing more effectual. In effect, new categories, more pluralistic in nature, may emerge. We may end up examining what I coin social-expressivism in this text, or expressivist social-epistemicism, or feminist social-expressivism, and so on.

In *The Web of Meaning*, Janet Emig speaks of the "tacit tradition" from which our work in composition research arises, the implicit knowledge and language shared by scholars and thinkers within our discipline. She notes that "certain kinds of knowing and doing, summed, qualify as emblems of membership and participation" (147). Emig urges us to examine these tacit traditions from which we arise. In the case of expressivist and social-expressivist rhetorics, "certain kinds of knowing and doing" have been passed down to us, not only through the writings of the romantics, but by subsequent educators and thinkers not usually considered romantics. Nonetheless, many of these educators shared some of the "root metaphors and governing paradigms" of romantic thought on education and learning.

In this book I make a two-pronged argument based on the tacit tradition that I bring forth: (1) that the recent denigration of the expressivist theories of composition is often based on misconceptions of expressivist theory and practice as well as incomplete knowledge of the tradition from which they arise; and (2) that social-expressivist rhetorics that arise from the intellectual tradition I examine here are already at work in the field, but that they need to be more fully articulated and enacted.

As a woman interested in both feminist and composition theory, I see part of the purpose of this book as deconstructing the rigid categorical alignments under which compositionists have worked for the past several years. Critics of expressivism are involved in a power struggle within their own discipline and within the larger field of English Studies. As compositionists we have had to fight and argue our way into disciplinary status. This hunger for power and authority within English Studies leads to the desire to create hierarchy and to establish one self-contained "best" theory that will stand out as worthy of a true field of academic study. The result has been the construction of oppositions in which expressivism is relegated to the position of weak "other." This study collapses the walls that scholars like Lester Faigley and James Berlin have built between expressivism and social-epistemicism. I argue here for the ignored version of expressivism—a social-expressivism—that the current taxonomy keeps invisible.

Social-expressivism blurs the categorical lines between social theories and theories of individualism. Social-expressivism stresses the need for teachers to focus on writing for discovery, writing to discover self and voice, and development of power and authority of one's own writing. But it also focuses on those things that social-epistemicism is being praised for: positioning the self within the world and writing for change. The current definitions of social-epistemic rhetorics imply a deterministic scenario in the classroom where the subject is acted upon and acculturated by his or her environment and constructed by material conditions and through language. Current critics of expressivism envision an expressivist subject who both refuses to participate in the social world altogether and who is somehow internally constructed separately from social influences. A social-expressivism, however, with roots already embedded in the tradition from which expressivism arises, suggests that all subjects negotiate within the system; they act and are acted upon by their environment. In order to be effective citizens and effective rhetorical beings, students must first learn how to carry out the negotiation between self and world. A first step in this negotiation must be to develop a clear sense of one's own beliefs as well as a clear sense of how one's own value system intersects or not with others, and how, finally, to communicate effectively. I am not suggesting that the subject, or self, is monolithic, centered, or rational. The self that confronts one's own beliefs and examines her interaction with culture is particularly plural and decentered, because the self is constructed differently in various times and in multiple classes and cultures. Previously scholars in the field, and particularly critics of expressivism, have ignored how the romantics and later theorists who carry on parts of a romantic tradition have incorporated both theories of individual selves and social selves into their educational theories.

Perhaps a social-expressivism has not previously been articulated because scholars in composition studies are inclined to make passing remarks about romanticism without much knowledge of what it entailed as a movement. Most critics, when citing expressivists' debt to the romantics, cite only the organic theory of composing, their focus on self-expression and voice, and writing as a means of discovery. They also claim that expressivists ignore the social, the ways that writing works in the world, and the ways that the world works on (through) the individual.

Critics seem only to remember the self-imposed isolation the romantics felt and the deep tie to nature that appears severed from the material conditions of civilization. Lester Faigley (1986) mentions expressivism's tie to romanticism through his citation of M. H.

Abrams and the expressivist emphasis on "integrity, spontaneity and originality." He never explains, however, what these mean in terms of romantic philosophy and expressivist theory and pedagogy. This one-sided view of romanticism results not only in a less than satisfactory understanding of expressivist composition theories as they stand now, but also in a less than satisfactory understanding of the ways in which expressivism and social-epistemicism overlap. A lopsided understanding of romanticism, and thus the tradition from which expressivism grows, blinds us to the possibilities for social-expressivisms.

My perspective is historical to the extent that I construct an intellectual tradition, and it brings British romanticism, primarily romanticism as it stems from Wordsworth and Coleridge, to the forefront of romantic pedagogies and expressivist rhetorics of the nineteenth and twentieth centuries. I am interested in the ways in which "certain kinds of knowing and doing" are re-represented in the educational philosophies of writers such as John Stuart Mill, Matthew Arnold, and John Dewey, and in the current rhetorics of Donald Murray, Peter Elbow, and Ann Berthoff. In the work of these compositionists, we can find at least one tacit tradition and an historical lineage from which expressivist and social-expressivist rhetorics grow. This lineage and my discussion of those generally labeled expressivist will show that the "expressivism" currently talked about in composition circles rarely exists as it has been conceived.

Fortunately, historians in the field of composition like Robert Connors, James Berlin, Sharon Crowley, and Cheryl Glenn are embarking on historical work which will contextualize current rhetorical theories. Their scholarship will help to establish composition as worthy of disciplinary status in a more productive manner than categorizing too tightly. Moreover, these historical inquiries and examinations of various traditions will reveal that our different theories and approaches share many of the same influences. For instance, while I might invoke Dewey as a player in expressivist history, he might as likely be called upon as an historical player in social-epistemic or cognitive theories. Dewey is often seen as the forefather of social construction since his belief that learning is a social process is basic to all of his educational philosophy. He believes in collaborative learning, and also that as humans we are shaped by our culture (Dewey 1969):

> through the influence of the social environment each person becomes saturated with the customs, beliefs, the purposes, skills, hopes and fears of the cultural group to which he belongs. The features of even his physical surroundings come to him through the eyes and ears of the community. (295)

Since Dewey is a social philosopher, strict categorical demarcations would deny his additions to the intellectual traditions of expressivism. But this is so only if we let strict categorical divisions deny the supplemental relationship between composition theories and thus perpetuate the unfruitful binary oppositions.

To gain a full sense of the importance of the tradition I talk about as it relates to the teaching of writing, it is important to understand that the milieu from which expressivism arises is broader than just a concern for the teaching of writing. For current expressivists such as Elbow and Murray, good writing is not separate from a strong education that celebrates the imagination and the growth of holistic selves as well as the growth of good writers. Writing is not an action that takes place severed from the complex interaction and dynamics taking place within the student as a whole, nor is it severed from the cultural milieu and historical moment.

Ties between romanticism and public discourse and/or the teaching of writing have been few in number and usually too bent on pointing to the perceived failures of expressivism. There has been only one positive, large-scale attempt to place expressivist rhetorics and rhetoricians within an historical framework—Mark Waldo's dissertation "The Rhetoric of Wordsworth and Coleridge" (1982). The most crucial difference between Waldo's perspective and my perspective is that his is strictly psychobiographical in approach. My approach is directly shaped in response to the current taxonomy operating in the field whose creators are predisposed to define expressivism in negative ways and social-epistemic theories in exonerated terms. At the time Waldo wrote his dissertation, proponents of social-epistemicism had not yet diminished expressivism in order to make room for their theories and approaches to the teaching of writing.

In *A Theory of Discourse*, James Kinneavy (1971) discusses the importance of Wordsworth and Coleridge to an understanding of the expressive aims of discourse, but he ultimately views the discourse aims of expressivism in a negative light, and he sees these discourse aims solely as self-expressive. The late James Berlin has given us the most recent historical sketch of expressivist rhetorics, but, like Waldo's and Kinneavy's, it is unsatisfactory. Not only do I find it too rigid, but it is cursory in its examination of such romantic complexities found in current expressivism as discovery, experience, reflection, and imagination. In their article Fishman and McCarthy (1992) opened the door for fuller and more detailed studies like mine. Our claims, however, are both similar and dissimilar. Fishman and McCarthy see that we must broaden "our understanding of romanticism" in order to understand expressivism fully

(649). They also disagree with the understanding of romanticism and expressivism as generating isolated and lonely writers. They return to eighteenth century German romanticism for their study, however. I return to the English romantics. While the Germans certainly influenced both the English and the American romantics, I believe a look at expressivism through the British poets is more fruitful, since they were much more directly influential on American educational thought than were the Germans.

Fishman and McCarthy merely touch on the credulous view of romanticism and expressivism that an ahistorical understanding yields. I, however, take this issue head-on by examining expressivism's intellectual traditions. What this allows me to do is to show the relationship between expressivism and social-constructivism. While Fishman and McCarthy's article begins to show the rapport between expressivism and social-constructivism, they do so in a very truncated way, as the boundaries of an article-length study dictate. What is most disturbing about their article is that they short shrift social-constructivism just as they claim social-constructivists have done to expressivists. Social-constructivism is much more than a mere demand for "disciplinary language" as they claim in both their introduction and conclusion. Social-constructivism, like expressivism, is complex and historically rich; the authors do a disservice to a reconsideration of expressivism by reducing social-constructivism. My study allows social-constructivism its full complexity while still historicizing expressivism and showing the relationship between these two composition theories and practices.

Maureen Neal's article, "Social Constructionism and Expressionism" comes closest to my position. She forthrightly states that "we need to stop understanding these theories as exclusive theoretical rivals . . ." (42). Neal argues that there are both points of contradiction and connection between social-constructivism and expressivism. To ignore the points of connection denies that these two theories, taken together, offer more to actual classroom practice. While I agree whole-heartedly with Neal, my book does not stop at suggesting that there are points of intersection between social-epistemicism and expressivism. My project reclaims what anti-expressivists have left out in their versions and narratives of expressivism.

What I will ultimately argue is that expressivist rhetorics are often simplified and reduced to appear far more ineffectual and anti-social than they actually are. This simplification has been easily accomplished and the current rigid taxonomies so uncritically accepted for at least two reasons: (1) expressivist rhetorics have not yet been satisfactorily placed within an intellectual tradition, and (2) a strict categorization or taxonomy of rhetorical theories allows

social-epistemic proponents to deny the ways in which expressivism enriches social theories and pedagogies—the ways in which
expressivism is already "social." With these starting points in
mind, then, I begin the task of examining the traditions and value
of expressivist and social-expressivist rhetorics.

This text itself is somewhat romantic or expressivist in form;
some readers are sure to object. It is not one linear argument or telling of history tidily packaged. I weave my history thematically
through such topics as general educational philosophy, imagination
in the classroom, and the part that reflection and experience play in
the teaching of writing. Thus, my telling of this tradition is not linear and strictly chronological, but rather a continual movement
from present to past and back to present.

I have structured my discussion as follows: Chapter One is an
overview of how we arrived at the current taxonomy that identifies
three clearly separate rhetorics vying for position within composition studies: cognitive, expressionistic, and social-epistemic. Here I
also reveal the disparaging myths surrounding romanticism that
are, in part, responsible for our currently denigrated and misinformed understanding of expressivism. I introduce the charges
against expressivist rhetorics as leveled by neo-classicists, cognitivists, and social-constructivists.

Chapter Two begins with a brief discussion of the recent film
Dead Poets Society as a way of exemplifying the greater educational
milieu, held over from the nineteenth century, which sparked the
expressivist demand for radical change in writing instruction. The
bulk of the chapter establishes the parallels regarding the educational practices that launched the romantics', the later educational
philosophers' like Mill and Dewey, and the twentieth century
expressivists' new theories in opposition to traditional practice.
Also, this chapter, and the next three chapters, begin to illuminate
the path from romanticism to social-expressivism.

Chapter Three examines an important, but too often ignored,
component of expressivist thought—the imagination. I trace the
evolution of the romantic imagination from Wordsworth and Coleridge directly to the educational practices and theories of composition scholars like Berthoff, Murray, and Elbow.

Chapter Four examines crucial ingredients for expressivist pedagogies if they are to move students toward the growth of imaginative intellects. I explore the ways discovery, perception, experience,
and reflection arise from the romantic tradition and are practiced by
current expressivists.

Chapter Five makes clear the social aspects already embedded
in expressivist theory and practice. I look at common charges
against expressivism and romanticism that stem from misreadings

of both. In rereading expressivism in a fuller historical context, I argue for a social-expressivism that is not arhetorical, apolitical, atheoretical, anti-intellectual, or lacking in a social understanding of self and the construction of knowledge.

Chapters Six and Seven focus on feminist approaches to the teaching of writing and expressivist practice in multicultural classrooms. In Chapter Six I turn to a deeply personal feminist analysis. I argue for the ways in which social-expressivism is amenable to feminist theories and pedagogical practices. Considering expressivist rhetorics in terms of gender issues helps to uncover what is problematic as well as useful for feminist teaching and women students.

In the final chapter, Chapter Seven, I do not come to any tidy and happy conclusions about social-expressivism as a whole or social-expressivism and the cross-cultural classroom. Instead, I reveal gaps that anyone like myself who wishes to make expressivist practices work in culturally diverse classrooms must consider. I conclude with questions, not answers.

Chapter One

Whose Categories Are These Anyway?

The writing theories and pedagogies practiced by such scholars as Donald Murray, Peter Elbow, and Ken Macrorie were firmly and rightly labeled as romantic in nature by the 1970s. While discussing the "current-traditionalist" paradigm that would remain firmly entrenched through the early 1980s, Richard Young (1978) suggested that as new research in the field of composition began to change the complexion of that current-traditional paradigm, two ultimately incompatible theories emerged from within it. One theory emphasizes the composed product and the other focuses on the composing process: he claims that our discipline was in crisis because the incongruity was irresolvable. The theoretical stance stressing the product also privileges "the analysis of discourse into words, sentences, and paragraphs; the classification of discourse into description, narration, exposition, and argument; the strong concern with usage (syntax, spelling, punctuation) and with style (economy, clarity, emphasis); the preoccupation with the informal essay and the research paper; and so on" (31). Young calls the opposing stance "vitalist." Its assumptions are "inherited from the Romantics"; it recognizes the composing process as important, and stresses the "natural powers of the mind and the uniqueness of the creative act" (31). By 1980 Young is arguing that these positions are completely incompatible, and to underscore their theoretical differences, he labels one the "new classicism" and the other the "new romanticism."

Since the early 1980s, others have identified what they believe to be various theoretical postures within the field of rhetoric, relabeling and redefining them to fit their own understanding of these views. Lester Faigley, narrowing his discussion to that part of the

1

rhetorical triad which focuses on composing, suggests that "current-traditional" rhetorics are currently out of favor and that the two major competitive perspectives on composing come from within the process movement of rhetoric. Relying on James Berlin's discussions of the present rhetorical scene, Faigley (1986) identifies these two outlooks on composing as a "cognitive view," which he sees as arising from the American movement in cognitive psychology, and an "expressive view," which he sets within the tradition of British romanticism since it views good writing as having "integrity, spontaneity and originality—the same qualities M. H. Abrams uses to define 'expressive' poetry in *The Mirror and the Lamp*" (529). He also acknowledges the emergence of a social view that is akin to Berlin's definition of a social-epistemic rhetoric. In a nutshell, the social view of rhetoric rejects the idea that writing is an activity that springs from a private construct.

Three Rhetorical Theories

James Berlin has most influenced our understanding of current rhetorical theory. His two monographs, *Writing Instruction in Nineteenth-Century American Colleges* and *Rhetoric and Reality in American Colleges: 1900–1985*, along with "Rhetoric and Ideology in the Writing Class," have virtually defined current rhetorics and their theoretical and pedagogical properties. Berlin is almost single-handedly responsible for the concrete divisions we perceive between expressivist rhetorics, social-epistemic rhetorics, and cognitive rhetorics.

In his earlier work on nineteenth-century writing instruction, Berlin (1984) had delineated three operative rhetorics for those years: classical, eighteenth-century, and romantic. Classical rhetoric "defines the real as rational" and posits that both the universe and the human mind are guided by rules and reason (4). He links the decline of classical rhetoric in American colleges to the overthrow of English rule since this rhetoric was so clearly seen as akin to an English way of life. This made room for the eighteenth-century rhetoric imported from Scottish colleges. As Berlin sees it, Americans in the nineteenth century "embraced Scottish Common Sense Realism" (6). Late in the century, after the transcendental movement of Emerson and Thoreau, romantic rhetoric flowered. In this rhetoric the composing process itself becomes a way of knowing or making meaning. "Reality" for romantic rhetoric, Berlin suggests, is situated not in "the realm of the senses and the perceptive faculties, but in the interaction of observer and observed" (10). Berlin makes it clear that of these three nineteenth-century rhetorics he strongly favors the romantic (12).

In his discussion of twentieth-century writing instruction, Berlin (1987) again defines three main categories that create his rhetorical scene. He has broadened these categories into "objective," "subjective," and "transactional," and shows how the more specific current-traditional, expressionistic, and social-epistemic rhetorics develop out of the three. The objective theories are those which posit reality as an empirically determined material world, and the writer's object is to relay that world as accurately as possible. Within this category Berlin includes current-traditional rhetorics, as well as behaviorist, semanticist, and linguistic rhetorics (x). Subjective theories, according to Berlin, find truth within the individual or within a context that is available only through the individual's internal perspective—"reality is a personal and private construct" (143). This is the rhetoric that is related to his earlier romantic rhetoric; he suggests that its roots, at least in America, are found in Platonic idealism as modified by Emerson and Thoreau and notes that the various rhetorics that spring from it are commonly called "expressionistic." His final category, that of transactional theories, is based on an epistemology that "sees truth as arising out of the interaction of the elements of the rhetorical situation: an interaction of subject and object or of subject and audience or even of all the elements—subject, object, audience, and language—operating simultaneously" (15). At this juncture, Berlin no longer favors expressivism and finds much to fault in romantic rhetorics. His preference is now for what he specifies as social theories of rhetoric.

I suspect that Berlin's dramatic shift from a position favoring romantic rhetorics to one preferring social-epistemic rhetorics has to do with the field of composition's power struggle within English Studies and the academy at large. To articulate untainted social theories for the teaching of writing aligns composition studies with the more favored and currently high-powered literary theories. Also, like most of us in the field, Berlin recognizes the "truth" in the position that knowledge is socially constructed and that gender, class, and race matter. What disturbs me, though, is Berlin's abrupt dismissal of expressivist rhetorics. How could he not see the ways in which expressivist pedagogy and theory are also part of his new-found position? I would argue that he does this by separating practice from theory. He leaves actual teaching approaches completely out of the picture by focusing solely on the language of expressivism in a narrowly conceived way. In practice, for instance, collaborative learning, journal writing, multiple drafting, and looking at the "self's" relationship to the world are just a few of the aspects of expressivism that remain a part of social-epistemic approaches to teaching writing. Rather than acknowledging any social-epistemic nature within expressivism, Berlin refrains from damaging his own argument by suggesting that there is a "psychological-epistemic rhetoric." This rhetoric, however, he dismisses as a form of expressionism, thereby sidestepping any analysis that might prove expressivism "social" in the ways reserved only for social-epistemicism (Berlin 1988, 488).

In "Rhetoric and Ideology in the Writing Class," the article that cements the way the discipline looks at current rhetorics, Berlin updates the ideas he expressed in *Rhetoric and Reality*. Once again he divides things three ways and comes up with cognitive rhetoric, expressionistic rhetoric, and social-epistemic rhetoric. Citing Linda Flower and John Hayes as the best-known proponents of cognitive rhetoric, he summarizes their stance as one in which "the most important features of composing are those which can be analyzed into discrete units and expressed in linear, hierarchical terms, however unpredictably recursive these terms may be. The mind is regarded as a set of structures that perform in a rational manner, adjusting and reordering functions in the service of the goals of the individual" (482).

Berlin presumes that expressionistic rhetoric developed during the first two decades of the twentieth century. But, like Young, he too traces it back to the romantics when he says that it is a "descendant of Rousseau on the one hand and of the romantic recoil from the urban horrors created by the nineteenth-century capitalism on the other" (484). He finds it closely tied to theories of psychology that argue for the inherent goodness of the individual. In fact, the existence of this rhetoric is "located within the individual subject. . . . [Writing] is an art, a creative act in which the process—the discovery of the true self—is as important as the product—the self discovered and expressed" (484). The names that Berlin associates with expressionistic rhetoric are Ken Macrorie, Walker Gibson, William Coles, Donald Murray, and Peter Elbow.

The third rhetoric (social-epistemic)—and the one that Berlin now favors—is distinguished by a belief that the "real is located in a relationship that involves the dialectical interaction of the observer, the discourse community (social group) in which the observer is functioning, and the material conditions of existence" (486). He argues that the individual is not a private self, as the expressionists might say, but that the self is a "social construct." "There is no universal, eternal, and authentic self that beneath all appearances is at one with all other selves," he says, simplifying the romantic roots of expressivist rhetorics for purposes of showing social rhetorics as superior (487). He goes on to argue that the "self is always a creation of a particular historical and cultural moment," but he never acknowledges that some romantic theorists might also hold this assumption (487). The greatest advantage that Berlin sees in social-epistemic rhetoric is that it views knowledge as an "arena of ideological conflict: there are no arguments from transcendent truth since all arguments arise in ideology. It thus inevitably supports economic, social, political, and cultural democracy" (487). Rhetoricians that Berlin cites as advocates of the social-epistemic or social constructivist rhetoric include Richard Ohmann, Kenneth Bruffee, Lester Faigley, David Bartholomae, Patricia Bizzell, and Karen Burke LeFevre.

The Aversion to Romanticism

Here, then, is a sketch of the history that has led us to the taxonomy currently most accepted in the field of composition. As Berlin's article ages, indeed as I age, I grow to increasingly appreciate his argument. Rhetoric is "always already ideological" (Berlin 1988, 477). To not have acknowledged this, as Berlin has demanded that we do, would keep us blind to the ways our theories and pedagogies are limiting and damaging. Implications for race, class, and gender would remain well hidden, and we would remain without the needed reflective revision and reworking of our theories and practices. In view of this, there are reasons for viewing expressivism in the negative light that Berlin does. Indeed, expressivist rhetorics were already under attack from the more traditional scholars in the field by the time Berlin cemented this current view of our taxonomies. The classical approach to rhetorical theory and pedagogy, for instance, as represented by such current theorists as John Gage, considers the romantic view unsuitable for composition pedagogy because it is premised on the romantic assumption that successful writing is a mysterious process or act of genius. Classical critics believe that proponents of romantic pedagogies assume that students improve their writing through subjective means—through "inspiration" or "self-discovery." This inner and individual focus, they claim, comes at the expense of intellectual rigor. What is meant by "intellectual rigor" and the value of certain kinds of "intellectual rigor" is, of course, debatable. Advocates of current-traditional or neo-classical rhetorics envision intellectual rigor primarily as clear, tidy, analytical, logical, and linear writing. Along similar lines to the argument that romantic rhetorics lack rigor, theorists of various persuasions have accused neo-romantic rhetorics of anti-intellectualism, and of thus making a poor theory on which to build a pedagogy.

This view is based on a long history of aversion to romanticism. Jacques Barzun (1961) has pointed out that the twentieth century has harbored an "anti-Romantic animus" (xi). When we consider how pervasive and relentless the disparagement of romanticism has been, it is not surprising that a theory of rhetoric which has been identified as a descendant of romanticism should come under attack as well. Much of the aversion to romanticism, however, seems based on caricatures of the romantic poets, caricatures which have their roots in false images perpetuated either by the poets themselves or by the satirical portraits of romantic contemporaries like Thomas Love Peacock.[1]

Peacock's sympathies were with neo-classical critical principles and he adroitly parodied a number of ideas popularized by Wordsworth and Coleridge. Feigning Wordsworth's voice, Peacock (1971) manages to portray the Lake Poets as idealistic nature freaks who have no use for society, and who walk around being showered with "poetical impressions":

> Poetical impressions can be received only among natural scenes: for all that is artificial is antipoetical. Society is artificial, therefore we will live out of society. The mountains are natural, therefore we will live in the mountains. There we shall be shining models of virtue, passing the whole day in the innocent and amiable occupation of going up and down hill, receiving poetical impressions. . . . (495)

From a passage like this arises the false sense that the romantics were merely "nature poets" who saw themselves as virtuous souls miraculously removed from the realities of a decaying society. While the romantics were idealistic and even promoted a caricature of themselves as brooding, isolated, and lonely poets, they were actually less so than either they or Peacock suggest.

Peacock goes on, this time in his own voice as literary critic, to suggest that the romantics lacked reason and intellectual rigor, and to denigrate the imagination to a form of "fantasy": "[the Lake Poets] remaining studiously ignorant of history, society, and human nature, cultivated the fantasy only at the expense of the memory and the reason" (495). He also offers a scathing interpretation of the romantic focus on feeling: "The highest inspirations of poetry are resolvable into three ingredients: the rant of unregulated passion, the whining of exaggerated feeling, and the cant of factitious sentiment" (486).

Barzun's cultural history of romanticism, *Classic, Romantic, Modern*, explains that extreme views of romanticism like Peacock's became accepted through unfounded generalizations that romanticism is stupid, anti-intellectual, fanciful, irrational, sentimental, an exaggeration of individuality, and overly emotional.[2] Modernists like Pound and Eliot continued to keep these generalizations alive, promoting further the twentieth century's negative view of romanticism. It is not uncommon for our culture to disdain those things it perceives as romantic. Dreamers or utopian thinkers, hopeful in spite of dour circumstances, are labeled as "hopeless romantics." Irrational, mysterious, or fanciful things are frowned upon and contemptuously referred to as "romantic." In spite of romanticism's impact on our world, we are still a culture that values logic, reason, and hard facts, and that devalues imaginative thinking and intuition. This dichotomy is deeply embedded in Western culture—it defines that which is "romantic" as frivolous and silly, and it defines "non-romantic" as reasonable and sound. While these generalizations are not always fair or even accurate, they do exist. Since composition studies, and even the rhetorical theories underlying writing instruction, are a twentieth-century phenomenon, it is to be expected that rhetorical theories identified as romantic would be saddled with some of the same unfounded generalizations.

Expressivist pedagogues, like their romantic forebears, value the emotive, the intuitive, and the imaginative. Understandings of (and discussions on) expressivism end up infused with the same negative generalizations that permeate our twentieth century culture's view of romantic tenets. Expressivist rhetorics are, after all, a product of their historical and cultural time. The expressivist emphasis on imagination, creativity, and process, for instance, has often resulted in a charge of anti-intellectualism. We can see how this has leaked into discussions on composition when Richard Young reminds us that a "frequently heard accusation against the new romanticism" is its lack of academic and intellectual "rigor" ("Arts, Crafts, Gifts, and Knacks" 56). This general accusation took on additional force when some expressivist rhetoricians dropped all reading from their writing courses and advocated that the students' own writing be the primary text in the class.

Donald Murray, for example, taught writing courses at the University of New Hampshire where the only required readings were the texts generated by the students in the course. Other readings were dropped in response to the traditional Freshman English course, which was not specifically a writing course, but was taught as another literature course which required the typical literary analysis. Murray (1986) explains in his anthology of readings for composition classes that the typical approach to the teaching of writing did not, at the time he switched to using student texts, allow students to make any connection between the problems they faced in their own drafts and the finished products they were reading: "When I first taught Freshman English I had to follow a syllabus that forced the students to read prose models that the students—and I—could not relate to the problems they faced in their own writing" (xiii). Also, Murray was attempting to raise the status of student writing. He continues to believe that student writing is highly undervalued when continually placed in juxtaposition to "Literature." Murray argues that student writing is well worth serious consideration and readerly analysis. Although Murray's intent was admirable—to connect reading with the actual writing process and to put more value on student writing—he might well have accentuated the already prevalent belief that anything "romantic" lacks "rigor."

 Both those who favor neo-classical rhetoric and cognitivists who see writing as goal-setting and problem-solving have negatively appraised if not dismissed expressivism on the grounds that pedagogies which arise from the romantic traditions are premised on a view that successful writing occurs only through inspiration or genius. Unfortunately for writing teachers, this is another case where the romantics help to paint a caricature of themselves, so it is not surprising that others accept this as a "truth." Linda Flower, a leading proponent of cognitivist rhetorics, argues that the myth of the inspired writer arose from Coleridge's introductory remarks on how he composed the poem "Kubla Khan." "Coleridge's account of his experience," Flower explains, "contains four major elements of the myth of inspiration" (42): he suggests that the creative vision comes without effort, that it comes fully articulated, that it comes in a matter of moments, and that it cannot be repeated because it is a gift from the muse.

Extrapolating from Coleridge's mystifications directly to expressivism, then, Flower finds that expressivism falls short as an effective theory for writing instruction because this romantic "myth of the inspired writer" does not take into account cognitive processes and such writerly strategies as problem solving and goal setting, and because the myth breeds passivity in students who would believe in inspiration and the muse rather than in hard work and the practice of successful writing strategies.

John Gage (1986), too, a rhetorician who prizes classical rhetorics, argues that students learn to believe that "'Writers are born not made.' 'Writers are sensitive people, gifted with imagination'" (17). This belief, says Gage, is "mixed up with another general superstition, perpetuated by the culture, that writers are special people, an idea that has its origin in the romantic adulation of writers as a class. . . . The romantic belief is a strong one, and it helps to kill the motivation of students who have struggled with mastery of technique" (17).

Patricia Bizzell (1986), a social-epistemic rhetorician whose interest lies in helping students master the academic discourse they are required to negotiate, finds that her students accept the idea of writing as inspiration—the students seem to like the idea of "instant text production." She suggests that the idea that text can be produced this way is a "part of a more general notion in our culture, a sort of debased Romantic version of creativity wherein verbal artifacts are supposed to be produced as easily and inevitably as a hen lays eggs" (4).

Neo-classical, cognitive, and social-epistemic theorists fault expressivism, assuming that it perpetuates the myth of inspiration, based on the generally held notion that the romantics saw the act of composing as mysterious and inspirational. They are not completely incorrect, but to accept this simplified version of "romantic inspiration" not only ignores the complexity of what this meant to the romantics, but it also denies that inspiration is accessible to most if not all students through the cultivation of a certain kind of intellect—an encompassing intellect. There is value in these criticisms, however, in that they do point out some problematics for actual expressivist classroom practice. Our students are even more apt to simplify the notion of inspiration, reducing it to "instant text production," than professional scholars are. The result is very likely to be students who don't want to revise because what they have written was certainly inspired and thus as close to perfection as possible. Perhaps, as Gage suggests, those students who must struggle and continuously rework their writings do end up with their motivation stamped out for good.

The Argument Against Expressivism

While expressivism is being hit from all sides, the harshest and most invested criticisms are coming from proponents of social-epistemic rhetorics. They advance many of the same criticisms just discussed, but additionally, they find romantic approaches to the teaching of writing deficient because they seem to focus on the individual as opposed to the relationships among the writer, the community, and the social, political, and economic conditions of existence. A romantic rhetoric and pedagogy results in isolated, fragmented, politically ineffectual students and citizens. Berlin is especially hard on expressivist rhetorics on this issue. He argues that their pedagogies may result in the empowerment of individuals but that those individuals remain unaware of economic, political, and social issues (Berlin 1988; 1987).

The romantic conception of rhetoric also distresses Berlin and others because they see it as causing special difficulties for teachers. Berlin, for instance, suggests that teachers cannot even "instruct the student in the principles of writing" in this rhetoric because writing for the romantic is an act of finding truth through a "private act of intuition" (Berlin 1987, 13). He further suggests that students and teachers are not interested in adapting a message for an audience but rather are interested in helping each other identify and exorcize what is "untrue to the private vision of the writer" (Berlin 1984, 89). Things romantic are envisioned as private and antithetical to rhetoric. As Berlin (1984) explains this argument, "the romantics, with their insistence on the private and personal in discovering and communicating truth, deny the inherently communal nature of the art, thereby abolishing rhetoric's reason for being" (42).

As usual, Berlin's criticisms of expressivism are insightful. He cuts right to the bone when he declares that expressivist rhetorics can indeed be anti-rhetorical. The more time I spend in the public school classrooms and with inexperienced teaching assistants, the more I realize how easily this can happen in practice. For many teachers the focus on self-expression and personal empowerment is very alluring. To find your students, previously downtrodden and firmly believing they cannot write, suddenly proud, producing, and believing that they can actually have something to say is quite heady. Sometimes students and teachers get stuck in this place, seeming to forget that the rhetorical situation is complex. While this doesn't have to be the case, it is not as unlikely as I once believed. I have observed classes where teachers never ask their students to reshape these moments of self-expression for particular audiences. The students are not taught how to move their essays from what Flower (1981) calls writer-based prose to reader-based prose (121).

Berlin also strikes a nerve when he suggests that expressivists' focus on the individual ignores the ideological circumstances in which students write. I firmly believe, like Berlin, that individuals are socially constructed. Our students, and thus their writings, are products of historical, economic, and other cultural forces. I am dedicated to helping students gain the tools by which to read and change the world in which they live. I no more want to create "ineffectual citizens" than does Berlin. His charge that expressivism's privileging of the individual ignores the ways in which the "self is always a creation of a particular historical and cultural moment," and thus it somehow suppresses cultural democracy, is crucial. Any expressivist pedagogy that intentionally or unintentionally does so is in need of the scrutiny that Berlin has set in motion. There is no reason, however, why a social-expressivism could not bring analysis of one's self as it is shaped by culture, and analysis of how one's "private vision" is actually situated within culture, to a pivotal position in the classroom.

Often, however, to make their own cases stronger, critics simplify expressivist theories, excluding what is valuable about them from their own theories. If expressivist ideas are embedded in their theories, they do not acknowledge them as expressivist in form and nature. Pointing to or even creating flaws in expressivist theories and pedagogies makes it easier for social-epistemic rhetorics to look superior in every way. Unfortunately, this tendency to create a straw man sets up a problematic system of categorization so narrowly conceived that it ignores what romantic theory contributes to the discipline and even to social-epistemic theories themselves.

The desire to uphold strict categorizations is sometimes explained as a guard against dangerous pedagogy. As Neal (1993) points out, "James Berlin, for example, cautions against mixing pedagogical theories and warns that we may confuse, even damage, students when we use a bit of one in naive combination with a snippet of another" (42). While it may be wise for teachers not to work out of naïveté, this argument strikes me as overblown. I do believe teachers should be reflective about their practices and have some understanding as to why they do what they do. For these reasons I am a strong advocate of both the movement toward classroom-based research and the attempts to professionalize the teaching of composition among instructor ranks. Nonetheless, the fear of combining theories and practices may well arise for more insidious reasons—the grip that patriarchal power has over composition studies.

The Patriarchal "Other"

Significantly enough, the strategy of keeping these theories "pure" through sharp category distinctions is the same strategy that most cultures use to distinguish masculine from feminine. By categorizing and polarizing, the patriarchy creates binary systems of masculine/feminine and masculine/other. Feminist writers have uncovered just how pervasive this kind of binary system-making is. As Elizabeth Fox-Genovese (1991) points out, some feminists are "rejecting all of our assumptions about knowledge on the grounds that they represent an oppressive and outmoded 'binary thinking'"

(4). While other theoretical approaches, such as marxism and deconstructionism, also unveil Western culture's predisposition for binary constructions and the creation of "others," feminism seems to punch through these most consistently. It makes sense, though, that feminism plays such a large role here. After all, when the construct of "woman" or "feminine" is added to any equation, the patriarchy always places it—the equation—in the most extreme "other" position. While black men may be forced into the position of "other" in a society where whites hold power, for instance, the black woman, because she is a woman, is one step further removed on the ladder of hierarchy and power. Likewise a poor man of any race is clearly the "other" in our capitalist society, but an indigent woman is even more the pariah and lacks power in even more essential ways.

Binary or dichotomous thinking grounds itself in difference and inequality, not difference and equality, thus perpetuating these various hierarchies. In composition studies this binary structure is embedded in our need to select an "other" in order to maintain a power position for any particular category. Once we have categorized in this way it is easy to set up dichotomies in innumerable ways—neo-classical vs. expressivist, cognitive vs. neo-classical, social-epistemic vs. expressivist, process vs. non-process, current-traditional vs. all others and so on. The loudest voices in composition currently see all approaches other than social-epistemic as the "other." It is expressivism, however, that poses the largest threat to social-epistemic rhetorics. It has a large following among what Stephen North (1987) calls "practitioners," and until the recent rise of social theories, expressivism occupied a large section of the rhetorical kingdom. It did so, in fact, for twenty years or more. While current-traditional, neo-classical, and cognitive theories and pedagogies still have many practitioners, publication and scholarly debate have focused more stridently on expressivism and social-epistemicism.

What we have come to recognize as the "process movement" in composition arose with expressivism in the 1960s. Expressivism, the first of the "process" rhetorics, took hold in reaction to pedagogies that relied on mechanical correctness and rote memorization. It is a direct reaction to the current-traditional model in composition which denied this notion of writing as a process. Expressivist theories grew up alongside feminism, and there are certain compatabilities between feminist approaches and aspects of the process movement which are particularly expressivist in nature. Perhaps one of the reasons expressivist and romantic theories are so easily placed in the position of the "other" is that they are perceived to contain many aspects of what our culture has identified as feminine: a focus on the personal, the emotive, and expression for the self (or a private domain) as well as for a public domain.

Feminist theory, as Cynthia Caywood and Gillian Overing (1987) point out, challenges the "inherently authoritarian nature of the patriarchy" (xii). The patriarchy, they say, values certain forms of discourse over others:

> the expository essay is valued over the exploratory; the argumentative essay set above the autobiographical; the clear evocation of a thesis preferred to a more organic exploration of a topic; the impersonal, rational voice ranked more highly than the intimate, subjective one. (xii)

Expressivism values the autobiographical, the intimate and subjective voice, and the organic development of a topic. This leads me to question whether the negative assessment of individual "truths," the criticism that expressivism ignores audience, and the decrying of the individual that social theories call for might not be just a slightly reshaped version of patriarchal and traditionally masculine values. Is the negative critique of expressivism tied to this "otherness," these more "feminine" facets? It is interesting that the majority of voices touting the social-epistemic rhetoric and poking accusing fingers at expressivism are male. Berlin, of course, stands at the forefront. I am not suggesting that all males are consciously moving us toward patriarchal control. Nor am I suggesting that women in the field do not merit many of these same criticisms. I do think, however, that gender plays a role here since it appears that most of the categorization and binary oppositions are put forth by male colleagues.[3]

A consideration of gender also seems crucial since gender awareness has not been a particularly strong issue thus far in composition studies. It has only been recently that gender issues have received any attention. Patricia A. Sullivan (1992) argues that this is the case in part because "women have been at the forefront of composition's struggle for autonomy [and this] also has bearing on why composition has thus far been relatively exempt from the kinds of feminist critique leveled at other disciplines: women have been present and influential from the start" (38). In spite of representative numbers of women scholars, however, most of the debate and research have centered on generalities that ignore gender.

Even if feminist critiques continue to challenge the hierarchical divisions that create inequality and false oppositions, I am not overly optimistic about breaking free of all dichotomies that bind us. While deconstruction has taught us to unravel binaries and categories, we simply continue to replace them with new ones, as

Jacques Derrida (1976) insists we must always do. My discussion here certainly reflects my own participation in this system-making. There is no way to deny that I am categorizing in ways that are probably limiting to the current compositionists that I talk about. It is important to note that just as Blake, Wordsworth, Coleridge, Byron, Shelley, and Keats did not label themselves romantics, Elbow, Murray, and Berthoff do not label themselves expressivists. It is others who define them in this way and I am guilty here by continuing to talk of them as expressivists or social-expressivists.

None of these scholars wishes to be pigeon-holed, nor in reality can they so easily be constructed as one thing or the other. They resist our categories and labels in various ways: Donald Murray remains silent on categorical assignments and continues to talk and write about what works for him as writer and teacher of writing; Peter Elbow does not write about expressivism nor defend his views but continues to reshape and rethink his thoughts on the teaching of writing as well as blaze new trails in assessment theory; and Ann Berthoff moves forward in her own scholarship, without comment on where she has been placed in the categorical camps, by looking to philosophy, poetic pasts and presents, and liberatory pedagogies to form a theory and practice for composition.

Beyond Categorization

I do see some positive aspects to our cultural proclivity for categorization, however. It does, after all, allow us to organize a plethora of ideas, theories, and philosophies so that we might talk about them in coherent ways. It is helpful to me, for instance, to talk here about expressivist vs. social-epistemic, and romantic vs. nonromantic. This aids in my desire to remind readers of the positive aspects of expressivist theories and pedagogies, to place them within a tradition, to disinfect the term "romantic" from some of the associations that have hampered a more positive view of current expressivist rhetorics, and to widen the term "romantic" for those who conceive of it too narrowly.

The danger lies in the predilection to categorize or dichotomize in order to maintain power over another. In tracing, however, certain ideas that have typically been labeled "romantic" through such "non-romantics" as Mill, Arnold, and Dewey, and by expanding the boundaries that are repeatedly used to describe expressivism, I hope to be more fluid than those who are reacting against expressivism have been able to remain.

In part I am arguing for composition scholars to embrace a complex mixture of our many rhetorics in both theory and practice. I am not recommending that we do so naïvely. To blend theory and practice requires that we examine closely what we are doing. To allow for the ways in which expressivism and social-epistemicism connect requires that we stop the knee-jerk reactions against expressivism in order that we might rediscover and reimplement what is valuable about it. To do so may also put a crimp in our tendencies to tidily place things in strict categorical terms; it may make agonistic intellectual debate less effectual and dialogue and theory sharing more effectual. In effect, new categories, more pluralistic in nature, may emerge. We may end up examining what I coin social-expressivism for the rhetoric that I favor, or expressivist social-epistemicism, or feminist social-expressivism, or social-cognitivism, and so on.

Derrida's logic of supplementation is helpful in explaining my position here. We might think of it this way: social-epistemic rhetorics do not exist without expressivist rhetorics and vice-versa. In Derridian terms, nothing exists unless it is supplemented. Neo-classical and current-traditional rhetorics did not exist until they could be juxtaposed against each other or against expressivist rhetorics, and social-epistemic rhetorics did not exist until expressivist rhetorics were defined. In other words, social-epistemic rhetorics were formed as a supplement of expressivist rhetorics. Supplements are not substitutes or identical things; they are, however, intricately intertwined. In this light, the strictly defined categories of neo-classical, current-traditional, cognitive, expressivist, and social-epistemic are false categories. Thus far, in the field of composition studies, scholars have focused on what Derrida (1976) calls the "absence" of the thing being supplemented rather than the "presence." This allows for expressivism to remain an "other," and an undervalued "other" at that, since ignoring what expressivist theory contributes to, or how it supplements and is supplemented by social theories ensconces social-epistemic rhetoric comfortably in a power position.

I do not make my arguments, then, from a position that accepts the firm lines of difference among categories. While I am trapped by the language of category and dichotomy in my defense and history of expressivism, I urge readers to unbind yourselves from the categories and allow for a rich, pluralistic mixture of our rhetorics that more accurately reflects our actual theories and practices. This is what I must do to position myself within the theories and pedagogies of contemporary composition studies. I fall between the cracks of categorization. Colleagues have claimed that I can't possibly be an expressivist since I agree that all writing situations (and knowledge) are governed by a cultural milieu. Likewise, I have been labeled an expressivist and anti-social-epistemic because of the value I find in such ideas as personal and authentic voice and writing for and of the self. In actuality, my positionality within the theories, pedagogies, and rhetorics of the field—my "self" so to speak—is a series of supplements which rely both on Derrida's notion of "presence" and "absence." I am neither a self-contained expressivist nor a self-contained social-epistemic. Like most, if not all, of us who spend week after week in the composition classroom, my practice is a complex blend of theories that our current taxonomies discourage or completely deny. It is time to move and speak beyond these categories.

Notes

1. Peacock's essay, "The Four Ages of Poetry," is what prompted Percy Shelley's solemn response in "A Defence of Poetry."

2. Barzun attaches an appendix to his study that lists some of the ways in which the term "romantic" is being used in modern conversation. These include "attractive," "exuberant," "ornamental," "unreal," "materialistic," "irrational," "futile," "heroic," "mysterious," "bombastic," "picturesque," "formless," "fanciful," and "emotional on principle."

3. Lester Faigley is to be commended for trying to break down the hierarchical oppositions that the categorization bolsters. In "Competing Theories of Process," he ends by asking for a complex mixture of the categories he delineates. What seems clear is that the oppositions still hold firm these many years later.

Chapter Two

The Dead Romantics Society: The Call For Educational Change

Neither romanticism nor expressivism sprang fully grown out of thin air. Neither were a priori categories. Rather, both evolved as reactions to other world views that were/are seen as mechanistic and rigid. The British romantics found themselves infused with a revolutionary spirit—now known as the "spirit of the age"— sparked by the upheaval and social unrest of the late eighteenth and early nineteenth centuries (Abrams 1953). Blake, Wordsworth, Coleridge, Shelley, and Byron issued a call for change on all political, social, and class levels. Both Wordsworth and Coleridge linked their demand for social and political change to educational theory as well as to poetica.

Likewise, American expressivists like D. Gordon Rohman, Ann Berthoff, Donald Murray, and Peter Elbow found themselves moved by the revolutionary spirit of the 1960s. They, like the romantics a century earlier, were champions for educational change. More specifically, expressivist writing theorists raised the cry to dismantle the current traditional approaches to writing instruction that so thoroughly simulates more general traditional pedagogies. As this history unfolds, we will begin to see specifically how expressivist theories are a continuance or reshaping of romantic educational ideas. Also, we will have a sense of how the theories current expressivists share with the romantics and with people like Mill and Dewey are in response to various contexts similar to those that sparked the original philosophies of the romantics and the subsequent romantic ideas of the later philosophers.

The current-traditional rhetoric that dominated writing instruction well into the 1960s, and still does in many public schools and in college writing courses, is a product of the more general educational climate surrounding it.

The educational philosophy at work prescribed the same skill, drill, and rote memorization enacted in both British and American school systems for centuries. While, occasionally, revolutionary educational proponents like Wordsworth and Coleridge in the nineteenth century and John Dewey in the early twentieth weakened the traditional approach, the conservatism always held on. So, in the 1950s, students were still expected to sit quietly in rows and view the teacher as all-knowing and all-powerful.

The recent film *Dead Poets Society* demonstrates the American educational conservatism of the time. In the film, student passivity and the drive for analytical objectivity is shattered when an alum, John Keating (played by Robin Williams), returns to teach literature at the academy. In contrast to the administration, Keating does not wish to have passive students; he does not see his students as vessels to be filled with knowledge. Everything that Keating does is radical in the context of the dry and uninspiring pedagogy that the academy endorses. The school attempts to ingrain conformity and reason at every turn, but not imaginative or creative thinking. The uniforms promote conformity. The boys go to bed at the same time, get up at the same time, and eat at the same time. Keating, however, tries to smash through this wall of conformity. He wants the students to find their own voices and not to be lemmings. This, of course, leads to an administrative questioning of Keating's teaching.

A few of the boys discover that, as a student, Keating had been a member of a group called the Dead Poets Society. Although Keating cautions his students about reactivating such a group, he does explain to them that the Society was a group of students who met in a cave, at midnight, to read and discuss poetry. A group of boys form a second generation of the Dead Poets Society, meeting, like the first, to drink, think, and breathe poetry. They begin to really *know* it, to feel it, to understand its greatness in a subjective way that differs greatly from the prescribed and objective steps to analyzing poetry for meter, rhyme, and greatness pushed by the administration.

As might be expected, Keating's pedagogy and the reestablishing of the Dead Poets Society eventually lead to Keating's firing by the administration. Keating's teaching set two opposing forces in motion through Neal, a major character in the movie: Neal's newfound ability to think and take action for himself, and the tyrannical systems of both Neal's father and the boy's academy. When Neal finds himself unable to return the nonthinking entity his father and the school expect him to be, but also unable to continue as an independent and critical thinker against their tyrannical force, Neal kills himself. Not surprisingly, the Headmaster and Neal's father blame Keating for Neal's suicide. The other boys at the academy recognize, however, that Neal's suicide results, not because of Keating's teaching methodologies, but because of Neal's tyrannical father and an educational system that suppresses self-expression and growth (as well as teachers like Keating).

While I agree with the students that it is the system, and not Keating, that finally pushes Neal to suicide, his death nonetheless raises an important issue: What risks arise with creating pedagogies that unleash the potential for thinking on one's own? It may indeed be death, exile, or imprisonment. When people are no longer empty vessels passively awaiting doctrinaire knowledge, no longer parroting back the unscrutinized "knowledge" that a government, a headmaster, or even a parent instills, the possibility for revolutionary action—whether personal and/or social—becomes a reality. And revolution is rarely desirable to those in power.

Paulo Freire's exile from Brazil is a case in point. Freire's liberatory pedagogy attempts to free those without power in countries controlled by dictators. His premise is that once the peasants can read and write the word, they can then read and write the world; by becoming literate through a pedagogy that encourages imaginative thinking and questioning of social and political ideologies (one that works very differently from the "banking concept" of education that merely indoctrinates people), then revolutionary change can be achieved and the unempowered become empowered. Suddenly, those previously easily controlled are now able to view their world critically and are able to think their way through and beyond the indoctrination. This works so well, in fact, that Freire was exiled from his own country.

Martin Luther King Jr. and Malcolm X, albeit radically different revolutionaries and thinkers, educated themselves in order to break loose from the manacles that their actual schooling helped to put in place. Because of their ability to imagine and critically think beyond the system that wished to contain them, they were both imprisoned by, and assassinated within, the supposedly greatest democracy in the Western world. Throughout history many great thinkers—and many unknowns like Neal—have found themselves facing suicide as a viable option to being imaginative and critical thinkers in a system that does its best to shut down free thinking through discipline and a traditional pedagogy as in the case of the boys academy in *Dead Poets Society*, or through death, imprisonment, or exile as in the case of [Rushdie,] King, and Freire.

It is not all bleak, however. [Rushdie still lives and writes.] Paulo Freire still teaches and publishes. Students fortunate enough to have found teachers like Keating are envisioning and working toward better ways of living in a complex and demanding society. There are many who go on to make radical social changes as did Martin Luther King Jr. Once the change has begun it is next to impossible to stop. *Dead Poets Society* closes, for instance, with the Headmaster attempting to restore a traditional pedagogy to Keating's classroom. Whether this is possible is questionable now that the boys are no longer [just] passive students but rather are their own thinkers; the movie closes with this question left hanging. As Keating leaves the room, the boys who choose to do so stand on their desks and defy the Headmaster's repeated command to "sit down." This signifies to Keating that they *will* continue to see things in new ways, from their own perspectives. I believe that the outward shell of the Headmaster's traditional pedagogy might be enacted in his classroom, but those young men will continue to educate themselves in the manner set in motion by John Keating— a teacher who values creativity and the imagination over drill work, rote memorization, and the robot-like students they create.

I do not mean to suggest that Keating's pedagogy is unproblematic. Any class, race, or gender analysis is sure to raise worthy questions. The movie's boys academy is, after all, economically and racially elitist as well as sexist. As Lil Brannon (1993) has argued, *Dead Poets Society* is yet another male quest, the story of the male romantic hero (459). And this story, according to Brannon, serves male teachers but not female teachers. It is also possible to question whether the boys have merely replaced the Headmaster's authority with Keating's—accepting the latter's without reflection. But while it may not be perfect, and it is in need of critique, especially feminist critique, Keating's radical pedagogy did begin chipping away at the concrete foundation of the damaging traditional pedagogy sustained by the Headmaster.

However truly radical Keating's pedagogy, it remains that *Dead Poets Society* [deftly] portrays the conservative nature of American education in the 1950s. Although "progressive" and "new" educational philosophies, especially those associated with John Dewey, were not obsolete in the fifties and sixties, they no longer held center stage. Technology continued to advance and helped once again to solidify traditional pedagogies. Russia's launching of Sputnik in 1957 pushed the United States fully into the technological race. America was now in a rush to catch up. As often happens, the fastest results occurred, on a surface level, through the cram and memorization that comes through the traditional teaching model. As the nation progressed as a leader in technology, education did reap some benefits. Yet, there were negative outcomes from this technological growth as well. Teaching practices literally became more automated and mechanical, encouraging the student passivity displayed in *Dead Poets Society*.

William Van Til, the Chair of the Department of Secondary Education at New York University during the early 1960s, noted that the ideas that had occupied John Dewey were no longer widely spoken about, and teaching practices seemed to revert to a traditional view of the student as a vessel to be filled with knowledge. This time, however, the traditional approach had a new technological twist: it was "engrossed with the application of technology to education, by means of educational television, language laboratories, courses on film, and programmed learning through teaching machines" (Van Til 1960, 67). "Programmed learning" had become a part of some American classrooms, promoting again a mechanical view of teaching and learning. This general mechanical approach to teaching was not without influence in writing instruction as well. As Berlin (1987) points out, the space age sent colleges into the business of becoming "training centers for the new specialists in business and government" (120). This resulted in universities that focused on research, ultimately harming the teaching of writing because of its place in the undergraduate curriculum (120).

Jonathan Kozol's book *Death at an Early Age* (1967) is a real-life counterpart to the fictional *Dead Poets*. Written about his experiences teaching in Boston during the 1964–65 academic school year, this narrative account unmasks the conservative educational system in action. The climax of Kozol's story is his firing from the school, one week before the end of classes, for reading a Langston Hughes poem to his students. Kozol's reading of Hughes was reason for dismissal because the poem reflects pain and suffering of blacks, but also it was "punishable because it was not in the Course of Study" (197). As told to Kozol, curriculum innovation would not be tolerated: "No literature, [the Principal] said, which is not in the Course of Study can *ever* be read by a Boston teacher without permission from someone higher up" (197). Kozol's experience was not an isolated case that could only have taken place in the Boston Public Schools. Herbert Kohl's *36 Children* (1967) and James Herndon's *The Way it Spozed to Be* (1968) further reveal the conservative stranglehold on education during the fifties and early sixties.

Writing instruction reflected this general educational conservatism. In the fifties, "current-traditional" rhetoric was in vogue, and by the 1960s most writing classes still focused on mechanical skill and "correct" style; any emphasis on process and the student's role in expression was rare. Writing was not seen as generative or as an act of discovering meaning. When students wrote they did not focus on invention or ideas but rather were taught to focus on the product and to practice writing in certain models or modes. Practitioners of current-traditional rhetorics did not concern themselves, at least on any large scale, with voice, passivity, imaginative thinking, or breaking away from conformity.

The pedagogies that we have come to call "romantic" or "expressivist" were, however, concerned with voice, imaginative thinking, and breaking from the conformity of the more traditional educational doctrines, however. As inheritors of romantic pedagogies, expressivist theorists began publishing extensively in reaction to the traditional approaches to education and their counterparts within writing instruction.

But the changes in education as a whole and writing instruction in the sixties were not solely supported by a few academics. There were also changes taking place at the larger societal level. By the mid-1960s America had changed drastically. We were embroiled in the Vietnam War, the fight for civil rights, and the beginnings of the modern feminist movement. The family was no longer sanctified as it had been in the previous decades. Many daughters and sons waged war against their parents over issues surrounding the length of hair, clothing, sexual activity, rock and roll, and the war.

Social upheaval was everywhere and many counter-cultures flourished. Peace marches, love-ins, the burning of draft cards, and the startling activities of Abbie Hoffman and the Chicago Seven happened simultaneously. College campuses were riotous. Students burned ROTC buildings, took over administrative offices, and demanded to play a role in university policy making. Four students died by National Guard rifle fire at Kent State. This decade of unrest could not go unnoticed by university faculty. Wayne Booth (1974), for instance, motivated by protesters at his college, put together several lectures about rhetoric now collected in his book *Modern Dogma and the Rhetoric of Assent*, and Donald Murray published "Finding Your Own Voice: Teaching Composition in an Age of Dissent" (1969). The traditional approaches to writing instruction began to waver as exemplified by Murray's and others' support of students channeling their yearnings for social change into the most powerful of all agents of change—the written word.

Illustrative of changes to come for writing instruction was D. Gordon Rohman's study (1965) on "prewriting," which refocused composition instruction from mechanics, style, and product to invention and process. The 1960s also saw Donald Murray and Peter Elbow begin talking about voice and self-discovery as necessary means to sound rhetorical communication. Ann Berthoff demanded that we "reclaim the Imagination" (1984) for the classroom and the teaching of writing. The 1966 conference at Dartmouth College on the teaching of English brought writing specialists from both sides of the Atlantic together. British expressivists such as James Britton joined American teachers in emphasizing self-expression and an active rather than passive model for the teaching and learning of writing.

The Romantic Past

If we shift to the romantic past, the historical parallels between expressivists and romantics are clear regarding the larger issues of education. Wordsworth and Coleridge reacted much like the fictional Keating and the current expressivists to the educational practices of their own day. Most educators of the time continued to uphold the longstanding belief that knowledge is best gained through the analytical study of books, mechanical exercises, and rote memorization. The educational policies they followed made learning a chore, something to dread. As James Fotheringham (1899) explains in his book on Wordsworth's *The Prelude* as a study of education, "the older educationists had made everything, or most things, hard, distasteful. They even seemed to act on the principle that the educational value of things in a course of training turned on their hardness, their unpleasantness" (35). There was simply no tolerance for those facets of education that Wordsworth and Coleridge spent much of their lifetime arguing for, as we shall see. Instead, the curriculum in English schools was strictly based on classical literature and languages and consisted of memorizing passages of literature. A student in the fifth or sixth form, for instance, would spend a great deal of time memorizing passages from Homer, Virgil, and Horace. What time was not spent on memorizing and reciting was spent writing Latin verses and composing "themes" in Latin.[1]

The theory underlying the instructional practices of reading and recitation garnered further support from the psychological theory of associationism put forth by Locke and Hartley. This view saw the mind as a kind of machine "in which were associated atomic particles of meaning" (Wardle 1976, 82) and worked on the assumption that if the simplest possible "elements" were stored in the mind, the teacher could impart his subject material in such a way that elements were associated together in useful connections. If one element were recalled, the others would be drawn from the mind one after another.

This approach to pedagogy was not completely without value. It relied on thorough preparation, and the material given was carefully analyzed. It also took into account the importance of experience and a developmental approach to learning. On the negative side, however, it represented much that Wordsworth and Coleridge found at fault in educational practices. Pupils, for example, became passive recipients of material given by the teachers. Most student participation was merely recapitulation and the student did not participate in any active search for meaning or knowledge.

Because of such practices, the early nineteenth century heard much discussion of education. Two popular educational systems of concern to Wordsworth and Coleridge that arose during this time are attributed to Andrew Bell and Joseph Lancaster. Although Bell and Lancaster were great rivals, their systems were quite similar, and the establishment of their respective systems spoke to problems that had arisen within the schools by the end of the eighteenth century. The masses were then entering the classrooms, and this changed the complexion of British schooling. Overcrowding was a continual problem that led to other difficulties such as meeting the needs of individual students, vast differences in students' literacy abilities, and disciplinary problems. Fundamental to both Bell and Lancaster was the reliance on a monitorial system because the schools were so overcrowded that a teacher could not handle all the students. They instituted two of the first monitorial systems in which a certain number of older pupils acted as tutors and much of the instruction was undertaken by them.

Despite many similarities, Bell and Lancaster differed greatly in their approaches to punishment. Bell left punishment up to the judgment of a student's peers (except in extreme cases) and preferred to focus on positive reinforcement. Lancaster, to the contrary, focused on severe punishments. Like the Headmaster in *Dead Poets Society*, he felt that force and discipline constructed an education. The Headmaster's punishments were quite severe (beatings with a paddle), but they seem tame next to Lancaster's. His disciplinary tactics included hanging six-pound logs about the necks of offenders; shackling their legs with pieces of wood; tying frequent offenders together by pieces of wood fastened around their necks; forcing them to walk backwards; and hanging pupils in a sack suspended from the roof for the amusement of other students.

It was the issue of punishment that most drew Wordsworth and Coleridge's ardent support of Bell, and Coleridge's continual rebuttals of Lancaster. Coleridge was publicly vociferous in his aspersions against Lancaster and his praise for Bell. In his Lecture on the

New System of Education at Bristol in 1813, he condemned Lancaster for mishandling discipline. Both Coleridge and Wordsworth understood that children need to play and that play time need not be isolated from learning. Coleridge dealt with other aspects of education in the lecture, but emphasized, in contrast to Lancaster, the need to teach children through love rather than fear and humiliation. Bell's system attracted Coleridge because the practice of the monitorial system was "a dynamic principle" that would arouse the "whole individual" into activity (Coleridge [1811] 1983, 60). This notion of a "whole individual" being coaxed into activity becomes crucial to later romantic pedagogies and rhetorics as set forth by the likes of Emerson, Dewey, and Fred Newton Scott.

The educational philosophies of Jean-Jacques Rousseau were also being tested in various forms. Perhaps Rousseau's greatest contribution, from an expressivist's position, was the first widespread consideration that human growth and education occur in developmental stages; he demanded that the child be valued as a child, not as a diminutive adult. Also, he disagreed strongly with the prevailing assumption that, because of Original Sin, children were predisposed toward evil—if left to their own, as the prevailing theory had it, children would simply fall the way of crime (Coveny 1967, 42). It had been the part of education to redeem these children, usually through strict discipline; thus, the well-practiced proverb "spare the rod and spoil the child." Rousseau viewed the child not as a passive receptor of external experience, but as an active soul, virtuous from birth (Coveny 1967, 42). This active soul and virtuous self, according to Rousseau, needed careful development and slow nurturing towards the demands of social existence.

While Coleridge's thoughts on education are scattered throughout his notebooks, lectures, letters, and marginalia, Wordsworth's are nicely drawn together in *The Prelude*. An account of the development of the poet's own philosophical and poetic mind, *The Prelude* is, among other things, a treatise on education. In fact, in its original design it was conceived as a work explicitly about education (Chandler 1984, 95), and we can find in it Wordsworth's statement of a plan for national education of the masses.

The Prelude follows the course of the poet's life, selecting the events and experiences that had significant influence in shaping his mind, personality, moral beliefs, and intellectual powers. In its completed form, the poem stands as an examination and condemnation of Wordsworth's notion of a misguided schooling. *The Prelude* includes not only a denunciation of the state's negligent and inept educational practices, but also of the many home education systems that had arisen in attempts to replace the formal systems both Wordsworth and Coleridge found so offensive.

Wordsworth was not specifically a follower of Rousseau, and there is little evidence that he seriously studied Rousseau's theories (Fotheringham 1899, 53). Yet, it is difficult to read *The Prelude* as a treatise on education without recognizing that Rousseau had helped set the stage for those educational philosophies that John M. Willinsky (1987) has identified as revolutionary and still highly influential to today's educational issues. Like Rousseau, Wordsworth spoke out against forcing children into premature adulthood; he believed the child should experience childhood and a slow and natural growth into the adult world. He also denounced the belief that children were evil, believing instead in their natural goodness and innocence. Like Rousseau, he recognized the importance of childhood, and respected it as necessary for proper psychological and educational growth.

In essence, Wordsworth and Coleridge argue that to reach a higher form of intellect—what I call the encompassing intellect and Wordsworth the philosophical mind—children must not be denied their childhood; they must exercise the imaginative and creative imagination in *conjunction* with a more traditional approach of mechanical exercise, memorization, and analytical reasoning. It is this inclination to favor only the analytical that sparked many of the more Wordsworthian and Coleridgean aspects of later educators such as Mill, Arnold, Dewey, and in our own time, Elbow, Murray, and Berthoff.

Charles Dickens' *Hard Times* ([1854] 1987), though written much later in the century, serves to help illuminate the kind of schooling Wordsworth and Coleridge were reacting against. This schooling Dickens laments is not unlike that which the fictional Keating battles in *Dead Poets Society*. And like the movie, *Hard Times* paints a satirical and fictional portrait of that "hard and distasteful" education, which is nonetheless based in reality:

> Now what I want is Facts. Teach these boys and girls nothing but Facts. Facts alone are wanted in life. Plant nothing else, and root out everything else . . .". The speaker, and the schoolmaster, and the third grown person present, all backed a little, and swept with their eyes the inclined plane of little vessels then and there arranged in order . . . Mr. Gradgrind . . . seemed a galvanizing apparatus; . . . charged with a grim, mechanical substitute for the tender young imaginations that were to be stormed away. . . . (47–48)

Dickens' language, "inclined plane," "vessels," "galvanizing apparatus," underscores the lifeless, mechanistic, noncreative, passive, and non-imaginative education that takes place in Mr. Gradgrind's school. This educational system "storms" the imagination away, so that when Gradgrind demands of young Bitzer, "Your definition of a horse," (50) the young student's answer is cold, calculated fact. He sees the horse in its parts, but not as a whole: "'Quadruped. Graminivorous. Forty teeth, namely twenty-four grinders, four eye-teeth, and twelve incisive. Sheds coat in the spring; in marshy countries sheds hoofs, too. Hoofs hard, but requiring to be shod with iron. Age known by marks in mouth.' Thus (and much more) Bitzer" (50).

Dickens' fictional account of these miseducated students is similar to that of real students that Wordsworth portrays in *The Prelude* and strikingly close to the fictional students in *Dead Poets Society*. The result of the commonplace schooling is a child "Full early trained to worship seemliness (50)." Like Bitzer in *Hard Times*, this student mimics the attitudes and inclinations of adults, thereby becoming the "diminutive adult" which Rousseau condemned as inappropriate and harmful. Wordsworth's wrongly educated student of *The Prelude* is lacking anything emotive, is purely rational and can "read" his way through all the subjects:

> . . . he can read
> The insides of the earth, and spell the stars;
> He knows the policies of foreign lands;
> Can string you names of districts, cities, towns,
> the whole world over, tight as beads of dew
> Upon a gossamer thread; he sifts, he weighs;
> All things are put to question[.] (V. 317–323)[2]

While this is clearly Wordsworth's view of a typical student of his day, it could as easily be a portrait of our current-day students who are taught to succeed on multiple-choice examinations and standardized tests yet show a startling inability to write, read, and think with any insight or perspective of their own. The problem for students "trained" in this manner, according to a Wordsworthian educational scheme, is that their intellectual abilities rely solely on memorization, analysis, and recapitulation (Waldo 1982, 52). In other words, if the child is kept from knowing what "Nature teaches" and is confined to a curriculum that excludes creative and imaginative life experiences, including those beyond the schoolroom walls, then school becomes a prison and the student a prisoner assigned to death row. As Wordsworth writes in *The Prelude*:

> In lieu of wandering, as we did, through vales
> Rich with indigenous produce, open ground
> Of fancy, happy pastures ranged at will,

> We had been followed, hourly watched, and noosed,
> Each in his several melancholy walk
> Stringed like a poor man's heifer at its feed,
> Led through the lanes in forlorn servitude;
> Or rather like a stalled ox debarred
> From touch of growing grass, that may not taste
> A flower till it have yielded up its sweets
> A prelibation to the mower's scythe. (V. 235–245)

In these lines, Wordsworth accuses the educational philosophy of his day of having made students passive, ineffective, and unable to reach their potential as philosophical beings. Foreshadowing Mill, Dewey, and current expressivist composition theorists, a Wordsworthian educational theory suggests that the potential for the intellect, or philosophical mind, will remain unfulfilled if the student only learns through books and rote exercises, and if the imagination is not nurtured through experience, perception, and interaction with nature. The student of the passage above is deficient. He may know geography, politics, and science, but because he has merely absorbed information, he lacks imagination, the essential element for a fully developed intellect; like Dickens' Bitzer he can analyze that information but cannot synthesize it, since synthesis requires an active imagination. The closing books (XII and XIII) of *The Prelude* strongly emphasize that the method in knowledge and education should be constructive and synthetic, not analytic. Only if education nurtures the child and an active mind will students reach what the romantics believed to be the most encompassing intellect.

Things had not changed much by the middle and later part of the century. America, too, seemed plagued with similar educational problems. British and American philosophers concerned with educational problems—people like Mill, Arnold, James, Dewey, and Whitehead—set forth their educational philosophies in reaction to social and historical circumstances akin to those which spurred the romantic poets toward the reactions and general tenets I have pointed to. For instance, Victorians like Mill and Arnold were still responding to, and in some cases reacting against, an establishment characterized by unenlightened schools, a bureaucratic government, churches that seemed aloof from many concerns of common life, and an industrial system that exploited its workers—including women and children—and that imposed a drab materialism on daily life (see Walker and Munn, for example). As the nineteenth century wore on, those concerns that set romantic philosophies in motion reached an even higher pitch. There was little or no change in national schooling, the government was slow to act even though social changes demanded quick political reform, and industrialization reached its peak.

Mill, Arnold, and Alternatives to Traditional Education

Both Mill and Arnold were deeply concerned with the state of the government, the problems that arose with industrialization, and the educational system. To bring these two Victorians into my history begins the stretching of categorical delineations that I mentioned earlier. They both seem antithetical to an expressivist tradition at first glance. Mill, of course, bears the stamp of utilitarianism, which aimed to test the usefulness of institutions in light of reason and common sense. Yet, he learned from his nervous breakdown and from Wordsworth and Coleridge that reason is not the be-all and end-all.

Wordsworth and Coleridge played a major role in shaping Mill's educational philosophies. Mill was a voracious reader; he read Wordsworth, as he tells us in a celebrated passage of his *Autobiography* [1863] (1969), and he was intimate with Coleridge's works, including the *Biographia Literaria*. In a letter to John Pringle Nichol dated April 15, 1834, Mill [1834] (1967) wrote that "Few persons have exercised more influence over my thoughts and character than Coleridge has . . ." (304). Although John Stuart Mill probably did not read Wordsworth's *The Prelude* when it was finally published in 1850 (Mill 1969, ix), he did read Wordsworth's other poems and the Preface to the *Lyrical Ballads*, which are also about education, at least in the broad sense of the cultivation of the imaginative mind.

Mill had several specific connections with Wordsworth. He first acquainted himself with Wordsworth's poetry in 1828 while in the throes of a severe mental depression and breakdown. According to Mill, it was Wordsworth's poetry that first alerted him to the fact that the educational path his father, James Mill, had led him down had neglected the feelings. Later, in 1829, Mill defended Wordsworth's worth as a poet in a debate. In 1833 he wrote a literary essay lauding not only Wordsworth's poems, but the poet's ability to cultivate emotion and feeling in his readers. In 1831 Mill met Wordsworth and considered this meeting one of the highlights of his life.

There are striking resemblances between Wordsworth's autobiographical poem and Mill's *Autobiography*. Although nearly every essay written by Mill talks about education in some capacity, like Wordsworth's *The Prelude*, Mill's *Autobiography* speaks in depth about education and the role of the imagination in the growth of the philosophic mind.

It is in the *Autobiography* that we learn of the specific shape Mill's childhood education took. Educated under the sole tutelage of his father, his days were spent studying "what are considered the higher branches of education" (19). By the age of eight, Mill was reading Herodotus, the *Memorials* of Socrates, and Diogenes Laertius in the original Greek. He began Latin at seven, logic at twelve, and introductions to political economy by age thirteen. The educational experimentation James Mill conducted on his son has many of the attributes the romantics found detrimental to the education of the young. In an earlier draft of the *Autobiography*, Mill revealed that his education was forced through fear rather than educed through love: "It was one of the most unfavourable of the moral agencies which acted on me in my boyhood, that mine was not an education of love but of fear" (Mill [1863], 1969, 66). In the later version of the text he recalls that his father was "often, and much beyond reason, provoked by my failures in cases where success could not have been expected" (19). While Mill's father might not have suspended logs about his son's neck as Lancaster did his students, he nonetheless governed his son's education through fear and intimidation.

Both Wordsworth and Coleridge bristled at the custom of using fear as a catalyst to learning. Coleridge was especially vocal on this issue, and Lancaster's tendency to discipline students with inhumane punishments provoked Coleridge's fiery ire. In his *Lecture on the New System of Education* (Coleridge [1813] 1967–71), he condemned Lancaster and his extreme punishments intended to infuse fear. In *Lecture on Shakespeare XI*, Coleridge argues that education is an active process that begins with love, and that from the seed of love obedience will naturally arise. When students "obey," or are not disruptive out of their own desire for active engagement with class work, a community is constructed where learning can move forward rather than being continually stymied by the teacher's need to discipline. Mill's formative years of education had been structured for the sole purpose of building an analytic intellect. His education failed to create feelings in "sufficient strength to resist the dissolving influence of analysis," while the whole course of his "intellectual cultivation had made precocious and premature analyses the inveterate habit of [his] mind" (Mill [1873] 1969, 84).

The structure of this analytical education relied solely on rote memorization and "cram." Just as Wordsworth and Coleridge had before him, Mill decried this kind of pedagogy. In "On Genius," for instance, [1834] (1967) Mill bemoans the widespread tendency to teach this way: "Modern education is all *cram*—Latin cram, mathematical cram, literary cram, political cram, theological cram, moral cram. The world already knows everything, and has only to tell it to its children, who, on their part, have only to hear, and lay it to rote (not to *heart*)" (44).

Although in this essay Mill advocated an education similar to that of the ancient Romans and Greeks, it is on the grounds that education at that time consisted "not in giving what is called knowledge, that is, grinding down other men's ideas to a convenient size, and administering them in the form of *cram*," but on "a series of exercises to form the thinking faculty itself, that the mind, being active and vigourous, might go forth and know" (40).

In Mill's mind, an education of cram and memorization led to students who could do no more than parrot back the facts force-fed them by instructors. Mill argued that rote memorization resulted in pupils unable to form an opinion of their own. In "On Genius," Mill wrote: "At school, what is the child taught, except to repeat by rote, or at most to apply technical rules, which are lodged, not in his reason, but in his memory? When he leaves school, does not everything conspire to tell him, that it is not expected he shall think, but only that he shall profess no opinion on any subject different than that professed by other people?" (43).

Like Coleridge and Wordsworth, and the fictional John Keating, Mill knew that the more positive educational experience for students is "not to be indoctrinated, is not to be taught other people's opinions, but to be induced and enabled to think for themselves" (304).

In the *Autobiography*, Mill stresses even further the problems that arise in an education of cram:

> Most boys or youths who have had much knowledge drilled into them, have their mental capacities not strengthened, but overlaid by it. They are crammed with mere facts, and with the opinions or phrases of other people, and these are accepted as a substitute for the power to form opinions of their own. And thus, the sons of eminent fathers, who have spared not pains in their education, so often grow up mere parroters of what they have learnt, incapable of using their minds except in the furrows traced for them. (20)

This is clearly the educational path Neal walked before Keating entered his life in *Dead Poets Society*. We might also think this passage a perfectly drawn portrait of Mill and his education, since, after all, he was educated to carry devoutly on the ideas of his father and Bentham. Mill did so without much reflection until after his breakdown and return to health. Throughout his writings Mill comments that he had not a creative mind or genius like his father and Bentham, but that he had a mind trained only for analysis.

Matthew Arnold also shared a deep concern for teaching and the state of education with Wordsworth, Coleridge, and Mill. Wordsworth was particularly influential on his thought. He cited Wordsworth as one of four leading influences on his thought and life, and he refers often to Wordsworth in his letters, notebooks, and essays, and celebrates Wordsworth in a laudatory essay. Wordsworth was also a close friend of Arnold's father and the older poet spent a fair amount of time with the Arnolds.[3]

Social theorists will not miss that Arnold upheld "high culture." His vision for education was one expressly for a special class of elite men. Ian Hunter recognizes Arnold as a carrier of romantic pedagogical ideas as his argument in *Culture and Government* (1988) makes clear. He suggests that the romantic tradition, as it relates to the teaching of literature at any rate, is riddled with problems. Hunter argues that

> Despite some recent claims concerning the ideological function of criticism, Arnold at no point advocated that it be deployed in the popular school (recitation and paraphrase were as far as he went in this regard) or that it be used in the training of teachers. And we shall see that despite Arnold's own axiom that "culture seeks to do away with classes," criticism for Arnold was in fact that which qualified him for membership of a special purpose-built class . . . In other words, romantic criticism and culture possessed no intrinsic generality or democratic drive that operationalized them at the level of the population or realised them in "society" through the teaching of English in schools. (5)

Romantic ideology as we see it here is clearly gendered and classist. This romantic legacy may be one reason why feminists find comfort in the social-constructivists' conscious attempt to bring pedagogy into the realm of the "mass writer" as opposed to the "class writer" of Arnold's high culture.

I am not convinced, however, that the romantic "literary" pedagogy Hunter speaks of has been enacted in most expressivist theories and pedagogies. Clearly I find expressivist approaches more democratic than has been previously understood by anti-expressivists. In the history of current expressivism itself, Murray's resistance to turning the writing classroom into a literary criticism classroom where students read literature and write literary interpretations in an attempt to join "high culture" is a conscious step toward addressing this specific problem. The expressivist agenda has not been to train an elite class of students for a particular caste, nor has it been to train and prepare a disadvantaged class to move upward into an elite class. In fact, to my way of thinking, this charge more accurately fits proponents of academic literacies who see our job as preparing students to enter into the special caste of the academic elite through a "mastery" of academic language.

Arnold's tenure as School Inspector began in 1851, and, although he did not really want the appointment, he went on to make it his life's work. His observation of educational systems included not only English schools, but those on the continent as well. In 1865 the Schools Enquiry Commissioners assigned him the duty of investigating the educational system for the middle and upper classes in France, Germany, Italy, and Switzerland. Like Wordsworth, Arnold held great interest in a national education, and his time as School Inspector resulted in many arguments for the changes he saw as necessary to ensure a system of education that was workable for the English masses.

As Arnold toured the schools of the continent and Britain, he saw still in place many of the problems that moved Wordsworth and Coleridge to take a stand on the state of national education in England. Like Coleridge, he railed heartily against an educational system that tried to force knowledge of a factual kind into the minds of children at too early an age.[4] In his report on the French schools, Arnold praised the French system for recognizing the intellectual limitations of children by not pushing competitive examinations upon the pupils, and he condemned the English system for its misuse of exams. The English school system's insensitivity to the intellectual limitations of young minds, in Arnold's view, had the same effect that Mill objected to in what he calls the "education of cram" (Arnold 1964). Inappropriate testing had damaging results:

> The French have plenty of examinations; but they put them almost entirely at the right age for examinations ... To put to little boys of nine or ten the pressure of a competitive examination ... is to offer a premium for the violation of nature's elementary laws, and to sacrifice, as in the poor geese fatted for Strasbourg pies, the due development of all organs of life to the premature hypertrophy of one. (92)

This premature "hypertrophy" means that the students will never reach a higher intellect capable of judgment, comparison, and synthesis.

When Arnold speaks harshly of examinations he is not condemning them entirely. In fact, his observations of German schools, where exams were completely dismissed, convinced him that examinations can be useful. His negative criticism of the examinations given in the English schools is that of Coleridge and Wordsworth before him— they are used to the wrong ends. In his Reports on Elementary Schools, Arnold (1964) points out that exams do not necessarily test any real knowledge that students might or might not have.

He recalls children getting through the Revised Code examinations in "reading, writing, and ciphering, without really knowing how to read and cipher":

> To take the commonest instance: a book is of a certain standard; all
> the year the children read this book over and over again, and no
> other. When the Inspector comes they are presented to read in this
> book; they can read their sentence or two fluently enough, but they
> cannot read any other book fluently. . . the circle of the children's
> reading has thus been narrowed and impoverished all the year for
> the sake of a result at the end of it, and the *result* is an illusion.
> (219–220)

In other words, knowledge for knowledge's sake was sacrificed to a
system that requested the memorization of a few facts and techniques coughed up upon request. Learning, in effect, had come to a
standstill.

Arnold (1964), through his firsthand observations of the English
schools, records further damage done by a system that merely pro-
pels children through it while relying too heavily on examinations
and not enough on natural growth.

> Nervous exhaustion at fifteen is the price which many a clever boy
> pays for over-stimulation at ten; and the nervous exhaustion of a
> number of our clever boys tends to create a broad reign of intellec-
> tual deadness in the mass of youths from fifteen to twenty, who
> the clever boys, had they been rightly developed and not unnatu-
> rally forced, ought to have leavened. (92–93)

Arnold's concern with an "unnatural" intellectual growth recalls
Coleridge's [1813] (1969–71) belief that education should be an act of
educing, of calling forth; "as the blossom is educed from the bud, the
vital excellencies are within; the acorn is but educed or brought forth
from the bud" (Vol. 5, 585). Arnold's argument is also reminiscent of
arguments made by Wordsworth in *The Prelude*, published the year
before Arnold began his tour as Inspector. In a well-known passage
from Book V of *The Prelude*, Wordsworth celebrates the escape his
Hawkshead experience allowed from such an education:

> . . . yet I rejoice,
> And, by these thoughts admonished, will pour out
> Thanks with uplifted heart, that I was reared
> Safe from an evil which these days have laid
> Upon the children of the land, a pest,
> That might have dried me up, body and soul.
> (*The Prelude* [1850] 224–229)

Arnold recognizes, in the "nervous exhaustion" of students, Mill's
education of "cram" and the same debilitating educational system
that Wordsworth luckily escaped. He felt that the British examinations not only did not test any significant knowledge, but, worse,

that they resulted in "intellectual deadness." If wrongly and untimely administered, examinations obscure the "true aim" of schools: "to develop our mind and to give us access to vital knowledge" (Arnold 1964, 299).

Education by Rote in the U. S.

John Dewey, a key figure in expressivism's past, faced historical circumstances in America that were counterparts of those the romantics, Mill, and Arnold faced earlier in the century in England. Between the years 1865 and 1918, America developed from a primarily agricultural country to a modern industrialized nation. This rapid expansion of industrialization resulted in many of the same atrocities that drew the attention of outspoken British poets, historians, and philosophers like Blake, Wordsworth, Coleridge, Shelley, Mill, and Arnold. Like workers earlier in England, Americans suffered the same exploitation and abuse that characterized the industrial policies of nineteenth-century England (see Link and McCormick).

By the time Dewey was formulating his philosophies for education, America had become less agricultural, more industrial, and a budding world power. The rapid change in America, as in England, was not without its consequences for education. Schools often reflected the ideology of American capitalism by pushing for an education of efficiency, production, and discipline in order to produce a work force that could continue to fuel America's prospering industry. A systematic coverage of various subjects and a mastery of facts, concepts, and principles acquired through drill had become the established and institutionalized norm. As Dewey's philosophical stance grew to include ideas from pragmatism, progressive education, empirical and objective psychology, and democracy, he offered an alternative to the established system of schooling.

Dewey shares a distaste for traditional pedagogies with his predecessors. He also finds an understanding of imaginative processes necessary and important to classroom instruction, reinforcing Coleridge and Wordsworth's, as well as Mill and Arnold's, insistence on the importance of the creative imagination within the educational arena. Dewey, too, took issue with pedagogies that curtailed students' abilities to think and that failed to nurture voice and student interest. Without doubt, Dewey would much have preferred John Keating's classroom to the traditional one that the Headmaster in *Dead Poets Society* tried so firmly to enforce.

Dewey ([1940] 1969) argues against a method of education that saw the mind of the student, in a metaphor that Coleridge might particularly have liked, as a "phonographic disc upon which certain impressions were made by the teacher, so when the disc was put on the machine and the movement started . . . it might reveal what was described upon it" (242). In antithesis to this traditional schooling, Dewey argued for a child-centered curriculum and progressive schools. In arguing for his progressive schools, Dewey (1964) writes that they "exhibit as compared to traditional schools a common emphasis upon respect for individuality and for increased freedom; a common disposition to build upon the nature and experience of the boys and girls that come to them, instead of imposing from without external subject-matter and standards . . . Emphasis upon activity as distinct from passivity is one of the common factors" (170).

This passage advances three of the basic elements crucial to an educational theory grounded in romantic philosophy: the importance of the individual; the importance of personal experience; and an emphasis on activity as opposed to passivity.

Dewey's ideas for progressive schools did not include eight hours of sitting passively at desks memorizing facts. Just as Wordsworth suggests it is "murder to dissect," Dewey rejects the analytical approach to learning about a subject like botany, wherein students are "pulling these flowers to pieces and giving technical names to the different parts" without an understanding of the plant as a whole. And to understand it as an integral whole, the student must see the plant as it is in nature, must see its relation to, and interaction with, the soil, water, sun, and air. Dewey fights student passivity and a pedagogy of cram and rote drill in order to put a stop to the molding of students like Dickens' Bitzer in *Hard Times*.

We can see, then, the ways in which Wordsworth and Coleridge, and philosophers as divergent as Mill, Arnold, and Dewey are the intellectual ancestors of current expressivists. Strong reactions (calls for change, imaginative thinking, an understanding of emotive processes in learning, and personal experience) against a mechanistic and dehumanized general education system link them in thought and practice.

Notes

1. Occasionally, a school would allow other subjects to creep into the curriculum, and geography and algebra might be taught.

2. Citations from *The Prelude* will be the 1850 edition unless otherwise noted.

3. At one time Wordsworth even helped the young Arnold study for an examination. (Gottfried 1963, 6)

4. Coleridge argued that the growth of the intellect takes place in progression, that the child begins with a capability limited to appreciating only "A, and B, and C; but not ABC=X" (Coburn 1979, 204).

Chapter Three

The Imagination for the Classroom

One of the best-known facets of romanticism is the emphasis placed on the imagination. This major component of romantic thought resurfaces throughout the intervening years between Wordsworth and Coleridge and current expressivists. The imagination becomes, in fact, one of the crucial historical ties between romanticism and expressivism. The romantics, educational philosophers who have lobbied for the imagination in learning and classroom practice, and expressivist compositionists, share a common belief that the development of a mind that synthesizes as well as analyzes requires a certain kind of schooling. It must rely foremost on the nurturing of the creative imagination.

For expressivists, the schooling of the imagination is a part of their overall theoretical perspective. To Ann Berthoff especially, the imagination is crucial to a sound pedagogy or theory of rhetoric. She often makes her ties to the romantics forthright by calling on Coleridge. He is, according to Berthoff (1981), "our best guide in developing a philosophy of rhetoric" because he has, in her view, created a plausible and useful theory of the imagination which is pertinent to the teaching of writing in the broadest sense (64).[1] Berthoff argues for the "reclaiming of the imagination" because positivists have relegated it to what they call the "affective domain." Berthoff understands, however, that, in its complexity, the romantic imagination does not pertain solely to emotion and feelings as opposed to thought.

Like Coleridge, she sees the imagination as a way of knowing and making meaning. Its domain includes both thought and feeling. The imagination, in Berthoff's scheme, is synonymous with the "active mind." It is akin to Arnold's "vital knowledge" and Mill's "vigourous" mind. She defines and redefines the imagination, throughout her various works, in Coleridge's language: it is "the shaping spirit"; it is a "doer, an agent"; it is the "form-finding form-creating power"; it is, she says, as Coleridge wrote "in one of the most famous passages in the literature of criticism . . ., 'the living power and prime agent of all human perception'" (Berthoff 1981, 28).

The Development of the Imaginative Mind

Berthoff's forerunners, Wordsworth and Coleridge, both warn that without a curriculum that fosters the imagination, students are "manufactured" full of factual knowledge but can end up empty of any thoughts or ideas of their own; they are more apt to have passive minds. It is the imagination that provides for an educated and fully operational mind capable of embracing both the passive principles of analysis and the active principles of synthetic creativity. Wordsworth sees the imagination as a power that shapes and creates, not only by dissolving and separating unity into number, but also by "consolidating numbers into unity" (Wordsworth [1815] 1984, 754). It perceives through "wise passiveness" while at the same time imprinting itself on the world.

Coleridge also sees the imagination as integral to learning and the cultivation of a learned mind although he defines it somewhat differently. He speaks of two interlocking forms of the imagination, the primary imagination and the secondary imagination. The primary imagination is "all of perception" and is accessible to everyone. The secondary imagination is creative, and has the power to reconcile opposites: "it dissolves, diffuses, dissipates, in order to re-create . . . to idealize and to unify" (Coleridge [1811] 1983, 304). It is cultivated and put into action by conscious will, and works upon material received by the primary imagination. Again, what is important to this immediate discussion is the conjoining of two different operative principles—the principles both Wordsworth and Coleridge regard as necessary for the well-rounded and educated mind: the passive and the active.

In his desire to reconcile these opposites, Coleridge adopts the figure of the androgyne as a controlling image throughout his prose writings. He uses this image because it allows him to underscore metaphorically the importance of fusion between disparate faculties. In Coleridge's (1835) scheme a great mind reconciles the active and the passive, and thus is androgynous.

> I have known *strong* minds with imposing, undoubting, Cobbett-like manners, but I have never met a *great* mind of this sort. And of the former, they are at least as often wrong as right. The truth is, a great mind, must be androgynous. (51)

This "androgynous," or imaginative and synthetic, mind is similar to the mind that Paul Armstrong (1988) describes as inventing "new ways of fitting things together by recognizing and even creating new analogies, new patterns of similarity and difference" (31). The result of recognizing and creating these new patterns of similarity and difference is an ability to create new concepts—to form a point of view. In other words, the imagination is essential, along with reasoning and analytical powers, to the growth of a full intellect—a creative, synthesizing intellect.

A passage from the *Biographia Literaria* is helpful in illuminating Coleridge's desire to have both passive and active processes become an element in the educative mission of fostering encompassing intellects. Using the water spider as an example, Coleridge describes the imagination in terms of its two parts:

> Most of my readers will have observed a small water-insect on the surface of rivulets, which throws a cinque-spotted shadow fringed with prismatic colours on the sunny bottom of the brook; and will have noticed, how the little animal wins its way up against the stream, by alternate pulses of active and passive motion, now resisting the current, and now yielding to it in order to gather strength and a momentary *fulcrum* for further propulsion. This is no unapt emblem of the mind's self-experience in the act of thinking. There are evidently two powers at work, which relative to each other are active and passive; and this is not possible without an intermediate faculty, which is at once both active and passive. (In philosophical language, we must denominate this intermediate faculty in all its degrees and determinations, the IMAGINA-TION. . . .) (124)

Both Wordsworth and Coleridge felt that if schools neglect one of these powers—and traditionally the "active" has been disregarded—then the imaginative mind will not come to fruition.

Wordsworth's and Coleridge's theories of the imagination set older, more classical theories on their ears. Their ideas have been highly influential and long lasting in poetics. Their theories also are instrumental in education and composition as Ann Berthoff's invoking of Coleridge testifies. These romantic notions of the creative imagination influence much thought, both poetic and educational, of many who followed: Mill, Arnold, Emerson, Dewey, and I. A. Richards, for instance. In *The Mirror and the Lamp*, M. H. Abrams (1953) points out that Mill's essays on poetry define poet and poetry in terms almost identical to those of Wordsworth and Coleridge. Others have recognized that one of Mill's (1969) major aims was the same as that of the romantics: "the improvement of society through . . . the internal culture of the individual" (viii). Mill's thoughts on poetry and on the growth of individuals are pertinent to education as a whole. Moreover, his ideas are tangentially related to issues on the teaching of writing because what Mill says about poetics, poets, and growth reflects the need for a complexity of imaginative thought, feeling, and analysis that ultimately lead to good thinking and, thus, a chance for good writing.

The imaginative readings that Wordsworth believed an integral part of childhood growth and that Coleridge lamented having had taken from him were for the most part denied to the young Mill. In the *Biographia Literaria*, Coleridge talks at length about the importance of stoking the fires of the imagination with readings. Coleridge, as a young boy, read fairy tales and adventure stories. His father, however, found this unbecoming to his son and to the type of education he felt Samuel should have. As an adult Coleridge (1797) makes an argument for these readings as important in the shaping of the encompassing intellect:

> From my early reading of fairy tales and genii, etc., etc., my mind had been habituated to the Vast, and I never regarded my *senses* in any way as the criteria of my belief. I regulated all my creeds by my conceptions, not by my *sight*, even at that age. Should children be permitted to read romances, and relations of giants and magicians and genii? I know all that has been said against it; but I have formed my faith in the affirmative. I know of no other way of giving the mind a love of the Great and the Whole. (*Selected Letters*)

Like most children when left to their own imaginative pursuits, Coleridge entered into the world of play and fantasy where he would act out exciting adventures (Waldo 1982, 98). Coleridge's father, however, was tyrannical when it came to "correct" education and what he deemed such unmanly pursuits. As Coleridge writes in a letter to Poole (October 9, 1797), when he observed his son acting out readings in imaginative play, he burned the books (503).

Although Mill never claims that his father barred him from imaginative readings, James Mill neither gave his son books like *The Arabian Nights* nor created room for such reading in his curriculum. Mill recalls that the only times he had access to tales of fantasy and adventure were on the rare occasions that family friends would give him books like *Robinson Crusoe* or *The Arabian Nights*. As an adult, Mill lamented that the modern system of education had deleted the literature of chivalry and romance from the curriculum. In an essay of 1838, Mill ([1838] 1967) mourned that "for the first time perhaps in history, the youths of both sexes of the educated classes are universally growing up unromantic" (53). Mill lauded books that stimulate the imagination with heroic people, and keep alive the "chivalrous spirit."

Fostering Imagination in the Classroom

Arnold, too, felt keenly the lack of pedagogies that specifically engendered the imagination in students. He never gave up hope that schools would begin to favor more imaginative classroom work. He saw the role of the teacher as doing "as much towards opening their mind, and opening their souls and imaginations, as is possible to be done with a number of children of their age and in their state of preparation and home surroundings" (Arnold 1969, 238). As Mill described it, the teacher's role was to prepare students to "go forth and know."

Arnold, like Wordsworth and Coleridge, makes clear that the curriculum should advance this vital knowledge by "educing" active participation from students. He writes of elementary education that "a great deal of the work in elementary schools must necessarily be of a mechanical kind" (226). But, in order to counterbalance the mechanical aspects of the curriculum, Arnold argues for "creative activity to relieve the passive reception of knowledge" (226). He suggests that the exercises he finds in the kindergartens are useful for sparking creativity in the younger grades. He recommends drawing and singing, for instance, as valuable activities. Whereas Wordsworth, and Coleridge to a lesser extent, would claim a student's interaction with nature and reading a part of this counter-balance, they do not suggest specific classroom activities. Arnold, however, focuses more on the actual pedagogical techniques as his position of School Inspector requires of him. Thus Arnold speaks of drawing and singing in the early curriculum.

It is unfortunate that in American schools these "useful" means of firing up creativity rarely go beyond the kindergarten classroom. While we seem willing to tolerate noise, movement, and creativity from five-year-olds, we will have none of it from first graders and older students. I am, of course, generalizing, but it still remains that far too many schools expect students to sit quietly and passively at their desks. Talking "out of turn" is sometimes punished by forced writing on the board ("I will not talk in class"), by being kept in from recess (one of the few ways our students get the exposure to nature and play that Wordsworth finds crucial), or by being kept after school (making school itself the punishment). Often student outbursts are signs of enthusiasm, excitement, or even epiphany. It is natural, as human beings, for students to want to voice what has struck them, what they are thinking. To shut these natural responses down is to eventually stamp out any desire for learning or creativity. To use writing as punishment seems extremely counterproductive. Is it any wonder that our students often think of writing as a boring and negative activity?

I am not suggesting that there is never a time for reprimand or quiet. What I am suggesting is that teachers who tolerate an active classroom where excitement and a multiplicity of sometimes chaotic voices are allowed help to alleviate unwanted and inappropriate outbursts. To foster the active principles and nurture the imaginative mind that Coleridge and Arnold speak of, it is crucial to allow students the freedom to move occasionally about the classroom, talk with each other, and read aloud to each other. The work that Donald Graves and his colleagues at the University of New Hampshire have done suggests that allowing interaction among students promotes reading, writing, and thinking skills. Collaborative learning is proving to be a successful way for students to gain critical thinking and problem-solving skills (both of which require imaginative ability). This is successful at all grade levels, including college. Classroom activities like these "relieve the passive reception of knowledge," as Arnold puts it. They promote creativity and learning in more fruitful ways.

Arnold also suggests that, as the pupil advances through the years, reading, and particularly the reading of poetry, should be added to the curriculum as a creative activity. Maxine Greene, one of the most insightful educational philosophers writing today, agrees. She suggests, however, that not only students, but teachers as well, need to reacquaint themselves with poetry. What she finds in the voices of Wordsworth, Whitman, Blake, Emerson, and Stevens are passion and possibility. For teachers to hang on to passion and possibility is necessary in a world where we are in need of what Greene calls a "critical pedagogy." A limiting discourse that keeps us from envisioning alternatives to "unwarranted inequities, shattered communities, unfulfilled lives" constrains American education (Greene 1986, 427). "How," queries Greene, "are we to justify our concern for their [students' and teachers'] awakening? Where are the sources of questioning, of restlessness?" "How," she wonders, do we inspire the young "towards what might be, what is not yet?" (427). The answer lies in opening up that limiting discourse that surrounds education, through the power of possibility that poetry stirs within us and our students (see also Bogdan 1992).

Since poets move us to "give play to our imaginations" they awaken us to "reflectiveness, to a recovery of lost landscapes and lost spontaneities" (428). Like Arnold, Greene sees value in reading poetry because it stimulates creative activity. If teachers can find passion and possibility in poetry, we can be inspired to pass on this passion to our students through transformative pedagogies, as well as through poetry itself. Passionate herself, Greene argues that we need to "teach in such a way as to arouse passion now and then. . . . These are dark and shadowed times, and we need to live them, standing before one another, open to the world" (441). This path lies through our reclaimed and enlivened imaginations.

Arnold desires the same movement toward creativity, imagination, and the encompassing intellect as Wordsworth and Coleridge did, and as Maxine Greene and Ann Berthoff and other expressivists do now. Like them, Arnold believes this movement is achieved, at least in part, through literature, which, he argues, has a humanizing and moving effect. As he makes clear, Arnold [1860] (1969) was not against pupils reading, but against them reading "dry scientific" writings of an "inferior order" (215). He argues that, in the everyday subjects of the curriculum (reading, writing, grammar, geography, history, etc.), the teacher's design of instruction should be governed by the "aim of calling forth, by some means or other, in every pupil a sense of pleasurable activity and of creation; [the teacher and student] should resist being made a mere ladder with 'information'" (227). In the same report, Arnold insists that the teaching of poetry is a valuable and necessary part of the curriculum because it is the one thing that can ensure the stimulation of creative activity.

Arnold believed that, in a curriculum where memorization is the major instructive mode, the mind is dulled unless there is an exercise of "pleasurable" and "creative activity . . . quite different from the effort of learning a list of words to spell, or a list of flesh-making and heat-giving foods, or a list of capes and bays, or a list of reigns and battles, and capable of greatly relieving the strain from learning these and of affording a lively pleasure" (226). Although we need not agree with Arnold that poetry is the only or best way to make all—including the imaginative—"principles operative," his point is nonetheless important: that at least some of the mechanical exercises and lectures must be replaced with activities that open the mind and soul through "vital knowledge." In a report on the elementary schools, Arnold [1874] (1969) reminds his readers that "the animation of mind, the multiplying of ideas, the promptness to connect, in thoughts, one thing with another, are what are wanted" (221). This statement of Arnold's could easily be attributed to

Wordsworth or Coleridge, so close is it in thought and phrasing to many of their statements on learning and the imagination.

John Dewey's writings reveal his faith in the romantic version of the creative imagination as well. Dewey [1934] (1987) cites Coleridge on the "esemplastic Imagination" as a beginning point for his own definition of the imagination (272). Dewey notes that Coleridge's definition used "the vocabulary of his generation" that referred to the faculties and imagination as separate. Although he disagrees with Coleridge's "verbal mode" in this definition, Dewey agrees with Coleridge's meaning of the "imaginative experience" (272). Dewey sees the imagination as animating, feeling, and actively composing an "integral whole." It designates a quality that animates and pervades all processes of making and observation. It is a way of seeing and feeling things as they compose an integral whole. It is the large and generous blending of interests at the point where the mind comes in contact with the world. When the old and familiar things are made new in experience there is imagination (271).

Dewey's language echoes Coleridge's [1817] (1983) explanation of the primary and secondary imagination: we can pair Dewey's "animates," "pervades," "observation," and "blending of interest" to make "old" things "new" with Coleridge's creative imagination.

Likewise, Dewey foreshadows Ann Berthoff's "shaping spirit" and "form-finding form-creating power," while also recalling Wordsworth's Preface to the *Lyrical Ballads*.

Dewey's statement "when the old and familiar things are made new in experience there is imagination" is an apt understanding of Wordsworth's project in the *Lyrical Ballads* (Dingwaney and Needham [1815] 1989):

> The principal object, then, proposed in these Poems was to choose incidents and situations from common life, and to relate or describe them, throughout, as far as was possible in a selection of language really used by men, and, at the same time, to throw over them a certain colouring of imagination, whereby ordinary things should be presented to the mind in an unusual aspect [.] (734)

Wordsworth is reconstructing the familiar language of the "common man" so we can experience it anew; he has, in Dewey's terms, taken "old and familiar things" and made them "new in experience." By casting over the common language of the common man a "certain colouring of imagination," Wordsworth's mind has, as Dewey writes, "come in contact with the world" (271).

Dewey's earlier work, *Psychology* [1887] (1967), which he calls a book "expressly for use in class-room instruction," looks, by its table of contents, much like an argument for faculty psychology.

But, as he writes of perception, memory, imagination, thinking, intuition, feeling, and the will as interrelated processes, it begins to look more like a romantic manifesto. Here he distinguishes among the "Mechanical Imagination," "Fancy," and the "Creative Imagination." "The Mechanical Imagination," he says, "proceeds by the laws of association and dissociation," while the Fancy "throws itself about all things, and connects them together, through the medium of feeling . . . . It affords keen delight rather than serves as an organ of penetration" (Dewey [1887] 1967, 171).

Different still, according to Dewey, is the Creative Imagination. It does not work in isolation. It "makes its object new by setting it in a new light" (171). He argues that the Creative Imagination "separates and combines," and that these separations and combinations are "filled with a direct and spontaneous sense of the relative values of detail in reference to the whole" (171). Dewey's (1987) descriptions of the imaginative experience and the lesser powers of the Mechanical Imagination and the Fancy are essentially those of Wordsworth and of Coleridge. If we recall Wordsworth's discussion of spontaneity, of "separating unity into number" and "consolidating number into unity," as well as Coleridge's "dissolving" in order to "unify," we quickly see how romantic thought shapes Dewey's.

The Expressivist Approach to Learning

Expressivist rhetoricians are especially drawn to the ways in which the romantics fostered the thinking and creative abilities of students. They share with their historical forefathers a desire to cultivate the imagination in their writing students. Richard Young (1980), although he admits that we lack "the historical studies" that permit generalizing with confidence, notes that the expressivist position seems

> a reaffirmation of the vitalist philosophy of an old romanticism enriched by modern psychology. It maintains that the composing process is, or should be, relatively free of deliberate control; that intellect is no more in touch with reality than non-logical processes; and that the act of composing is a kind of mysterious growth fed by what Henry James called "the deep well of unconscious cerebration (1934, 23)." Above all, it insists on the primacy of the imagination in the composing process. (55)

Teachers such as D. Gordon Rohman, Donald Murray, Ann Berthoff, and Peter Elbow certainly do include "unconscious cerebration," "spontaneity," and "primacy of the imagination" as central to their theories and pedagogies.

In 1964, Albert Wlecke and D. Gordon Rohman published the results of a federally funded research project on prewriting that would firmly place expressivism as central in theoretical and pedagogical debates. They tested a pedagogical model in which students focused on the writing process rather than a product. The students practiced prewriting, journal writing, meditation, and analogies. As Rohman's article (1965) based on this research makes clear, this pedagogical approach stimulates discovery, spontaneity, originality, and last but not least, the creative imagination.

Prewriting for Rohman is tied to generative thought, a kind of thought he describes as "that activity of mind which *brings forth* and develops ideas, plans, designs, not merely the entrance of an idea into one's mind; an active, not a passive enlistment in the 'cause' of an idea" (106). Thus prewriting is a creative act, defined in terms kindred to the romantic imagination. In fact, in their study on prewriting, Rohman and his colleagues "sought ways for students to imitate the 'creative principle' itself which produces finished works" (107). Much like Arnold's call for non-mechanical exercises that will introduce "creative activity," the prewriting activities attempt to stimulate the imagination, the "dynamics of creation," so that good writing can occur.

At least in the eyes of the researchers, this study in prewriting did make a difference in student thinking and writing. However the definition of "good writing" is highly subjective and, for teachers of college composition, is highly contingent on their own pragmatic and theoretical perspectives. So, while someone like I might agree with Rohman's assessment because voice, individual perspective, creativity, and messy and complex thinking on paper are valuable signs of good writing to me, another teacher of different persuasion might view the results of Rohman's study as indicating clear failure. I base my position here, however, on my belief that writing should not be viewed merely as a set of rules and forms, nor taught as something that can be severed from an educational plan that fosters emotive and analytical processes, imaginative thinking, and whole human beings. The teaching of writing for expressivists is inexorably tied to this larger context.

According to Rohman, "good writing" itself is an imaginative act that closely resembles Coleridge's description of the creative imagination: "The meaning of writing is the meaning of the combination, the pattern that the meaning of the many words makes when fused by a writer's consciousness in the moment of 'discovery'"

(107). Good writing comes from shaping, through a combinatory act (secondary imagination), patterns determined in an experience (primary imagination), an experience discovered through prewriting. Worthwhile writing, says Rohman in a truly romantic fashion, is that discovered "combination of words" that allows for "fresh and original" insight.

To help students "imitate the creative principle itself," Rohman and his colleagues employed the keeping of journals, the practice of religious-like meditation, and the use of analogy as teaching techniques. The use of analogy, writes Rohman, enables us "to know anything in our present simply because we have known similar things in our past to which we compare the present. Each act of present 'knowing' associates the present with the past as another instance" (111). This associative or analogical "knowing" is a way of "rearranging and reassembling the focus of our experience" (111). Thus, this use of analogy is creative. Rohman further argues that analogy "provides practice with the concrete world of the five senses" (111). If the student writer participates in a "personally-experienced encounter with his subject freshly seen from the perspective of a new analogy," he has the stuff with which to make his subject fly. In other words, analogy can help the student, as Wordsworth puts it, to "throw over" an incident "a certain colouring of imagination," and thereby lead to poetry in the poet's case, and good writing in the student's.

Donald Murray is a composition specialist whose theories and practices have deep roots in a romantic tradition. He makes explicit that making meaning out of language is an imaginative act; he sees writing as active and creative. Murray argues that, for these reasons, writing must go against traditional classroom practice and pedagogy. Like others who favor romantic pedagogies, he believes that real learning rarely takes place in classrooms that focus on rote memorization and passive reception of facts. Students do not learn, and certainly do not learn to write in the ways that expressivists value, under the circumstances or method of teaching that Dewey calls the "phonographic disc" method in which teachers' impressions are "described" upon the student's mind.

In Murray's (1989) view, writing calls on innumerable imaginative processes—it is ever moving, ever changing perception, collecting, focusing, and ordering. Writing makes "meaning out of chaos" (24). The language that Murray (1984) uses when he speaks of this act of meaning making is akin to the romantic imagination: "Words . . . allow us to play with information, to make connections and patterns, to put together and take apart and put together again, to see what experience means. In other words, to think" (3). Murray's passage echoes Wordsworth's definition of the imagination as a "modifying power" capable of "consolidating numbers into unity, and dissolving and separating unity into number." It is very close to Coleridge's definition of the secondary imagination that, Coleridge claims, shapes perception and experience into patterns and connections by fusing and taking apart.

Expressivist rhetoricians believe that the writing classroom is the ideal place to strive for an education of the imagination. Like most rhetoricians since the rise of the New Rhetoric, they view language itself as creative and knowledge constructing. Rhetoric is epistemic. This belief in the creative capacities of language was a major concern of earlier romantics as well. Their influence on this matter underlies much thought of rhetoricians since the 1960s, even those we normally place in categories other than expressivist.

I would argue, for instance, that Francis Christensen supplements his work on sentence and paragraph construction with romantic theories of language even though he is often defined as a "formalist," a term usually used in opposition to expressivism (Gere 1986, 31). In Christensen's [1963] (1984) "A Generative Rhetoric of the Sentence," he expresses his discontent with the traditional approach to the teaching of sentence-production.[2] He suggests that "tear-out workbooks and four-pound anthologies" are ways of avoiding the hard work it would take to make a difference in student understandings of language. It may not seem likely, at first glance, that a discussion of the grammatical unit of the sentence, written such a great distance in time from Wordsworth and Coleridge, would bear their influence. But the method Christensen would like to see in place of workbook drills is romantic in theory. "We need," he argues, "a rhetoric of the sentence that will do more than combine the ideas of primer sentences. We need one that will *generate* ideas" (Graves 1976, 110).

Christensen perceives language as the romantics do: as productive and creative. He suggests that when writing is successful it is not merely ornamental and static. Thus, Christensen offers the cumulative sentence as the foundation for generative writing because it is "dynamic rather than static, representing the mind thinking" (111-112). The representation of the "mind thinking" is a key romantic idea and Christensen's position here is the one articulated by Wordsworth and Coleridge in response to the eighteenth-century view of language. It is their belief that language is creative, and their poems, in effect, are the linguistic representative of "the mind thinking."[3] It is for this reason that Wordsworth rejected the use of personification in his own poetry. Wordsworth insisted that when he did use personification he was not using it for ornamentation. If used, it grew naturally out of the passion and the language and context of the creative moment. Thus, the personification becomes dynamic; it is not merely static ornamentation.

In his discussion of the grammar of the sentence, Christensen relies on organic analogies to establish that the cumulative sentence mirrors live and productive language in action. The cumulative sentence, says Christensen [1963] (1984), is "probing its bearing implications, exemplifying it or seeking an analogy or metaphor for it, or reducing" it to details. Thus the mere form of the sentence generates ideas" (112). Coleridge's (1956–71) position on language also relies on an organic theory. In the Preface of *Aids to Reflection* he reminds us that words are "living powers," (Walsh 1958, 61) and, in a letter to Godwin, that words are "parts and germinations of the Plant," they are "Things, and living Things too" (626). In his argument against a traditional grammar and for a generative one, Christensen is searching for a theory and method that reveals "the language as it operates" rather than one that "leaves everything, to borrow a phrase from Wordsworth, 'in disconnection dead and spiritless'" (112).

For expressivists, to "reclaim the imagination" from the romantic tradition and from a historical lineage that includes many philosophers and educators is to build a pedagogy based on the belief that language, and thus writing, is a generative and knowledge-constructing act. To view student writing merely as a product that conducts knowledge, rather than as a process that constructs knowledge, is simply wrong-headed. While most current theories of rhetoric acknowledge that a product-centered theory and pedagogy for writing kills language, denying its generative nature, it is the expressivists who best understand what part the creative "active principles" play here. It is because of this that the imagination remains central to their theories and pedagogies.

I cannot argue that the rhetoric describing the romantic vision of the imagination suggests a mind or imaginative intellect shaped by culture. Rather, the rhetoric suggests that the imaginative mind shapes culture but not the contrary. This need not stop us, however, from revising this romantic position in light of what social-epistemicism teaches us. It is simple enough to understand that the imagination is both shaping agent and shaped object. I would also argue that this initial flaw in the rhetoric describing the romantic vision of the imagination need not deter us from examining the romantic and expressivist contribution to such important educational movements as whole language and write-to-learn. John M. Willinsky (1987), for instance, argues that the romantics, particularly Wordsworth and Coleridge, are the root of what he calls the New Literacy. An important aspect of the New Literacy is the whole language movement, and important aspects of whole language include creativity and the imagination.

Indeed, the curricula in whole language classrooms attempt to stimulate the imaginative faculties "as the means to enriching their [students'] perception and their cognitive claim on the world" (Willinsky 273). The approach taken in whole language classrooms relies not on the drills and skills that the romantics and neo-romantic rhetoricians work directly against, but, rather, this approach works through a holistic view of the student as a being who learns progressively and through a process. Thus activities for the classroom spark insight, creativity, and imaginative processes.

Expressive and process writing, and a focus on voice and self-discovery, are main tenets of this creative work. The work of expressivist compositionists directly influences whole language theories. James Britton is surely a key player here, but so are others. The National Writing Project, a leader in training teachers in whole language and process writing theories, uses the texts of teachers trained by expressivists as central learning tools of their program. Lucy Calkins, for instance, a teacher whose works are widely circulated by the NWP, worked with Donald Graves. Likewise, Tom Romano's *Clearing the Way* (1987) remains a crucial text in Writing Project libraries. Romano is a protégé of Donald Murray.

The influence of expressivism resides not only in Willinsky's New Literacy and in the whole language movement. It is distinctly present in writing-to-learn theories as well. The work of Britton, the man perhaps most responsible for bringing the term "expressive" to the consciousness of educators and compositionists, is the starting point for our current cadre of writing-to-learn and writing-across-the-curriculum theories and pedagogies. At the foundation of Britton's work is an understanding of the role the imagination plays in learning. The imagination is the basis for language growth and thus is specifically tied to writing.

Arising from Britton's understanding of the role of the imagination is his well-known triad for language use that he distills from the work of linguists and sociologists: expressive, transactional, poetic. The expressive is the forming discourse for both the poetic and the transactional. In other words, the expressive leads to the other forms of discourse and remains an integral part of them. The three form a continuum or spectrum. Thus, Britton's taxonomy is not prohibitive; rather, it is dynamic and active.

Britton lays out this triad in an article that's title reflects a direct tie to current writing-to-learn theories—"Writing to Learn and Learning to Write." Britton (1982) argues that the expressive plays a crucial role. Britton quotes linguist Edward Sapir and then elaborates on

Sapir's quotation: "'language is learned early and piecemeal, in constant association with the color and the requirements of actual contexts.' In other words, we pick it up as we go. 'Early and piecemeal,' never loses its ability to revive the actuality of the contexts with all their colors and all their requirements" (96). Or, in current writing-to-learn theoretical terms, the expressive (language close to the self, an attempt at discovery) and the student's knowledge and personal context can, perhaps should, be the starting point. From this point, the student can move toward the contexts of the issue or discipline he or she is studying. Britton himself gives us examples of how "referential," in this case discipline specific, discourse "makes its best start in the expressive" (94), when he reports Jacqueline's written response on the making of oxygen (94) and the ten-year-old boy from Suffolk's writing about making coal gas (99).

Since Britton stresses fully the importance of writing across the spectrum of the three discourses, it is perhaps wrong to assume that he sees poetic writing as most important. Nonetheless, the poetic is the most clearly infused with creativity and the imagination. The poetic is not, however, simply poetry. It is a wide-ranging discourse that incorporates most fully that which the romantics and neo-romantic compositionists argue so strenuously for as a necessity for real learning. Further, Britton (1982) defines it as "a construct, not a means but an end in itself" (107). Transactional language, on the other hand, "is language that gets things done, language as means" (107). For writing-to-learn theory, then, poetic language acts as a tool for learning in any discipline because it is a means by which students partake in connective thought and discovery.

Art Young's (1983) study of poetic language use in an introductory psychology class illustrates how writing-to-learn based on Britton's classifications might work. The students in the class were asked to do expressive, poetic, and transactional assignments on the subject of schizophrenia. The students' expressive writing took the form of journals, the transactional took the form of the traditional and more formal paper, and the poetic took the form of poems and a short story. The poetic assignments resulted in spurring creativity that in turn helped students "understand schizophrenia from the inside." Not surprisingly, the transactional writing helped the students organize their thoughts (some of which arose from their poetic work) and prepare to communicate these thoughts to an audience. Young's study glimpses writing-to-learn theories in actual practice.

James Britton, however, is not the only compositionist to set the foundation for writing-to-learn theories. Perhaps he is the only one acknowledged because he himself makes the direct connection with the title and consequent arguments in "Writing to Learn." Nonetheless, Elbow, Murray, and Berthoff also have direct ties to the theories underlying the write-to-learn and writing-across-the-curriculum (WAC) movements. Toby Fulwiler, (1991) composition's leading expert on WAC and writing-to-learn, notes that a writing-to-learn practice grows out of the following:

1. Expressive writing where students are allowed to explore their own beliefs through informal writing assignments and where they work to find their own voices.
2. Open-ended assignments where students are invited to ask and answer questions that seem pertinent to them.
3. Collaborative learning groups where students work together to pose and solve problems about their writing or the subject under study.
4. Real world writing where instructors provide the opportunity for students to write about what seems real and useful.
5. Response to student writing that is honest and supportive while asking questions and making suggestions rather then giving commands, correcting, and grading.
6. Faculty write with the students, thereby participating in the work of the class with the students. Students witness the more experienced teacher/writer generating ideas and shaping those ideas into coherent thoughts. (183–184)

All of the points Fulwiler articulates are central to expressivist classrooms. Indeed, they were first introduced into writing theory by expressivists, including Elbow and Murray.

The teaching methods behind write-to-learn pedagogies owe much to expressivist theory. Writing-to-learn relies on concepts such as experience, discovery, perception, reflection, and creativity, which as I will examine more fully in the next chapter, are romantic in nature. While Elbow, Murray, and Berthoff are not consistently linked to movements like write-to-learn and whole language as is James Britton, the underpinnings of their theories for teaching writing depend on theorizing experience, discovery, perception, and reflection. As the next chapter argues, their focus on these ideas is directly tied to theories of the imagination; but, perception, experience, discovery, and reflection move the theories of the imagination beyond the academic setting to a practice and theory of larger consequence. The expressivist focus on the imagination is not only about classroom practice, but about creating a learning context through classroom practice that carries over to a full educational experience.

Notes

1. Berthoff is not as consistently placed in the expressivist camp as are Elbow and Murray. Berlin tags her as a social-epistemic, clearly acknowledging the social aspects of her theories. Unfortunately, he ignores her expressivism, and thus the social-expressivism that she works from. I am sure that she will strongly resist being categorized as an expressivist. I do not intend to be limiting here, however. In fact, Berthoff's inability to be placed, and contained, under any particular label illustrates my point about the ways in which expressivist and social-epistemic rhetorics supplement each other.

2. The version I am using is collected in Richard L. Graves' *Rhetoric and Composition: Sourcebook for Teachers.*

3. My oversimplification here does a disservice to the romantic view on language. Their theories are complex and insightful. Three essays that I find helpful in understanding romantic theories of language are A.W. Phinney's "Wordsworth's Winander Boy and Romantic Theories of Language," Jonathon Ramsey's "Wordsworth and the Childhood of Language," and Gene Ruoff's "Wordsworth on Language: Toward a Radical Poetics for English Romanticism." Also of interest is Isobel Armstrong's *Language as Living Form in Nineteenth-Century Poetry.*

Chapter Four

Vital Links: Discovery, Perception, Experience, and Reflection

Expressivist rhetoricians believe that the imagination thrives in more of us than just the great poets or brilliant students. Rather, as the previous chapter points out, they believe that particular pedagogies and certain acts of writing foster the imagination—what Wordsworth calls the philosophical mind—in most students. As with earlier romantic pedagogies, expressivist classroom practices contain some identifiable elements that ensure the growth of the mind and the writer, including discovery, perception, experience, and reflection. These elements are crucial aspects of expressivist and romantic educational theories because of the role they play in the nurturing of the encompassing intellect. While scholars might recognize that expressivists have ties to romanticism through these elements, they have not examined these ties in depth; nor have they seen fit to point out what is valuable in these particular romantic connections.

The Writing Process

The actual practicing of discovery, perception, experience, and reflection is a complex and rigorous intellectual interaction. For those who do not understand the discipline and rigor behind the practices that engender this interaction—a common problem because of our ahistorical understanding of expressivism—the pedagogical techniques can seem frivolous and "romantic" in the most debased sense. While this expressivist approach often draws the sort of skepticism that John Keating's pedagogy drew from his more traditional colleagues in *Dead Poets Society*, it nonetheless is based in sound theory and practice. As John Dewey ([1940] 1969) argued, these are processes "requiring activity of mind rather than merely powers of absorption and reproduction" (242).

While the interests, theories, and pedagogies of expressivists vary, they share certain characteristics and assumptions, most of which became apparent in the 1960s with the advent of the New Rhetoric and an interest in writing as a process. Expressivists hold the belief that writing is a complex process and that writing pedagogy should focus on this process; they contend that our students will not learn to write well until they understand writing as a process. This is not to say that the written "product" is not important. They argue, rather, that a poem, a story, an essay, or a research paper does not mysteriously appear, in finished form, on the page or screen in front of us.

Their theories differ from other process-oriented writing theories such as neo-classical and cognitive approaches, however, in that an expressivist does not see the process in terms of linearity (as neo-classicists are likely to), nor in terms of hierarchy and discrete units clearly separable into stages (as cognitivists are inclined to). Linda Flower (1981), the leading proponent of cognitive approaches for writing instruction, has written that her goal is to make "unconscious actions a little more conscious: to give writers a greater awareness of their own intellectual processes, and therefore the power and possibility of conscious choice" (vi). Flower finds the expressivist attempts to cultivate the imaginative intellect ineffective because they result in a model for composing that is too muddled and too dependent on "inspiration". For her, the expressivists' rather global approach to the writing process remains unarticulated, and thus unconscious.

Yet expressivists, like cognitivists, try to make "conscious" how "unconscious actions" of the writing process work. Having students write about and examine their writing and thinking is an attempt to articulate the more unconscious aspects of writing; certainly Donald Murray's pedagogical use of professional writers' ideas and writings about their works is an attempt to make conscious the actual working out of the writers' imaginative and composing processes.

It is not in trying to make conscious the unconscious, then, that expressivists and cognitivists differ; it is in how to make this transformation take place. Flower, to bring forth the hidden aspects of composing, separates the process of writing into "distinctive parts" (vii). She builds a model of composing that appears to take place in stages, although she does realize the recursive nature of these stages. More important, however, Flower sees the process of writing as goal-oriented and for purposes of problem-solving. While expressivists do not object to Flower's use of scientific methods to research the ways in which writers compose, nor to the ideas that writing can be used to solve problems and can be highly goal-oriented, they do object to a pedagogy founded on the hierarchical models that represent her vision of the composing process. They object even more strongly to the view of the process of writing as always needing to be about goal attainment and solutions. Expressivists fear that this separation of the process into parts and stages can lead students and teachers to view writing in an overregimented and simplistic light. They see the process more often as a means of questioning and discovering than of attaining preset and deterministic goals. In an expressivist's eyes, sometimes holding off on predetermined goals and letting discovery become the goal itself enriches both writing and thinking. This does not mean that discovery need always be the goal.

Expressivist pedagogies, which enact a blending of discovery, experience, perception, and reflection, help in making conscious the complexity and recursive nature of composing. The cognitivist approach, some expressivists believe, tends to sever the affective realm from the cognitive, creating the potential to reduce the complex intellectual and imaginative aspects of writing to a mechanical set of writing strategies. Writing, for expressivists, is an act of the whole being; it is through reflecting, questioning, feeling, experiencing, reasoning, and imagining that writers become writers. While this might seem an ambitious and ideal approach to writing instruction, I would argue that it is just such an ideal that we need to hold to fully educate students in a system that often denies the emotive, creative, and imaginative aspects of the intellect.

As I have argued, the expressivist theories of such scholars as Rohman, Berthoff, Murray, and Elbow, like those of the romantics and their nineteenth- and early twentieth-century followers, arose in reaction to a conservative educational system. This system denied the more creative aspects of the intellect and promoted a theory of writing instruction that privileged passive learning, rote drills, and the written product over the process. Thirty years after Murray, Elbow, and others began their work, we are still facing a less than enlightened educational system and expressivists are still working against this system, each in his or her own way. Rather than standing in front of a classroom filling passive students with grammatical rules and the "correct" reading of a work of literature, these teachers are placing students in an active and participatory role in their own learning processes.

Ann Berthoff's students, for instance, work in dialectical notebooks, responding in writing to what they read, think, and observe. Rather than being told how to read and write, her students develop, through work in the double-entry notebooks, their own methods for critical reading and writing by engaging in "reflective questioning." Peter Elbow uses groups for developing a critical method of reading and writing. Students working together in these groups engage in dialogue about the texts being written and read. Ideally, they are actively thinking, reflecting, questioning, and discovering.

Likewise, Donald Murray subverts the traditional teaching model by making the student/teacher conference the center of his pedagogy. When the student enters into a discussion with Murray she is the "expert" and she makes decisions about her own writing. Through this close one-on-one dialogue, she learns to probe, question, reflect, and discover for herself. She may indeed be an inexperienced "expert," and she may make many ineffective decisions about her work. But, as Murray would argue, it is in these false starts and failed attempts that real discovery, real learning, and thus real writing, take place.

Wordsworth, Education, and the "Vital Soul"

There is a strong historical precedent for the stance that expressivists take on such elements as discovery, perception, experience, and reflection. These romantic ideas show up in many different incarnations and in the discussions of educational philosophers as varied as Rousseau, Pezzalozi, and Arendt. Wordsworth and Coleridge have fully articulated the role that these other elements play in education and the imagination. For Wordsworth, nature plays an important part in setting perception and experience into motion. In much of his poetry he proclaims, in what might seem an extremely radical stance to his readers, that the child will benefit from the wisdom and education fostered outside the schoolroom walls. Interestingly enough, as we shall see, later educators like Dewey and Berthoff return to nature as important to an educational enterprise, although they do so in much less radical ways.

In "The Tables Turned" Wordsworth ([1798] 1989) counsels readers to leave study and books and come into the woods where the real learning will take place:

Books! 'tis a dull and endless strife:
Come, hear the woodland linnet,
How sweet his music! on my life,
There's more of wisdom in it. . . .

One impulse from a vernal wood
May teach you more of man,
Of moral evil and of good,
Than all the sages can. (377)

This extreme stance is more easily understood, however, when we recall what was passing as education inside the school walls— pedagogical practices relying almost exclusively on recitation and memorization of facts.

Wordsworth's stance on education seems to call for "quitting" books and wandering about in nature. We cannot escape, however, the irony of Wordsworth's counsel to stop reading while, at the same time, he is communicating his theories to us through the written word. This, of course, seems to negate his dictum that we should give up books as an educational pursuit. What we must remember, however, is that Wordsworth's relentless and apparently one-sided demand for an education of nature is in some ways a rhetorical ploy. In other words, in poems like "Tables Turned," "Expostulation and Reply," and parts of *The Prelude* as well, Wordsworth ([1798] 1984) is carefully choosing and selecting those experiences that made his education different from the traditional one (377; 495). He employs a rhetorical strategy that allows him to emphasize what he saw as the detrimental lack of imaginative schooling practiced by most schools of his day. Like Arnold, Wordsworth did not condemn books and reading unconditionally, as a cursory study of his works might suggest, but only insofar as they were misused for educational purposes both in formal school systems and in amateur practices at home.

Considering Wordsworth's supposed stance against books, it is especially interesting that, while at Hawkshead, he read vociferously. In 1885 the son of Hawkshead Headmaster, Thomas Bowman, recalled things his father had said about Wordsworth and reading. Wordsworth (Thompson 1970) wanted books, "all sorts of books; Tours and Travel, which my father was partial to, and Histories and Biographies, which were also favorites with him; and Poetry—that goes without saying. . . ." (343–344). What, then, prompts Wordsworth to suggest that the reading required by schools is damaging to the intellect? In large part it was that the study of books was forced indiscriminately on children. As Arnold later argued, much of this reading was of the "dry, scientific" sort. Wordsworth read out of excitement and because he yearned for knowledge. As Stephen Gill (1989) notes in his biography of Wordsworth, Hawkshead made books available to all of its students, not only through the library proper, but through the Boys Book Club which Wordsworth promptly joined, and the Headmaster's personal library. In his earliest years of school, Wordsworth read "all Fielding's works, *Don Quixote, Gil Blas,* and any part of Swift that I liked; *Gulliver's Travels,* and *Tale of a Tub,* being much to my taste" (28). What is strikingly different for Wordsworth, in comparison with most school children of his day, is that he was able to pursue his own interests as well as those expected by the school. "The importance of any school," however, "lies not so much in the formal curriculum or even in the quality of the teaching as in the encouragement it offers to a pupil's own interests and the possibilities it opens up" (28).

Even though Wordsworth found plenty of time for play, the Hawkshead curriculum was strenuous; the school was considered one of the best in England. Every year several Hawkshead boys went to Cambridge, and many were exemplary scholars. Wordsworth not only received a solid background in mathematics and natural philosophy, but he gained a firm grounding in the classics as well. This foundation, however, was not built through tiresome exercises in verse compositions in Greek and Latin and rote learning, as it was at most schools (27). As Gill suggests, Hawkshead's approach to learning must have worked with Wordsworth, for he had a passionate love of Virgil, Ovid, and Homer, all of which he read at school, he was affected deeply by the beauty of classical literature, and he enjoyed poetry as more than an "academic chore" (27). The reading and study required of Wordsworth became a pleasurable activity, rather than a chore, because he was granted time for play as well as work. He stimulated his imagination through jaunts in the country, through the stories of the old woman he lived with (Dame Tyson), and through readings of his own choice. The pursuit of experience, emotion, and an active education became the main ingredients to his success. He was not merely crammed full of facts.

Wordsworth's academic studies and his imaginative pursuits animated by what he calls "vital feeling" or the "vital soul" (Fotheringham 1899, 31), led him to promote the educational philosophy that holds that the emotive and imaginative faculties in *conjunction with* the intellectual and analytical make for a mature and encompassing intellect.[1] The "vital soul" is crucial to Wordsworth. It is the aspect of the self(ves) that perceives, creates, and feels. It is "the ground of all real education, and the free expansion of the 'vital soul' is the true end of education. . . .There is no real and right growth for the human mind without depth and cordiality of feeling" (31–33). In fact, an inability to develop the vital soul spells certain death for the encompassing intellect. It seems to me that this is what John Keating knew. The development of what Wordsworth calls the "vital soul" was the impetus behind the original formation of the Dead Poets Society at the boys academy.

Wordsworth's "Lucy" poems, though very complex and not amenable to a single interpretation, might be read as eulogies for the death of the vital soul. In "A Slumber did My Spirit Seal," for instance, if we understand Lucy to be emblematic of the soul, the slumber that closes Lucy off from the "touch of earthly years" also seals her off from the "vital feelings of delight" (Wordsworth [1800] 1984):

> A slumber did my spirit seal;
>   I had no human fears:
> She seemed a thing that could not feel
>   The touch of earthly years.
> No motion has she now, no force;
>   She neither hears nor sees;
> Rolled round in earth's diurnal course,
>   With rocks, and stones, and trees.

In the passive state of slumber, the vital soul is unable to perceive, to feel, to create; thus, the mind lacks one-half of the equation needed to make it the all-powerful faculty of Wordsworth's philosophic mind.

The vital soul is a natural element for children and, unless educated out of them, it provides children with passionate feelings such as hate and love. According to Wordsworth, the vital soul and all the passionate feelings that are a part of it are necessary for a full education. And with these come

> Simplicity in habit, truth in speech,
> Be these the daily strengtheners of their minds;
> May books and Nature be their early joy!
> And knowledge, rightly honored with that name—
> Knowledge not purchased by the loss of power!
> (*The Prelude*, [1850] V: 421–425)

Peter Elbow (1973) seems to agree with Wordsworth that these passionate feelings have a place in the education of our students. Elbow never shies away from anger, for instance. Instead, he urges students to tap into the power of anger and let it drive their language. And yet, Elbow knows that, while anger should not be denied or shoved away, there are times it can be detrimental to communication. Thus he argues for pouring that anger into language and onto the page during freewriting sessions before the actual drafting of a written text.

It was Wordsworth's desire in much of his poetry and prose to
show how most educators had gone astray, even damaged the intellect of their students, by barring students from emotion, experience,
and imagination. If the analytical mind is severed from the passions
and the imaginative intellect, knowledge comes at great cost—lost is
the higher intellect, the "encompassing intellect," which melds
both reason and imagination.

The growth of the philosophic mind does not end in childhood,
but continues, forever in progression, until death, a concept we now
name lifelong learning. It is not surprising, then, that Wordsworth's
interest in the instruction of pupils does not end with grammar
school. Wordsworth's years at Cambridge served to reinforce what
his Hawkshead schooling had taught him about learning and the
fostering of a complete intellect (Schneider 1957, 39). His tenure at
Cambridge spurred him to articulate what he found wrong with the
university program and to continue arguing for his own ideal vision
of the university where the fertilization of the encompassing intellect proceeded.[2] Again, it is *The Prelude* that lends most insight
into Wordsworth's thoughts on higher education and the growth of
the mental faculties.

Although Wordsworth certainly did not find his time at Cambridge a total loss, there was much he found lacking. In Book V of
The Prelude [1850] he "condemned" (Schneider 1957, 39)

> The guides and wardens of our faculties,
> Sages who in their prescience would control
> All accidents, and to the very road
> Which they have fashioned would confine us down
> Like engines[.] (*The Prelude* [1850] 354–358)

Cambridge was such a place for Wordsworth. The system was too
controlling. He comments directly on this:

> I did not love,
> Judging not ill perhaps, the timid course
> Of our scholastic studies; could have wished
> To see the river flow with ampler range
> And freer pace[.] (*The Prelude* [1850] III: 496–500)

The result of this tightly controlled educational practice was to
leave Wordsworth divorced from his scholarly activities:

> many books
> Were skimmed, devoured, or studiously perused,
> But with not settled plan. I was detached
> Internally from academic cares (*The Prelude* [1850] VI: 23–26)

Wordsworth blamed Cambridge for placing knowledge at risk: the structure there initiated and honored competitive strife while actively discouraging some students from a true desire to learn. This competitive gamesmanship was rewarded with various kinds of prizes, and the prizes became more important to the students than actual learning. This is, unfortunately, a situation I face often enough with my students. With undergraduates, learning and knowledge tend to be secondary to the letter grade; this is a major catalyst for cheating. The fraternities encourage this focus on the prize, as opposed to knowledge, by granting privileges to those members who maintain a certain grade point average. The problem, however, is that they do not care how members achieve these grades. It is common practice for members to sell test answers and essays to other members. Also, many parents subvert the learning process by bribing their children—if their grades are high enough they will receive money, or perhaps a new car. This inspires the worst kind of competitive strife, cheating, and a forfeiture of real learning.

Even more disturbing is the fact that the nasty competition Wordsworth alludes to is also alive and well at the graduate level. Students often seem intent on competing with each other for the teacher's attention, the highest grades, and the esteemed position of "brightest student." When these students become set on competing with each other, they forsake the pursuit of knowledge for arguing in unproductive argument designed to make themselves look better by making their colleagues look foolish, and by striking an attitude of already knowing all there is to know. The result is an abrupt halt to the most beneficial kind of classroom interaction and intellectual pursuits. The process of learning is lost to unnecessary competition and one-upmanship.

Perhaps the most atrocious outcome of this competitive system, in Wordsworth's view (Schneider 1957), is its effect on the quality of teaching. Under a routine of competition for prizes, students at Cambridge were not obliged to study unless they desired a prize, and thus tutors were not obliged to teach them (25). Since students were in pursuit of prizes and not knowledge, professors ceased to function as teachers. Believing that the prizes themselves were enough to stimulate learning, they "contented themselves with putting the proper material before them [students] in lectures, which were usually dull" (27). The teaching was poor, the students inappropriately inspired by prizes, not knowledge or learning for learning's sake.

Wordsworth would have none of this. He did not compete for prizes and consequently he took no honors at Cambridge. Wordsworth cut his own educational path and continued to walk it until he took his B.A. He read voraciously, but did not give up the nurturing of his emotional and experiential side for the narrowness of the Cambridge curriculum. He continued to enrich his vital soul through study, imaginative pursuits, and his beloved nature:

> Besides the pleasant Mill of Trompington
> I laughed with Chaucer in the hawthorn shade;
> Heard him,
> while birds were warbling, tell his tales
> Of amorous passion . . .
> Sweet Spenser, moving through his clouded heaven
> With the moon's beauty and the moon's soft pace,
> (*The Prelude*, [1850] III: 278–284)

Like many of us teaching at universities today, Wordsworth hoped for a system of higher education that would foster learning for its own sake. He longed for a broader curriculum, one that would inspire students to an active, imaginative, and lifelong desire to learn.

Coleridge and the Value of Self-Knowledge

Wordsworth is speaking of Coleridge when he writes of a friend raised in the city and denied the joys of the English countryside. Coleridge did not attend Hawkshead where Wordsworth found the luxury of expanding his imagination through interaction with nature. Rather, Coleridge studied at Christ's Hospital, a far more traditional school, where he was tightly governed by the hand of the Reverend James Boyer. Yet, despite the differences in their upbringing, Wordsworth and Coleridge held similar ideas and philosophies, not only about politics, poetry, and theories of the imagination, but about the importance of things like experience and reflection to the educational enterprise as well. Coleridge came to kindred conclusions with Wordsworth about the part played by creative activity, reading, self-reflection, self-knowledge, emotion, perception, and the imagination in the growth of a full intellect. One might argue that he arrived at these conclusions not only through his own limited imaginative childhood play, but through a vicarious sharing of the childhood of his friend William Wordsworth—a man Coleridge considered to have a truly great mind and an uncanny understanding of the human condition.

What was lacking in his own education prompted Coleridge to hope for better things for his children. In "Frost at Midnight" ([1798] 1985) he gives thanks that his son Hartley will not suffer the "cloisters dim":

My Babe so beautiful! it thrills my heart
With tender gladness, thus to look at thee,
And think that thou shalt learn far other lore,
And in far other scenes! For I was reared
In the great city, pent 'mid cloisters dim,
And saw not lovely but the sky and stars.
But *thou* my babe! shalt wander like a breeze
By lakes and sandy shores, beneath the clouds,
Which image in their bulk both lakes and shores
And mountain crags[:] (87)

Read literally, Coleridge was certainly blessing Hartley's opportunities to frolic amongst the pleasures of the natural world. He sees in his son's interactions with nature a chance to foster the "natural child," the passionate and experiential component of learning that Wordsworth claims such power for in his chronicle of the growth of the philosophical mind. It is no accident that these lines about learning appear in a poem so directly about the imagination: Coleridge means to draw attention to the importance of the imagination in the education of children. The "cloisters dim," which shut Coleridge off from the world of nature, are more than city dwellings. Coleridge was not merely "pent" physically, but mentally and imaginatively as well, and this he sees as detrimental to education and learning.

The "stern preceptor" remembered by Coleridge in "Frost at Midnight," ([1798] 1985) while recalling his father, probably refers more directly to James Boyer, Coleridge's teacher at Christ's Hospital (Waldo 1982, 105). In the *Biographia Literaria* ([1817] 1983), Coleridge writes ambivalently of Boyer and his educational techniques. Boyer followed the tradition of the time in that his instruction consisted mostly of memorization and drills. Student prose compositions were important only as grammatically correct products destined to fit a pre-determined form. They were to contain none of the subjectivity, emotion, or imaginative pursuit that later became a major tenet of romantic theories on literature. In fact, Boyer took great pains to keep the imagination of his students in check.[3] Coleridge ([1817] 1983) recollects that Boyer "showed no mercy to phrase, metaphor, or image, unsupported by sound sense, or where the same sense might have been conveyed with equal force and dignity in plainer words" (I: 9–10). Imaginative connections and analogies were an "abomination" to Boyer: "In fancy I can almost hear him now, exclaiming 'Harp? Harp? Lyre? Pen and ink, boy, you mean! Muse, boy, Muse? Your Nurse's daughter, you mean! Pierian spring? Oh! aye! The cloister-pump, I suppose!'" (10).

As different as Coleridge's education was from Wordsworth's,

Coleridge did come to hold a similar educational philosophy based on the idea that analytical practice and imaginative pursuits should be yoked together to obtain optimum mental powers. He also agreed with Wordsworth on how this educative goal could be reached. Coleridge joined ranks with Rousseau and Wordsworth in his belief that children should not be educated as though they were miniature adults. Therefore Coleridge also agreed with Wordsworth that the pursuit of knowledge takes place in progression, and that it is a great error to cram young minds with facts that pass as knowledge. Education should attempt to refine the sense of relation and connections because, according to Coleridge (Walsh 1958), "the comparing power, the judgment, is not at that age active, and ought not to be forcibly excited as is too frequently and mistakenly done in modern systems of education . . ." (19). To force academic pursuits and exercises, rote memorization, and factual information upon young children is a grave mistake. In a powerful analogy Coleridge (Coburn 1979) wrote, "Touch a door a little ajar or half open, and it will yield to the push of your finger. Fire a cannon-ball at it, and the door stirs not much: you make a hole thro' it, the door is spoilt for ever, but not *moved*" (81).

Coleridge would connect, I believe, the school system's tendency to rely on rote memorization to "memoria technica," a process that he decries as "artificial memory" in the *Biographia Literaria* ([1817] 1983). Memoria technica is an ancient technique of impressing places and images on the memory. The problem that Coleridge had with this is that, because it was solely passive, it neglected the role the will plays in memory: "But the will itself by confining and intensifying the attention may arbitrarily give vividness and distinctness to any object whatsoever; and from hence we may deduce the uselessness if not the absurdity of certain schemes that *promise* an artificial *memory*, but which in reality can only produce a confusion and debasement of the *fancy*." (127) It is the active participation of the will, as it relates to the act of remembering, that rote memorization fails to stimulate.

It is clear, then, that by education Coleridge meant more than gaining expertise or memorizing little-known facts; and he meant even more than the imaginative pursuits afforded by readings of the fantastic. Education also includes moral growth—preparation of the mind to make the best judgments for the good of society. It takes both aspects of education, moral and intellectual, to be fully educated, which in Coleridge's terms meant having the ability to see all things in fullness and relation to each other. As he wrote in the *Biographia Literaria*, "the educated man chiefly seeks to discover and express those *connections* of things, or those relative *bearings* of fact to fact . . ." (53). Ultimately this is Coleridge's definition of the encompassing intellect. As with Wordsworth, the mind is fully mature when it is synthetic and able to unify as well as analyze.

According to Coleridge, the ability to nurture the young mind into the encompassing intellect must include reflection, self-knowledge, and consciousness, all which lead to the melding of reasoning and imaginative powers necessary to the completely educated mind.[4] "Our intellectual life," he argued in a lecture on Shakespeare, passes "not so much in acquiring new facts, as in acquiring a *distinct consciousness*" (Coburn 1977, 25). Without a consciousness of self the moral intellect is stunted, damaging not only the individual, but society as well. He felt the lack of it could be harmful to others and often spoke to this issue. Speaking of the conflicts in human societies Coleridge asked, "Why is difference linked with hatred?" His answer was: from lack of consciousness of self (32).

This consciousness is, in turn, linked to reflection and self-knowledge. Self-knowledge is the ability to commune with the "very and permanent" self and it is a prerequisite for any knowledge. This "permanent" self is not a non-socially constructed self as critics of expressivism and romanticism are want to believe. While this self does appear Godlike as Coleridge's choice of the word "very" suggests, the permanent or very self is not innate and untouched or uninfluenced by the world that our selves reside in. By permanent, Coleridge means that self-reflection should become a fundamental part of one's self(ves). Self-reflection is so important to learning and to understanding that Coleridge demands it become like second nature.

Knowledge in its fullest sense, Coleridge (Walsh 1958) argues, is "not merely mechanical and like a carpenter's rule, having its whole value in the immediate outward use to which it is applied . . . all knowledge . . . that enlightens and liberalises, is a form and means of self-knowledge, whether it be grammar, logical or classical" (60). Coleridge's self-knowledge is much like Wordsworth's vital soul; it is attainable through a method of thinking, feeling, experiencing, imagining, and cultivating sensitivity. It comes from a combination of inner and outer awareness. Outer awareness is observation and interaction with environment—including one's society—and he calls inner awareness the art of reflection.

Reflection is a mode of personal experience; it is concrete. As William Walsh (1958) points out, it is not to be confused with reverie, "a lackadaisical, bemused sauntering in the company of a mere sequence of notions and images" (58). Rather, it is a very difficult and active process calling on "energy and thought" (58).

The educational philosophies with which both Coleridge and Wordsworth disagree err by ignoring the cultivation of a reflective self-knowledge. Rather than "educing" it from within, they try, says Coleridge, to "shape convictions and deduce knowledge from without by an exclusive observation of outward and sensible things" (58). This results in a mind able to distinguish between aggregate parts but not a vitally whole mind capable of making connections.

Learning the art of reflection includes reflective self-knowledge—examining one's own thoughts and actions—but since language and the written word shape us, it also includes learning to actively analyze language and question what we study, be it text, event, or world. As Coleridge wrote in the Preface to *Aids to Reflection:* "Reflect on your thoughts, actions, circumstances and—which will be of especial aid to you in forming a *habit* of reflection—accustom yourself to reflect on the words you use, hear or read, their truth, derivation and history. For if words are not things, they are living powers, by which things of most importance to mankind are activated, combined and humanised" (61).[5]

To reflect on "thoughts, actions, and circumstances" is to consider not only one's actions but the circumstances in which this self exists. This does not exclude cultural and historical circumstances. Through Coleridge's ideas on reflection we can begin to see the roots of a social-expressivism.

"The first question we should put to ourselves," alleges Coleridge, "when we have to read a passage that perplexes us in a work of authority is: What does the writer *mean* by all this? And the second question should be, What does he intend by all this?" (61). Coleridge suggests that, as readers, we should consider each part of the text in relation to the whole, what the author has written in relation to ourselves, and the intention of the author. Further, he suggests that reflection, whether on ourselves or on a text, can help lead to a refined sense of "distinction." For Coleridge, making distinctions, but seeing how those distinctions create a whole, or how they work together or against each other, is the sign of the truly educated mind. A "distinct consciousness" leads to an encompassing intellect.

Through his own learning experiences, his vast reading on the nature of knowledge, and his deep friendship with William Wordsworth, Coleridge came to believe that a child's intellect needs strengthening through excitement, imagination, nourishing support, reflection, a consciousness of self, and time. Education is an active process. If we approach education as "educing . . . the blossom . . . from the bud" in a progression that begins with respecting the capabilities of the young mind and the need for creative activity, as opposed to requiring the memorization and regurgitation of factual information, the imaginative power will come alive. With an education that truly educes the "vital soul," as Wordsworth calls it, "vital excellencies" in Coleridge's terms, of imagination, passion, reason, deep feeling, and moral intellect can be cultivated. As a passage in a letter of 1801 from Coleridge to Poole underscores, "deep thinking is attainable only by . . . deep feeling"[6] (Jackson 89).

Coleridge, like Wordsworth, firmly believed that a mechanized approach to education, which did not take into account the natural development of a child's mind and moral being or the importance of the vital excellencies, was gravely damaging. Echoing passages of Wordsworth's from *The Prelude* ([1850] 1983), Coleridge [1817] condemns those educators who deny the young mind its natural growth toward intellectual and moral power. Teachers are, he says, "instructed how to metamorphose children into prodigies; . . . prodigies of self-conceit, shallowness, arrogance, and infidelity" (I: 13). These students are not fully educated; they lack an imaginative intellect. They can repeat memorized definitions and facts, but are unable to do the kinds of reflecting, connecting, and discriminating that they ought to be able to do.

Mill and the Education of Feelings

What Wordsworth and Coleridge had to say about such things as the imagination, emotion, nature, reflection, and experience struck a chord for later poets, philosophers, and educators as varied as John Stuart Mill, Henry David Thoreau, William James, John Dewey, and Fred Newton Scott. Mill, for instance, talks about the detrimental effects his father's educational program had on him because it so completely suppressed interaction with nature and anything emotive.

In the *Autobiography* ([1863] 1969), Mill explains that his father kept him from outdoor recreation and shielded him from the "ordinary corrupting influence which boys exercise over boys," so that he might not be contaminated with "vulgar modes of thought and feeling" (22). Mill was not one of the "real children," rightly educated, that Wordsworth considered himself and the students that shared his Hawkshead education to be:

A race of real children, not too wise,
Too learned, or too good; but wanton, fresh,
And bandied up and down by love and hate;
Not unresentful where justified;
Fierce, moody, patient, virtuous, modest, shy;

> Mad in their sports like withered leaves in winds;
> Though doing wrong and suffering, and full oft
> Bending beneath our life's mysterious weight
> Of pain, and doubt, and fear, yet yielding not
> In happiness to the happiest upon earth. (*The Prelude*, [1850] V:
> 411–425)

Instead, Mill was Wordsworth's "miracle of scientific lore." Because of the "deficiencies" in his education, Mill found himself to be a social "misfit" (24) just like Coleridge. In a letter to Thomas Poole of October 9, 1797, Coleridge, describing how the deficiencies in his education made him a social pariah, could have been writing of Mill as well as himself: "I was fretful and immoderately passionate, and as I could not play at anything and was slothful, I was despised and hated by the boys. . . .I could read and spell and had, I may truly say, a memory and understanding forced into almost unnatural ripeness. . . . (*Selected Letters* [1797] 1987, 59)" Like Wordsworth and Coleridge, Mill believed that normal childhood play and interaction with other children added an essential ingredient to a youth's education. Mill himself, however, spent most of his time with adults like his father and Bentham.

Mill ([1873] 1969) was not only denied the company of youngsters his own age, but simple physical activity was limited for him as well. Although he took solitary walks daily, these were subdued and "in general of a quiet, if not bookish turn, and gave little stimulus to any other kind of mental activity than that which was already called forth by studies" (23).

Wordsworth was also known for his solitary walks, but he had a balance unknown to Mill, and indulged in play as well as deep thought; Wordsworth was the Winander boy hooting back at the owls, while Mill was the "miracle of scientific lore." Wordsworth opened himself up to nature. He observed nature's ways, allowed his experiences in nature to stimulate all of his senses. Mill was "utterly inobservant: I was as my father continually told me, like a person who had not the organs of sense. My eyes and ears seemed of no use to me, so little did I see or hear what was before me, and so little, even of what I did see or hear, did I observe or remember. . . ." (*Autobiography* 24). Because his senses were closed to nature he was unable to nurture the experiential and emotive aspects of his intellect.

However, from the vantage point of an adult restored to health through the cultivation of feelings, Mill remembered two Wordsworthian-like experiences from his childhood that "bettered" his education. At Bentham's residence in Somersetshire, where Mill spent a part of each year during the years of 1814 to 1817, Mill finally became aware of the importance of interaction with nature as a stimulant to feelings and, thus, to education. Bentham's home in Somersetshire was an abbey surrounded by the natural world; it was a place where Mill could have a freer existence. Mill saw the time spent at the Abbey as crucial to his education, because it was the first time he found himself in circumstances allowing him the luxury of communing with nature.

The second occurrence Mill (1969) writes of was a stay in France where "the first introduction to the highest order of mountain scenery made the deepest impression. . . .and gave a colour to my tastes through life" (37). As unemotional as this latter passage of Mill's might seem, it recalls Wordsworth's much more passionate telling of crossing the Alps. Perhaps of more direct interest is Mill's mention of the "colouration" of his tastes. What Mill is suggesting is that the mountain scenery excited his imagination, and, having excited his imagination, this particular scene stayed with him throughout life, stored in his memory the way Wordsworth's mind is "a mansion for all lovely forms." Mill's language is strikingly similar to that used by Wordsworth in his discussion in the Preface to the *Lyrical Ballads* [1815] on the Poet's ability to imbue ordinary objects with imaginative vision by throwing "over them a certain colouring of imagination" (*Poetical Works* 734).[7]

In 1828, Mill was suffering from severe depression and had begun to believe that his education and life had been for naught. Mill ([1873] 1969) comments that two lines from Coleridge were often in his thoughts: "Work without hope draws nectar in a sieve, / And hope without an object cannot live." It was Coleridge, wrote Mill, "in whom alone of all writers I have found a true description of what I felt. . . ." (84). This despondent state of thought and feelings made reading Wordsworth for the first time an important event in Mill's life. Wordsworth's poems were "a medicine" for Mill's "state of mind." The poems expressed feelings, and Mill had come to understand that feelings were crucial and that they were missing from his own life. He wrote that Wordsworth's poems stimulated his feelings and in them he "seemed to draw from a source of inward joy, of sympathetic and imaginative pleasure, which could be shared by all human beings. . . ." (83). Mill is arguing here for an education that weds an analytical mind to an emotive one, in order to foster the fully capable and creative mind.

Almost as though he could hear Wordsworth and Coleridge pointing to him as an example of everything wrong with education, Mill explains that his education did contain valuable aspects. Perhaps the most important to Mill is that his education was not as passive as we might be inclined to think. It was active in that, cording to Mill, his father never just doled out facts and answers; .e younger Mill was to express an understanding of his lessons ..nd to display an ability to connect ideas before his father would move on with the studies. According to Mill, his father did not want what he had learned to "degenerate into a mere exercise of memory" (20). Unlike Wordsworth and Coleridge, Mill does not object to being introduced to all the "branches of science and philosophy" as a mere child. In fact, he does not believe that any "scientific teaching ever was more thorough, or better fitted for training the faculties," than the mode by which his father taught him logic and political economy (19). Mill objects not to what he studied, but to what his education left out: normal childhood activity, an appreciation of beauty, and the cultivation of feeling and the imagination.

From Wordsworth and Coleridge, Mill understood that the mind cannot thrive if the analytical intellect is severed from imagination and feelings. Having learned this, Mill's *Autobiography,* as Jack Stillinger points out, "focuses on the role of the imagination in the growth of the Philosophic mind (xii)," and by the time Mill ([1867] 1969) gives the St. Andrews Inaugural Address in 1867, he insists that there are three interrelated parts that make up a full education: "intellectual education, moral education, and the education of feelings" (189). Wordsworth and Coleridge's hope for an education that will nurture an encompassing intellect inspired Mill to incorporate what he learned from them with his own educative experiences.

Dewey and the Organic Connection to Learning

Of all the educators influenced by Wordsworth and Coleridge, John Dewey seems to incorporate most fully their ideas on perception, experience, and reflection. Dewey (1934) writes forcefully in defense of experience and perception. "It is mere ignorance," he argues, "that leads them [critics of expressivism] to the supposition that the connection of art and esthetic perception with experience signifies a lowering of their [the words of art] significance and dignity" (25). Dewey argues as an expressivist when he suggests, in antithesis, that "Experience. . . . *is* heightened vitality" (25). In other words, experience is vital and it enables the creation of art and knowledge. Like Wordsworth and Coleridge, Dewey sees the act of experiencing taking place, at least in part, through "perception" and participation with the world. According to Dewey, the senses are the way in which a "live creature participates directly with the ongoings of the world" (28). Again, we are reminded of Arnold's call for "creative principles" and Mill's desire to "go forth

and know." This perception and participation, then, leads to expe
rience, which in Dewey's argument leads to art.

This category of experience seems less ambiguous for Dewey
than for his predecessors. In Wordsworth and Coleridge, for
instance, it is difficult to ascertain whether experience is directly
available at all times or whether it is something less tangible and
more mystical perhaps. Dewey, however, uses this term in ways
easier to discern. Experience does not necessarily preclude mystical
experience or some deep intuitive category. As it is for me, and for
some current expressivists, experience cannot always be ascer-
tained discursively. And yet, an expressivist's understanding of
experience as it relates to pedagogy might be closer to seeing experience as a heuristic, as a method for discovering things for oneself.
In Dewey's case this becomes clear when he urges classroom practice to include actual participation with the subject being studied.

Dewey also makes the case, as Wordsworth and Coleridge do,
that perception is more than mere nonparticipatory recognition,
more than senses being bombarded by an external world; it is not
completely passive. Dewey writes that "perception replaces bare
recognition." In this replacement there is "an act of reconstructive
doing and consciousness [which] becomes fresh and alive" (59). It
is this act of "reconstructive perception" that Wordsworth ([1798]
1969) writes of in "Tintern Abbey":

> with gleams of half-extinguished thought,
> With many recognitions dim and faint. . . .
> The picture of the mind revives again:
> . . . . not only with the sense
> of present pleasure, but with pleasing thoughts
> That in this moment there is life and food
> For future years. (53–65; 163)

What Wordsworth remembers and comforts himself with as he
stands on the banks of the Wye is the knowledge that through an
active perception in the present, he can reconstruct the perception
of the past, and his memory and experience can always become
"fresh and alive."

Dewey's (1987) "undergoing phase of experience" is receptive
but not passive. "It involves surrender. But adequate yielding of the
self . . . through a controlled activity that may well be intense" (59).
What Dewey has described here fits particularly well with Wordsworth's "wise passiveness" and "spots of time," where the poet
receives nature in all her power, surrendering to the force of "diz-
zying raptures" so that the world wheels by with great intensity.
When older and a poet, Wordsworth reconstructed his art from the
"yielding of self" to experience.

Also apparent in Dewey's explanation of undergoing experience as it relates to art is the importance of a spontaneous overflow of powerful feeling, which both he and Wordsworth find necessary for artistic expression. Dewey is not satisfied that the experience itself will lead to art; art is not just the overflow of spontaneous emotion, but contemplated spontaneous feeling. Dewey enlists Wordsworth to explain that it is the spontaneous overflow of "emotion recollected in tranquility" that leads to expression (75), a concept that we shall see is crucial to current expressivist theory as well.

Many of Dewey's educational ideas, as well as those about art, correspond to those of Wordsworth and Coleridge. Dewey did not, however, accept all aspects of romantic educational theory. He made a point of saying that he did not. He lodged explicit objections, for instance, to the analogy of the development of a seed into a full-grown plant, an analogy he ascribes to Rousseau but which was pervasive among English romantic poets.[8] Dewey ([1940] 1969) believed that the "growth of a seed is limited as compared with that of a human being . . . It has not got the capacities for growth in different directions toward different outcomes that are characteristic of the more flexible and richly endowed human young" (289). He also objected to the more "exaggerated parts of Rousseau's doctrines" that idealize and sentimentalize the child (69). Dewey does not accept "romanticism" when it is defined as "whim" or "arbitrary emotion," and although Dewey does not directly address these criticisms to Wordsworth and Coleridge, he surely would have objected to Wordsworth's belief in the child as a "philosopher."

Coleridge, however, was much more closely aligned to Dewey's way of thinking on this issue, and he himself takes Wordsworth to task. In the *Intimation Ode*, Wordsworth [1807] (1984) suggests that the child is by nature a philosopher. In Book XXII of the *Biographia Literaria* ([1817] 1983), however, Coleridge disagrees with Wordsworth and demands Wordsworth explain in what sense the child is a philosopher. Like Dewey, Coleridge finds this particular position on childhood a "sentimental idealization" and a "deification" of the child. Although Coleridge shares a belief in the natural development of the child with Dewey, Dewey differs not only from Coleridge but from Arnold and Mill as well, because of his readings in "experimental" and "emergence" psychology. He began to establish a theory of "developmental" psychology. This shows, once again, how taxonomies leak; we could argue for Dewey as an intellectual ancestor to cognitivist rhetorics as well as expressivist and social-epistemic rhetorics.

Dewey saw experience as the foundation for an education that honors active rather than passive learning, and which could eventually lead to the sort of educated intellect that Wordsworth calls the "philosophical mind." "Moral and intellectual powers increase in vigor," says Dewey ([1940] 1969), when a "spontaneous interest and desire to accomplish something are behind them" (79). In Dewey's educational scheme, experience becomes the motivation for learning. A typical evil that Dewey (1956) found prevalent in traditional schools was the lack of any positive motivation. Since "the lack of any organic connection with what the child has seen and felt and loved makes the material purely formal and symbolic" (24), the learner has no connection or interaction with the material and cannot learn in the full sense of the word. The student can merely parrot back what has been read or heard. As Coleridge argues, learning is organic, is "educed" and not externally imposed.

In *The Child and the Curriculum* (1956), Dewey argues that, if the "subject-matter . . . be such as to have an appropriate place within the expanding consciousness of the child, if it grows out of his own past doings, thinkings, sufferings . . . no device or trick of method has to be resorted to in order to enlist interest" (27). This is exactly Wordsworth's point when he writes disdainfully of his Cambridge education where academic prizes became the "trick of method." It is also Coleridge's point when he responds with such ire against the Lancastrian system of punishment. Dewey agrees completely with Wordsworth and Coleridge when he argues that information that is unconnected to a student's experience will not really be learned by the student. It remains alone and remote from the student. For Dewey, as for Wordsworth, Coleridge, Mill, and Arnold, experience generated through perception and an organic connection between child and subject matter is a more beneficial path to knowledge than the external method of drilling facts into passive brains.

Dewey also shares with Wordsworth and Coleridge the same educational means by which to gain the experience crucial to the encompassing intellect: interaction with nature. In "Democracy in Education," Dewey ([1940] 1969) suggests that to "free the processes of mental growth," "the child [should be taken] out of doors, widening and organizing his experiences with reference to the world. . . ." No real knowledge is gained about nature, for example, unless it is "nature study when pursued as a vital observation of forces working under their natural conditions, plants and animals growing in their own homes, instead of mere discussion of dead specimens" (71).

In a stance truly reminiscent of Wordsworth, Dewey ([1902] 1956) argues that "we cannot overlook the importance for educational purposes of the close intimate acquaintance with nature at first hand," because in this interaction with nature comes "continual training of observation, of ingenuity, [of] constructive imagination . . ." (11). It is this point that Wordsworth makes in the poem "Tables Turned" [1798]: To "hear the woodland linnet" has more of "wisdom in it," says the poet, than the "dull and endless strife" of books ill used. Also like Wordsworth, Dewey ([1940] 1969) believes that traditional schools misuse books. He aligns himself with Wordsworth when he remarks that it is not a "Philistine attack upon books and reading" that he has in mind, that the question is not "how to get rid of them, but how to get their value . . ." (29).

In a Wordsworthian educational scheme, miseducation occurs if books are not tied to experience, perception, imaginative activity, and interaction with the world. Because of his freedom to read what excited him, and because of the Hawkshead school that promoted an education of experience, Wordsworth was an avid reader, and, as Book V of *The Prelude* ([1850] 1954) points out, his readings were of great influence in the shaping of his philosophical mind. Wordsworth, in fact, fits the description of Dewey's ([1940] 1969) ideal for learning through reading: "the child should have a personal interest in what is read, a personal hunger for it, and a personal power of satisfying this appetite" (29).

Dewey realizes that nurturing a full intellect takes the growth of personal experience and interaction with nature, for without these, there is no nourishing of what Coleridge calls "vital excellencies" and Wordsworth the "vital soul." As Dewey ([1940] 1969) talks about methods of learning to read he is arguing that only a "vital relation" to the subject at hand will breed successful learning: most methods "lack the essential of any well-grounded method, namely relevancy to the child's mental needs. No scheme for learning to read can supply this want. Only . . . putting the child into vital relation to the materials to be read" (28). Learning that moves students toward an encompassing intellect must arise out of the cultivation of Wordsworth's "vital soul," Coleridge's "vital excellencies," and out of what Dewey calls "vital relations" and "vital observations." If this is neglected, the student will lack what Dewey has called "spontaneous interest" and will instead be "thrown into a passive, receptive, or absorbing" educational setting where full learning cannot take place (13).

Dewey ([1899] 1956) further incorporates romantic ideas in his view that "reflection" is a crucial aspect of the journey toward the encompassing intellect. He makes his belief in this matter clear in an essay entitled "Why Reflective Thinking Must Be an Educational Aim." Like Coleridge, he finds that the reflective mind is a prerequisite to the truly educated intellect: "A person who has gained the power of reflective attention, the power to hold problems, questions, before the mind, *is* in so far, intellectually speaking, educated. He has mental discipline—power of the mind and *for* the mind" (147).

Coleridge, in *Aids to Reflection* ([1825] 1884), makes similar points and urges his readers to reflect on thoughts, actions, and circumstances, because not to engage in reflection results in a mind unable to make connections, unable to observe the whole. And as Dewey ([1940] 1969) seconds, "reflective thinking is a process of detecting relations . . . " (247).[9]

Coleridge suggests that through reflection we will nourish a sense of "distinction" and cultivate a questioning and active mind. Dewey ([1899] 1954) makes an almost identical argument: "True reflective attention, on the other hand, always involves judging, reasoning, deliberation; it means that the child has a *question of his own* and is actively engaged in seeking and selecting relevant material with which to answer it, consider the bearings and relations of this material . . ." (148) [original emphasis].

The questioning that arises out of reflection leads to Coleridge's sense of "distinction" that is like Dewey's selecting of "relevant material." Finally, for Dewey (1964) as for Coleridge, self-reflection and reflective thinking are necessary ingredients to intellectual success. In "The Process and Product of Reflective Activity: Psychological Process and Logical Form," Dewey writes that something is "achieved through conquering, by personal reflection, the difficulties that prevent immediate overflow into action and spontaneous success" (257). As Arnold puts it, reflection and self-knowledge are prerequisites to action.

Romantic Links to Contemporary Writing Theory

These romantic notions of self-reflection have reached far beyond Dewey and his progressive schools. They are, for instance, crucial to the write- and read-to-learn strategies of the National Writing Project and many writing-across-the-curriculum programs. Writing-to-learn advocates see writing as discovery and reflection; initial writing exercises are tentative, clarifying, questioning. Write- and read-to-learn techniques allow students to examine conflicting claims, make observations, explore causal relationships, change their minds and start again. Like the romantics and Dewey, write- and read-to-learn supporters understand that learning is an ongoing process full of fits and starts, speculations and questions, combining and separating, and analysis and synthesis. These are the crucial links to the imaginative intellect for current write-to-learn theorists just as for Wordsworth, Coleridge, and Dewey.

As strongly as Dewey (1987) lobbied for the vital links to the education of the imagination that we are now finding in current write-to-learn pedagogies, he just as strongly objected to the "separation and compartmentalization of emotion and thought, practice from insight, imagination from 'executive doing'" (27). Dewey felt that the mind could not be educated to its fullest potential in traditional schools because methods relied on Mill's version of "cram": passivity, drills, and reason separated from emotion. Thus, like the romantics, he sought an education that fosters emotion and imagination in conjunction with analysis and reason.

Not only does Dewey ([1899] 1964) define the same problems with the school systems as do Wordsworth and Coleridge, but he offers the same solution when he suggests the "introduction of more active, expressive, and self-directing factors" (29). Dewey is incorporating romantic ideas into his own philosophy, and his educational arguments keep alive some of the ideas articulated by Wordsworth and Coleridge more than a generation earlier. Dewey ([1940] 1969) is passing on some of the most important concepts and ideas of a romantic philosophy on education when he argues that "It is a method of discovery through search, through inquiry, through testing, through observation and reflection—all processes requiring *activity* of mind rather than merely powers of absorption and reproduction" (242).

Such things as discovery and reflection, which have now also been adopted by writing- and reading-to-learn advocates, entered discussions on current composition theory and practice en masse, in the 1960s with the likes of Ken Macrorie, William Coles, James Britton, D. Gordon Rohman, Peter Elbow, Donald Murray, and Ann Berthoff. Expressivists built their theories on foundations similar to those of the earlier poets and philosophers. In fact, the crux of expressivist theory is a desire to create a pedagogy that not only cultivates writing capabilities, but develops students' minds to their greatest capacity. A pedagogy that works toward these ends, according to expressivist doctrine, relies on what I have identified in the philosophies of the romantics—and in Mill, Arnold, and Dewey—as discovery, experience, reflection, and imagination. These are the romantic ideas that have flourished in response to mechanical and passive educational philosophies and product-centered writing instruction. While neo-classical rhetorics and cognitive writing theories also arose in reaction to product-centered writing instruction, these approaches still viewed writing as a linear and hierarchical activity that could be analyzed in terms of separate units or stages. Expressivist theory, however, does not view the act of composing as linear or hierarchical, but rather as a blending of experience, reflection, discovery, analysis, synthesis, reason, and imagination. It is in this recursive blending of "vital" actions that we can see the romantic legacy.

For instance, the assumption underlying the practice of prewriting, as Rohman (1965) defines it, is that students can write well, with "originality" and "spontaneity," if they can just discover the "exceptional power of revealing experience by expressing it first to [themselves] (Pre-Writing), and then to others (Communicating) so that we recognize the experience as our own too" (108). He believes that prewriting allows the writer to discover experience. Rohman also assumes that writing is a "personally transformed experience of an event." Thus he suggests the technique of meditation as a method that might give students "an inner knowledge transforming their 'events' into 'experiences'" (109). What he is after here, though perhaps in a less extreme way, is the sort of mystical experience that Wordsworth retells in the boat-stealing episode of *The Prelude* ([1850] 1954).

Taking the boat onto the lake was merely an event, but Wordsworth's "meditative" powers, his ability to "transform" this event into an experience, brought the mountains alive and closing rapidly upon his back. This was an event that he transformed into an experience powerful enough to play a part in shaping the philosophical mind of the poet. Rohman sees the practice of meditation as achieving the effect of an experience no longer merely happening "to you but *in* you" just as it happened with the young Wordsworth. Since prewriting and meditation issue "from the same sort of dynamic interplay of self and world," the meditation leads to the imitation of the creative principle that Rohman assumes prewriting is.

The students that took part in Rohman's (1965) initial study also kept journals in which they wrote daily. They were given a long list of questions that would hopefully provoke them to discovery of "what they believed, what they felt, what they knew" (109). Rohman and his colleagues were attempting to guide the students into the kind of reflective state that Coleridge, Arnold, and Dewey demand of the educated mind. Rohman explains that "in the process of introspection, formalized by the daily writing in the journal, we hoped to mobilize the consciousness of every student writer" (109). In other words, his hope was to foster, through reflective writing, the "distinct consciousness" that Coleridge claims comes from the same source: self-reflection. And Rohman and Wlecke feel the results of the study indicate that this is possible.

Donald Murray (1989) also argues for the importance of experience, reflection, and perception. While reflecting on a piece of his own writing, for instance, he chronicles the progression from perception to the moment when the writing comes together:

> There is the surprise of *perception* that I *experience* when the character in my novel saw no color. There is the surprise of *recollection* when I heard that terrible cough left over from a previous war. There is the surprise of *connection* when I relate my surprise in writing . . . There is the surprise of celebration when we *re-create* something . . . the surprise of *pattern* when a whole complex of connections click into place on the page. [emphasis added] (9)

In this whole discussion of surprise we can see a list of terms that as a whole are clearly romantic in complexion: "perception," "experience," "recollection," "connection," "re-create," "pattern," "whole."

As the romantics argued, to see, feel, hear, smell, and taste the outer world enhances the growth of the self; to actively engage the senses tills the soil of the soul for the fertile harvest of experience. The ability to perceive through all the senses leads to what Wordsworth has called a more "lively sensibility, more enthusiasm and tenderness . . . a greater knowledge of human nature" ["Preface" to the Second Edition of the *Lyrical Ballads* (737)]. In "Frost at Midnight," ([1798] 1985) while speaking of the future education and mental growth of his son, Coleridge likewise stresses the importance of communing with, of perceiving through the senses, the mountains, lakes, and shores of the natural world. Along with this external world, "Frost at Midnight" portrays the poet's mind at work, looking inward, perceiving, as it were, the internal world of the selves.

Murray (1984), recognizing the importance of gaining experience through perception, has incorporated this romantic philosophy into his teaching. The full intellect, and thus the capable writer, is always receiving, says Murray. The writer actively places himself in strategic places so that he is always receiving and collecting (33–48). Murray's discussions of receiving and collecting are in some ways analogous to Wordsworth's "wise passiveness." Although this receiving through the senses can be merely passive, it is, as Wordsworth suggests, "wise" because the passive receptiveness is the basis for perceiving and experiencing, and being wisely passive leads to the growth of a great mind. Murray (1982) has said that the writing course is the practice of perception (117). In "Internal Revision: A Process of Discovery," Murray discusses what he calls "prevision": "This term encompasses everything that precedes the first draft—

receptive experience, such as awareness (conscious and unconscious), observation, remembering; and exploratory experience such as research, reading, interviewing, and note-taking " (73). Experience, the process of taking inward what the world offers, is an important step toward effective writing, and learning to perceive leads to experience.

For Murray, the reflective state is also a necessity in learning to write well. If we do not cultivate reflection, according to Murray, we will not be able to make meaning through language. Today's world does not often allow the time needed for the inward looks afforded by reflection, and thus Murray (1982) makes a point of starting the day with stillness in which he may "stare vacantly out the window, notebook open, pen uncapped" (21). If he bypasses the reflective state, the writing will not work. It will be like trying to make "mashed potatoes pass through a keyhole." In order for writing to work, we must return to that "reflective state" where we can "play with language, connecting and disconnecting, listening for voice" (8). While some writers can write easily without this premeditative state, as I will argue shortly, this is usually because one way or another they have found themselves with a mind trained to react in certain ways.

This reflective state results in Murray's state of surprise. Surprise for him is like Wordsworth and Dewey's spontaneity. It is when something suddenly arises from within us. It is finding the unexpected. It is putting ourselves in touch with the perceptions, feelings, and experiences that we have internalized. It is yet another form of self-discovery. And the "wonderful thing about surprise," says Murray (1989) in "Writing for Surprise," is that "the more you experience surprise the easier it becomes to experience it. Surprise breeds surprise. And you can learn to be patient at your desk waiting for surprise to land" (6). Once it has "landed," this surprise is likely to be the nugget for a good piece of writing.

It is important to note here that surprise in Murray's terminology, and spontaneity in the romantics', is not something that just happens if people are lucky, and does not happen if they are down on their luck. Rather, receptivity and reflection cultivate surprise and spontaneity. It comes out of perception, feeling, experience, and practiced reflection. And these come from opening the mind to experience. As David Perkins (1964) explains in *Wordsworth and the Poetry of Sincerity*, spontaneity "begins in a concrete immediacy, and goes on to ponder it in discursive terms" (23). Out of our experience, and reflecting on that experience, "the poetry builds toward a moment of insight, when a general truth seems to break upon the mind with compelling force" (23). Surprise for Murray is this "moment of insight" as it "breaks upon the mind." Thus, the habit of reflection allows for the mind, as Wordsworth ([1798] 1984) puts it in the Preface, to be "connected with important subjects" (735). Once the connection is made, Wordsworth can compose "blindly" (735), just as Murray lets his pen be "the blind man's cane."

Murray's privileging of surprise is also tied to the romantic idea of organicism. The writing should come as "easily as leaves to the tree" as Keats argues, from a "germ within" as Coleridge suggests, or as the "tree does from the vital principle that actuates it" as Wordsworth says. Not to let the writing take this organic path is to place the writer at risk. Murray cautions, for instance, that "we run the danger of closing down thinking, exploration, and discovery" if we impose a pre-established form on the surprise, the insight, or the writing. What we must do, urges Murray (1989), like the romantics before him, is trust to the organic nature of creating meaning—the organic nature of the imaginative act. It is a mistake to "pay too much attention to genre at the wrong time," he warns (45). Instead, we need to allow the surprise—the thought, the word, or the line— to "lead us to form. And it should" (45). Murray's belief is that if we have a theory and pedagogy of writing that cultivates discovery, perception, and reflection, we have a basis not only for surprise and spontaneity but for the imaginative act of making meaning out of language as well.

Peter Elbow has most fully defined the importance of freewriting for the teaching of writing, and it is Elbow who has most fully seen the ways in which freewriting is a catalyst for reflection, discovery, and the articulation of experience. As he describes it, freewriting is simply writing without stopping for five or ten minutes, simply letting the words tumble out and onto the page. The goal is not good, polished writing, but a stream of consciousness. The focus is on the process, not the product. If we write freely during the first stage of our writing process, according to Elbow (1981), we "will warm up *all* [our] faculties" (10). Elbow (1973) describes this process as "cooking" and "growing"—metaphors that would feel quite comfortable to the romantics. Once the faculties are warm, the possibility then exists for entire pieces of writing to "cook perfectly" in our heads. These pieces will "grow out of that magic which some excellent writers can call on at will: simultaneous creativity and critical thinking" (Elbow 1981, 10). Elbow's spontaneity evolving from freewriting is Murray's cultivated surprise. This spontaneity comes from stimulating what lies within our unconscious. Once we have tapped what lies below our consciousness, the good writing can begin to flow, just as Coleridge claimed it did for him in the creation of "Kubla Khan."

Elbow (1981) also claims that freewriting can help in the development of a writer's voice, and voice in writing implies, for him, "words that capture the sound of an individual on the page" (287). *"Writing without voice,"* he claims, "is wooden or dead because it lacks sound, rhythm, energy, and individuality" (299). Elbow's project for the contemporary writer is like that of the romantic poets for their poetry. They rejected, for instance, much of eighteenth-century poetry that they felt was "dead and spiritless," precisely because it lacked the "energy and individuality" that came from infusing the writing with the experiences, feelings, passions, and voice of the poet.

In his quest for what he identifies as voice, it is easy to assume that Elbow neglects quality. Elbow (1981) himself acknowledges that he faces these charges (300), but one way in which he finds freewriting valuable is that, even though it can turn out "careless, excessive, or self-indulgent writing," it can also nurture voice and lead to good writing. Thus, in his answer to the charges that he ignores quality, Elbow retorts:

> My theory of voice helps me trust my own taste and deal with the accusation that I don't care about quality. I now see that caring about quality has two different meanings and springs from two different temperamental approaches to writing. On the one hand caring about quality implies a hunger to stamp out terrible writing. A hunger to destroy defects, failing, excess, and ugliness. I don't have this hunger. I am content to let people write much that is bad. I try to let myself write badly too. On the other hand, caring about quality implies hungering for excellencies, wanting the real things, not settling for mere adequacy. That's me. I want the moon. (301)

Elbow is not ignoring quality. He is out to get what is "real" and moving—exactly, I would add, what the romantics wanted for their poetry. As Elbow unabashedly admits, he and his students produce much that is not topnotch writing, just as the romantics wrote a great deal of second-rate poetry. Nonetheless, Elbow's students do produce some good writing and the romantics have given us what many consider some of the greatest poetry of the English language.

Elbow also argues that there are many benefits that arise from student writers' search for voice. It leads them "toward new thought, feelings, memories and new modes of seeing and writing" (284). In effect, it leads to discovery on many levels. It also prompts reflective writing which leads to a "greater connection between their writing and themselves," which in turn leads to "growth or development" (284). Reflection occurs because the search for voice means exploring "angry feelings, perhaps depressed feelings, perhaps a particular area of their lives" (284). Coleridge felt that a lack of reflective thinking and writing led to stasis, but that active self-reflection led to mental growth; Arnold believed that the instructor's "prime direct aim is to enable a man to know himself and his world" in order to take any worthwhile action; Elbow believes that freewriting and the search for voice are catalysts to reflective thinking and writing which result in "growth or development" (284). The growth Elbow speaks of might come about through writing to voice anger, hurt, or betrayal. The crux here is feelings, and giving vent to feelings gives way to the sorts of healing and growth that Mill found in Wordsworth's poetry.

Elbow is careful to explain more fully what he means by feelings and emotions as they relate to good writing, however. He is aware that he may have "made real voice sound as though it is always full of loud emotion" (312). His message is not that writers must always be writing lots of "strong feelings," but that they must "experience" what they are writing about. He means something "much closer to 'should see and hear' than 'should feel strongly'" (333). Seeing and hearing, as Elbow refers to it, has to do with the ability to perceive and notice something and then do something with it through language. Elbow grants that feelings naturally occur when we experience something fully, but that strong feelings alone do not make good writing, and often, in fact, make bad writing. To be good, says Elbow, writing must come out of the "event or scene itself" (334).

I can imagine, at this point, assent that the feelings and experiences that Elbow speaks of are valuable for personal writing and narratives, but I can also imagine dissent in a belief that they are appropriate for more objective and academic styles of writing. If, however, we reexamine the key terms from these passages of Elbow's—"strong feelings," "experience," and the idea of strong writing coming from the "event or scene itself"—we find that they are perfectly apt for various disciplinary writing tasks. Why, for example, does a marxist literary critic choose to write an article about the virtues of her marxist readings, if it is not that she has "strong feelings" that reading in this light is important? Does she not "experience" herself, as best she can, as a marxist as she writes her article? Does her argument not arise out of the "event or scene" of marxism? To assume that Elbow's use of and intent for these terms is only applicable to personal writing is a misunderstanding and a far too limiting view of Elbow's theoretical stance. Indeed, strong feelings, experience, and the idea of the discourse arising from the event or scene are as crucial to an interesting and commanding academic essay as they are to a personal narrative.

Elbow further concentrates on ways of experiencing and ways of bringing about re-experiences, because, like Wordsworth, he believes that the ability to really experience something is educated out of children: "As children get older and more sophisticated, they get better at making the kind of *refusal* to experience that most adults are good at" (321). In poems like "We Are Seven," Wordsworth argues that the ability to imagine, to experience or re-experience, has vanished by adulthood. The adult in this poem insists that the little girl and her siblings are five in number, not seven, since two "in the church-yard lie." The child in the poem, however, re-experiences play as it was when her siblings were alive: she is able, as Elbow puts it, to "see, hear, and smell everything": "'Nay,'" says the child, "'we are seven!'" Like the romantics' desire to maintain the "fresh gaze of a child with the obstinate integrity of a man consulting his own experience, and hence thinking outside traditional categories or interpretations" (Perkins 1964, 65), Elbow wants his students to be able to experience in order to think and write well.

Ann Berthoff's (1981) discussions on the imagination, and the ways in which discovery, perception, reflection, and experience foster the imagination, are the most complex and fully articulated of the current expressivist theories. She argues that if we restore the imagination to its proper realm, we have the perfect theory on which to build a pedagogy for composition because it gives us a basis for generating a concept of "forming." The imagination's power lies in the many analogies "between writing and all other acts of mind whereby we make sense of the world" (4). The imagination, according to Berthoff, helps us "form the concept of forming," which in turn requires us to "coordinate and subordinate, to amalgamate, discard, and expand; it is our means of giving shape to contact" (4). For Berthoff (1984), language, or writing, is in itself a creative and forming act as well. "When we write," she says, "we represent our recognitions of relationships: that is what *composing* means" (1).

As with the romantics and Mill, Arnold, and Dewey, Berthoff sees the imagination as a crucial part of a fully capable intellect, and she relies on the romantic means of nurturing the imagination in her own method of teaching. She suggests that, as teachers, we must realize that "perception" is an important model for the "process of making meaning" (46). She argues that every composition course should begin with activities meant to stimulate observation, because the ability to see and re-see is vital to the imagination. Observation is extremely important because looking closely is active and engages the mind. Without an actively engaged mind, no composing will take place. She recommends writing assignments such as a detailed record of ten minutes of observation and reflection carried out daily for a week. Close "descriptions and speculations in response to a seashell, a milkweed pod, a chestnut burr, or any natural object" could reap a rich harvest for the mind. But we must remember to "think of perception as *visual thinking* " or, as Dewey would also argue, observation becomes a mechanical exercise for the sake of producing "vivid detail about nothing much" as opposed to what it really is: the "mind in action" (64).

A theory of imagination not only provides occasions for the practice of perception, in Berthoff's estimation, but it gives us a new way to approach language instruction, even at the very basic level of the sentence. She concedes that the "drill can teach youngsters—and college freshman—how to correct faulty sentences in workbooks," but drill is inadequate because it "cannot teach them to write substantial, readable sentences" (24). To really "compose" sentences and not just glue together "somebody else's pretend subsentences, we will have to know something about language as . . . a means of making knowledge" (24). Language, and thus writing, for Berthoff as for her romantic mentors, is alive and powerful. Writing creates meaning. It is an act of forming and shaping. It is the recognition of relationships. The process of composing is analogous to the imagination in action.

Berthoff offers the double-entry notebook as a pedagogical technique that arises from a theory of the imagination, and thus one that can teach students to "really compose." Her approach is to have students write continuously in a spiral-bound notebook. On the right side they make reading notes on "direct quotations, observational notes, fragments, lists, images—verbal and visual" (45). On the other side they make notes and observations about their original entries. The double-entry format, suggests Berthoff, "provides a way for the student to conduct that 'continuing audit of meaning' that is at the heart of learning to read and write critically. The facing pages are in dialogue with one another" (45). In the double-entry notebook Berthoff brings the processes of reading and writing together. She believes that writing in this way can help develop a critical method of reading as well as writing because it gives students access to watching a text come into being, in this case their own. It also encourages the habits of "reflective questioning in the process of reading" (45), which, we will remember, is what Coleridge ([1825] 1884) urges us to do in *Aids to Reflection*. If we do not consider each part of the text in relation to ourselves, through this kind of reflective questioning, then, according to Coleridge, we cannot cultivate the "educated mind" or what I call the encompassing intellect.

Berthoff also finds the double-entry notebook useful in that it sets up a dialectic in the juxtaposition of entries, which is important to Berthoff's method and theory of imagination because she believes that composing is a dialectical process. Through this dialectic students are able to generate new meaning. Here again her affinity with Coleridge is a strong one. Reflective and dialectical processes are embedded in the creation of art, in the voluntary action of what Coleridge calls the secondary imagination. For Coleridge this dialectic takes the form of the "reconciliation of opposites." As the mind engages in the creative act of finding "multeity in unity," it engages in a dialectic of self and world, matter and spirit, nature and mind, object and subject. As the mind engages in this dialectic, meaning is forged through a "progression of contraries." Berthoff's aim for the composition of new meaning through dialectic is similar. When students write, observe, and reflect about nature, about objects, about their world, about their reading, writing, and thinking in the double-entry journals, they are faced with the dichotomies between subject and object, self and world, mind and nature. As they return to their original entries to summarize, formulate, and find likeness in difference, they are performing the creative act of composing—forming new meaning.

If this dialectical process seems potentially chaotic for students, it is. In "Learning the Uses of Chaos," Berthoff (1981) argues that "learning to write is a matter of learning to tolerate ambiguity" (71). She notes that chaos is scary for both students and teachers, but that if we give in to it and understand it, it can enhance composing. "Meanings," argues Berthoff, "don't come out of the air; we make them out of a chaos of images, half-truth, remembrances, syntactic fragments, from the mysterious and unformed" (70). It is these sorts of "mysterious and unformed" images and remembrances from which Coleridge (*Political Works* [1798] 1912, 297–298) claims to have created the poem "Kubla Khan." And likewise, it is from chaos that the Kubla Khan decrees his "stately pleasure dome" within the poem. If, as teachers, we can encourage our students to accept chaos by cultivating Keats' negative capability as Berthoff argues we can, or as Coleridge has done in the creation of "Kubla Khan," [1798] 1912, 297–298), they begin to find meanings which "can be discerned taking shape within it" (70–71). Berthoff suggests that the way to do so is to design assignments that let student writers discover the potential of language by playing with it, working it, pushing it to its limits. This requires that we make room for non-graded, messy, and informal student thinking and writing. They must reflect on it and recognize that it is dynamic. If we can design courses that allow this, then students will learn to tolerate ambiguity and chaos. And since chaos generates language, argues Berthoff, students "can learn to write by learning the uses of chaos, which is to say, rediscovering the power of language to generate the sources of meaning" (70).

Ann Berthoff is one of the most philosophical of composition scholars writing today. She grounds much of her philosophy in the complex theories of knowing and creating that Coleridge set forth in the *Biographia Literaria* ([1817] 1983), and she continually relies on his definitions of the imagination. She (1981) understands, as Coleridge did, that in order to write or compose we must "learn to intuit," to "see how things are related," to "grasp" the "relationship of parts to the meaning of a whole" (57). She demands that we "reclaim the imagination," because once we have done so, we have a method for teaching that "recognizes the human need and ability to shape, discriminate, select" (29).

Because of our current ahistorical understanding of expressivism, scholars and teachers might have recognized that expressivists have ties to romanticism, but they have not examined the connections in depth, nor have they been willing to acknowledge what is valuable about these romantic ties. The romantic and expressivist privileging of spontaneity, for instance, is not usually understood as a skill that arises only as the result of practice and through cultivating a certain habit of mind. It is seen, to the contrary, as a "myth of inspiration" that is detrimental to student writers.

The theories and practices of these contemporary expressivists are a complex and valuable reincarnation of what is most worthwhile in the educational and poetic theories of the original romantics. None of the poets, philosophers, and teachers I examine here are carbon copies of each other, and my intent is not to suggest that they are. Rather, my intent is to illuminate a tradition of romantic thought and to suggest that many theories on education and writing have been supplemented, in invaluable ways, by some important romantic tenets. To do so expands the boundaries repeatedly used to describe expressivism. It allows us to see that current expressivists' romantic pedagogies foster in students the ability to create knowledge through writing. And particularly interesting, considering the pervasive view that expressivists are primarily practitioners and lack a theoretical center, is that they not only share assumptions held by the romantics, but that they share much of the same philosophical grounding as three men who are generally seen as profound thinkers and philosophers of the nineteenth and twentieth centuries. Like Dewey, expressivists understand that having experiences and being able to know and name those experiences play a vital role in the discovery and creating of writing and coming to knowledge. They share with many philosophers, poets, and educators of later years the belief that education must not deny experience, must not separate the emotive from the analytical, but instead must capture what is most vital: feeling, experience, reflection, creativity. And like the romantics before them, Rohman, Murray, Elbow, and Berthoff, in an attempt to counteract a pedagogy that views learning as passive and writing as a mechanical act, nurture the opportunity for students to reflect, question, and think deeply so that the imaginative mind, the "encompassing intellect," can flourish.

The traditions and philosophies of romanticism are clearly present in many of our composition theories and pedagogies, and not just those which have been labeled expressivist. They appear as well in write-to-learn theories and social-epistemic theories. An understanding of learning and writing as processes, a focus on reflective and critical thinking, a belief that writing acts as a source for seeking and creating knowledge, and the nurturance of student participation in the act of creating knowledge are important aspects of social-epistemicism, yes, but they are often claimed as social-epistemic in nature. Yet, these are all at the basis of expressivist theory as it arises out of romanticism.

Social-epistemicism is not a freestanding theory, pure and unattached to expressivist theory and romantic thought. As Albert O. Wlecke and D. Gordon Rohman argued at the 1990 Conference on College Composition and Communication in Chicago, there is much of modern society that is deeply rooted in romanticism. Moreover, as M. H. Abrams (1989) says of Wordsworth, "he has altered our consciousness and culture as well as the ways in which we perceive not only the natural world, but ourselves and others" (45). As the field of composition continues its exploration of social-epistemic theories, it will attempt to break free of many of these romantic ties. Perhaps some of these roots do need to be severed. But it would serve us better, I think, to acknowledge the ways in which expressivist and social-epistemic rhetorics supplement each other, and to recognize what expressivism has contributed to social-epistemic theories and pedagogies. There is, after all, much in expressivist theories and pedagogies, and in their heritage, that is worthwhile. In order to recognize this, and in order to envision the ways in which expressivist and social-epistemic rhetorics are not merely estranged theories that share no common ground, we must provide the historical contexts for expressivism as I have been doing here.

Notes

1. Mark Waldo's dissertation also points out that the crucial aspect of the educational philosophy Wordsworth is promoting is based on the conjunction of the imaginative and analytical.

2. Ben Ross Schneider Jr.'s book, *Wordsworth's Cambridge Education* (1957), presents a clear study of Wordsworth's attitudes and actions during his time at Cambridge.

3. Waldo offers a useful discussion of Boyer's effect on Coleridge.

4. Walsh and Waldo also note the importance of reflection to Coleridge's theories.

5. See also Walsh page 61.

6. Elsewhere Coleridge has said that the powerful intellect is one that discovers: "to invent was different from to discover—a watch maker invented a time-piece, but a profound thinker only could discover" (*Collected Works of Samuel Taylor Coleridge,* vol. V, 583).

7. Mill's explanation for the healing reads like a shortened version or paraphrase of Wordsworth's statement of purpose in the Preface:

> to choose incidents and situations from common life, and to relate or describe them, throughout as far as was possible in a selection of language really used by men, and at the same time, to throw over them a certain colouring of imagination, whereby ordinary things should be presented to the mind in an unusual aspect; and further, and above all, to make these incidents and situations interesting by tracing them, truly though not ostentatiously, the primary laws of our nature: chiefly, as far as regards the manner in which we associate ideas in a state of excitement. (Preface 734)

8. M. H. Abrams (1953) takes note of the importance of the plant metaphor to the romantics in *The Mirror and the Lamp.*

9. Dewey had read Coleridge's *Aids to Reflection* [1825] and occasionally quotes from this work.

Chapter Five

Toward a Social-Expressivism: Misreadings and Rereadings of Expressivism Past and Present

Romanticism and expressivism are often misread, or at least only partially read, by many compositionists. As I argued earlier, the twentieth century has indulged in an "antiRomantic animus" (Barzun, xi) which accounts, in part, for a need to reread expressivism and the romantic tradition from which it stems in a fuller and more positive light. In Chapter One I touched briefly on some of the ways in which this anti-romantic enmity reveals itself in accusations against expressivism. In this chapter I look more fully at the charges that neo-romantic and expressivist rhetorics lack rigor, are arhetorical because they are solely for self-expression and thereby ignore audience and the social contexts for writing, and are radically individualistic, resulting in a desire only for self-development and a naiveté about social and political realities. All of these attacks against expressivism are tied to a shortsighted view of the romantic and expressivist self. I either read more fully, or reread when necessary, both romanticism and expressivism to adjust the field's general understanding of romantic rhetorics in the face of disparaging attacks on expressivism. In so doing, a theory and practice for social-expressivisms arises from both the romantic past and the expressivist present.

Misreadings of the Romantics

As my earlier quotation from Richard Young's (1980) work suggests (Chapter One), invoking the romantic ancestry of expressivism has resulted in the charge that expressivism lacks intellectual rigor. A "frequently heard accusation against the new romanticism" is its lack of academic and intellectual "rigor" (Young 1980, 56). But, as Young also points out, this charge stems from a change in the role of teacher as purveyor of knowledge to explorer with the students "alert for the spontaneous, the intuitive, the innovative." This change in the teacher's role does not necessarily mean the classroom is devoid of rigor (56).

In part, these charges against romanticism, which is then often conflated with expressivism, stem from a narrowly defined vision of academic rigor. Generally the romantics are seen as anti-academic in terms of what most scholars mean by "academic": mastering academic canons of literature; mastering the ability to reason in specific ways; mastering the ability to analyze; mastering logical and linear forms of discourse within particular academic settings. The romantics, of course, privileged emotions, imagination, synthesis, less linear forms of discourse and logic, and the importance of a non-academic setting in which to learn—usually nature.

This version of what the romantics find important in education is accurate to a certain degree. While they did honor and focus attention on these "nonacademic" components of learning, the belief that this is their sole focus creates a lopsided version of the romantics' intellectual concerns and suggests they disavowed traditional academic activities completely. Shelley wrote insightful and knowledgeable essays on many subjects, including love, religion, and politics. Coleridge was a philosopher as well as a poet, and perhaps one of the most well read thinkers of all time. Moreover, his lectures on Shakespeare remain a standard in the traditional literary canon. In *Aids to Reflection* ([1825] 1884), he argues not only for reading, but for reflection, analysis, and synthesis of that reading—what I would call rigorous intellectual work.

Perhaps the more commonly accepted version of academic rigor seems missing in romanticism because of a misunderstanding of Wordsworth. If poems such as "Expostulation and Reply" and "Tables Turned" are read at face value, severed from Wordsworth's fuller philosophy, then it appears that he indeed might be privileging frolic with nature over intellectual activity. But Wordsworth was adamant about books and study, not only for himself, but in his plan for a successful national education as well.[1] Finally, a study of romanticism reveals that proponents of romantic thought had a thorough knowledge of what traditional academics have seen as the greatest works of science, history, art, and literature. Similarly, anyone who reads either Elbow or Berthoff, even summarily, would be hard put to miss how widely read both are in theory, philosophy, and literature.

While it is true that the romantics were not devoid of traditional academic knowledge such as the established canons of literary, philosophical, and scientific thought, it might also be true that neo-romantics and expressivists who do not believe in any one body of knowledge that everyone must read in order to be cultured are still charged with being anti-academic. To confuse the romantics' academic knowledge with that of the students' in our classrooms would be more than just problematic. But nor can critics of expressivism argue that expressivist classrooms are anti-intellectual or anti-academic merely because they arise from romanticism. Moreover, expressivists who do not believe in one academic canon for every student to "master" meet the so-called more progressive and leftist social, multicultural, and marxist compositionists at this juncture.

At any rate, what is of utmost importance to expressivists is not merely literary or rhetorical training isolated from the broader goal of nurturing encompassing intellects and whole beings. In other words, writing and thinking are not separate entities. Exercising emotive and analytical processes, driving towards synthesis, writing for discovery, and demanding reflexivity—all components of an expressivist-based classroom—are intellectually demanding. So, even if the goal of a pedagogy is not merely to master academic forms, this does not create an intellectually "soft" pedagogy. A fuller intellect fostered in our students can result in the ability to think and reflect deeply, and to create ideas and solutions. It is this ability that expressivists want for students, not merely the ability to repeat such memorized "facts" as dates and definitions, as Dickens' Bitzer does in *Hard Times*. As Ann Berthoff would argue, without an imaginative mind capable of "forming," composition becomes a mere act of drill rather than an act of making meaning.

When Flower, Bizzell, and Gage talk about the "myth of the inspired writer" as a negative romantic legacy, they illustrate my point about the way in which general myths surrounding romanticism have entered the conversations about current rhetorical theory. What is most problematic is that they do so by isolating this myth from any understanding of expressivist inspiration. It is true that many people have come to view artists and poets as special beings blessed with transcendent power. This probably does have its roots in romanticism, as Gage suggests. Perhaps this is because the romantic self-projections, the poet-figures in romantic poetry, emanate a carefully constructed blessed and special quality. Perhaps it is also because, as Flower points out about the introduction to "Kubla Khan," the poets liked to give readers the sense that their poems and creative visions just happened. Yet in larger works such as the *Biographia Literaria* ([1817] 1983) and the "Preface" to the *Lyrical Ballads* ([1815] 1984), Coleridge's and Wordsworth's theories on the making of poetry and the poet are less "adulatory." Although the poets did believe they had a greater "sensibility" than the general population, they were not as elitist as Gage implies; the romantics believed that this "sensibility" was something that could be cultivated in the general population.

Just as the accusation that the romantics believed in a myth of the inspired writer is not completely without justification, the accusation that expressivists similarly hold to a notion of good writing as inspired, as mysterious, and as some sort of gift is also not unfounded. Scholars like William Coles (1967), for instance, have suggested that writing is an art, and since art cannot be taught as a mere skill, we cannot really teach writing as writing (111). I agree with Coles that writing is much more than a skill and that if it is to be "good" writing, it should not be taught as though it were a skill for a formulaic procedure. The fact remains, however, that it is dangerous to conceive of writing as a gift of genius. A classroom where some students have God-given inspiration or genius, and others do not, is, by definition, oppressive and undemocratic. There are, after all, very few of our students whom we would classify as possessing "genius." Thus, if we have automatically created an underclass through some idea that good writing is the province of student prodigies, there is no hope in the writing classroom for the majority of our students. And yet, there are certain learnable aspects of artistry, when we think of it in the medieval sense. We can "democratize" art when we think of it as craft. Many elementary school teachers have begun this process by teaching the art of book binding so that students are publishing their own writing.

David Russell (1988) is another critic who sees undemocratic and oppressive ends as following inexorably from expressivist pedagogy:

> At the level of public policy, then, Romantic assumptions about composition have a particularly significant effect. If composition is an individual response to inner promptings, a mysterious process, then some will be prompted and some will not. Those who are not may be excluded. Sometimes that exclusion is direct: a student is not admitted, or admitted only to certain programs ... At other times the exclusion is more subtle: a student is excluded from an

education that empowers her to take a leadership role in society because an institution assumes that many (or most) of its students cannot write well enough to receive such an education, or that they cannot be taught . . . to write. (144)

I am not arguing against Russell's point that public policy is affected, sometimes for the worse, if institutions assume that good writing happens only through inspiration or if they assume that writing is not teachable. Rather, my point of departure is with what Bizzell hints at when she notes that the myth of instant text production is a romantic idea which has been "debased." I will be more blunt and call it an understandable misuse, but misuse nonetheless, of the term "romantic."[2] To misconstrue romantic ideas about genius and inspiration is to confine expressivists to a theory of composing that limits and perhaps damages students; it also allows critics of expressivism a convenient reason to dismiss expressivist rhetorics as too problematic to be useful.

If we return to the romantics in order to understand more fully what it means to be the "inspired writer," perhaps this issue will become less of a stumbling block. Critics might be less likely to cast out what is good about romantic rhetorics with what is bad, and perhaps it will offer expressivists new insight, not only into their heritage, but into the complexities involved with the composing of "good writing." We can also begin to correct, for our students, the misconceived notion of inspiration and genius so that they do not continue to believe in the idea of "instant text production," and so that "motivation is not killed" for those who have worked hard to "master technique" (Gage 1986, 17).

Critics of expressivism, or expressivists themselves for that matter, who equate expressivist theories with the notion that students must be geniuses or inspired beings to write well are confusing the education of the imagination, or encompassing intellect, with the production of a great poet or artist. Most poets have undergone an imaginative education of one sort or another. But this does not mean that an education of the imagination can only take place if you are a great poet, nor does it mean that imagination is available to some and not others. Wordsworth, for example, believed that the imagination is innate, as his poetry about children suggests, but that it is "educated" out of us. He believed that the imagination can be cultivated and nurtured in all people, and since the imagination is the key ingredient in genius, he believed that genius is also innate, but it needs to be drawn forth with the right kind of education.

Coleridge ([1817] 1983) was skeptical of Wordsworth's belief here because Coleridge held that all people have primary imagination but not all are capable of utilizing the secondary. However, the

secondary imagination can be put into motion by a mind self-
consciously aware of its own imaginative potential (XVII). Like his
discussion of the educated mind, Coleridge's claim that the imagination can be voluntarily invoked points to the romantic faith that
people can nurture an imaginative mind. In this light, the negative
criticism that an expressivist pedagogy does not work because our
students are not poetic geniuses is less credible. To critics who dis-
regard expressivist rhetorics because of a debased understanding of
romantic inspiration, I suggest that a context for expressivism, which
includes a fuller knowledge of its traditions, will offer an alternative
reading.

Ideally, the issue of inspiration takes care of itself through the
entire enterprise of cultivating in our students an encompassing and
imaginative intellect. In other words, when the mind is properly
prepared, inspiration becomes a habit, not an occasional gift from
the muse.

In *The Prelude* ([1850] 1954), Wordsworth wrote:

> for I neither seem
> To lack that first great gift, the vital soul,
> Nor general Truths, which are themselves a sort
> Of Elements and Agents, Under-powers,
> Subordinate helpers of the living mind:
> Nor am I naked of external things Forms,
> images. . . . (I: 149–155)

This passage identifies "general Truths," "external things," and the
"vital soul" as necessary seeds for the growth of the philosophical
mind. At least two of these core ingredients—"vital soul" and
"external things"—also become essential to the educational philosophies of later transitional figures between the romantics and
expressivists—Mill and Dewey, for instance. Likewise, they have
traversed time and are inherent in the theory and pedagogy of current expressivists such as Elbow and Murray. Each has made the
point that if we foster what Wordsworth calls the "vital soul" or
"living mind," we are promoting observation, perception, experience, discovery, feelings, and reflection. These, in their entirety,
allow Wordsworth to compose poetry that appears to be spontaneous and inspired, allow Elbow to tap into the "good writing that can
just flow," not just occasionally, but on a regular basis for almost
any writing task. In other words, inspiration for the romantics, and
for most expressivist rhetoricians, is not a phenomenon that is random and involuntary. As Coleridge says, the creative act is motivated by "voluntary will," and in the "Preface" to the Second Edition of the *Lyrical Ballads* ([1815] 1954), Wordsworth suggests that

it is practice that makes the poet different from the non-poet: "from practice . . . a greater readiness and power in expressing what he thinks and feels, and especially those thoughts and feelings which, by his own choice, or from the structure of his own mind, arise in him without immediate external excitement" (737).

The problem for a theory and pedagogy of writing, of course, lies in the fact that a writing course lasts ten to fifteen weeks—certainly not enough time to cultivate an encompassing intellect in students. Yet, it is Wordsworth's "practice" that expressivist rhetorics foster and hope to set into motion, not just for ten or fifteen weeks, but for a lifetime. However, when expressivists advocate prewriting, free-writing, searching for voice, and discovery as ways of inducing "good writing" from our students, incorporating writing into their lives, and initiating the continued growth of the intellect, we are saddled with the unwarranted criticism that the expressivist approach sees no writing "worth doing" but writing for discovery.

Maxine Hairston (1986), for instance, misreads expressivists on this point:

> They [Murray, Elbow, Coles, Berthoff] believe that we create mean-ing by writing, that meaning does not exist as a separate entity to be communicated by writing. They hold that the essential features of good writing are originality and an authentic voice. These teach-ers seem to believe that every time students write they should do Class III writing [what Hairston calls reflective writing], spending substantial time on discovery and working through several drafts to find out what they mean. They imply that no other writing is worth doing. (449)

Hairston is correct that expressivists believe "students should write to discover themselves and to make sense out of their world" and that we "create meaning by writing." None of the people she cites, how-ever, say that meaning cannot previously exist and be communicated in writing, nor do they imply that other kinds of writing are not worthwhile. They do not imply that the self being discovered is a self-contained self and not socially constructed. In *Writing With Power,* Peter Elbow (1981) spends many pages discussing writing strategies for tasks that do not lend themselves to discovery, drafting, and reflecting. What Elbow does argue is that doing reflective writing and writing for discovery whenever possible can make one a better writer and thinker, thereby helping in any writing task. Like Word-sworth and Coleridge, he is talking about "personal," "authentic," and "emotive" writing as necessary to the growth of self and mind, not saying that it is necessary for every written document. Like Mill, he realizes that splitting the emotive from the analytical has negative consequences.

Elbow addresses these misguided criticisms himself when he tells his readers that "in the short run there is probably a conflict between developing a real voice and producing successful pragmatic writing—polished pieces that work for specific audiences and situations . . . Deep personal outrage, for example, may be the only authentic tone of voice you can use in writing to a particular person, yet that voice is neither appropriate nor useful for the actual document you have to write" (307).

Elbow would argue that a quick five or ten minute freewrite might clear the mind of this outrage, thus facilitating the rapid construction of the appropriate text. The feelings are not denied but remain a counterpart to the analytical approach that produces the "appropriate" text.

I would argue, finally, that much of what creates the "vital soul," and thus creates the most fertile opportunities for successful writing, is teachable. We can, for instance, teach students to explore, if not fully understand, their passions, through such exercises as Peter Elbow's freewritings and through personal journal writing. We can take the important step of teaching them to reflect on their feelings, thoughts, observations, perceptions, and experiences as Ann Berthoff does with her double-entry notebook. Through these reflections students can begin to examine their positions within the social world that they interact with daily. There is much that we can teach, and if we take our cues from the romantics, perhaps we can envision and define a pedagogy that makes insight and inspiration a recurrent aspect of every student's daily thinking, and of the majority of their writing tasks, from the most mundane to the most artistic. If, on the other hand, we choose to teach writing as a skill of form and style and not as an act of thinking that requires using the creative and imaginative mind, there will be very few students indeed who will become "good writers."

It is difficult to discuss romanticism and expressivist rhetorics without "emotions" and "feelings" creeping into the conversation. It has become a generally accepted cultural assumption that to be "romantic" is equivalent to being excessively sensitive, sentimental, and emotional. Likewise, there is a general feeling that expressivist rhetorics are "touchy-feely," unnecessarily indulgent, and inappropriately tolerant of students wallowing in their own feelings. Admittedly, expressivists, especially Peter Elbow, do not balk at the idea of bringing personal feeling into the educational arena and the writing classroom; thus it is easy to see how this assumption continues to thrive.

Learning to write well relies a great deal on learning to write with voice. Elbow (1981) believes that the search for voice means exploring feelings: "angry feelings, perhaps depressed feelings" (284). This search for voice, in turn, is a catalyst to the sorts of reflective thinking and writing which result in "growth or development" (284). Elbow indicates that it is not just personal emotional growth that comes about through writing to voice anger, hurt, or betrayal, but intellectual development as well. Again, the personal and intellectual are yoked here because Elbow chooses not to separate writers and students into non-holistic elements. Writers are complex beings within which emotional, psychological, spiritual, analytical, and intellectual developments are related. His point is, finally, that these feelings, whatever they may be, are crucial. However, just as it is wrong to view the romantic poets as overly emotional, it is a mistake to assume that Elbow's students devote an entire writing course to indulging their feelings in inappropriate ways.

Elbow is not advocating raw emotions and feelings as good writing within the confines of what the academy is willing to accept, even though both are part of fully experiencing something. He is advocating the romantic version of experience and Wordsworth's and Dewey's belief that expression is at its best when an overflow of powerful emotion is recalled and recreated through language later, not at the moment of the overflow. That is, as Wordsworth (1815) puts it in the Preface to the *Lyrical Ballads* ([1815] 1984), "Our continued influxes of feeling are modified, and directed by our thoughts, which are indeed the representations of all our past feelings" (735). What is important here, but often forgotten or ignored, is that Wordsworth's poetry is not composed at the moment he is overwhelmed with raw feeling, but, rather, from a distance, while re-experiencing some event that yielded those strong feelings. This is exactly Elbow's point when he says that good writing arises out of the re-experience, the participation in an event. Peter Elbow (1981) is aware that people misconstrue the part emotions play in his rhetoric, and thus he makes a point to explain that writing is not just "loud emotion" (312), but rather, as Wordsworth argues, a "recollection in tranquillity."

To consider emotions within a romantic and neo-romantic context leads directly to a discussion of the many different misconceptions of the romantic and expressivist self. Critics tend to see the romantic and expressivist emphasis on personal feeling, greater sensibility, and experience as a mere reflection of the inner self and, therefore, meaningful only to the individual. The romantics' focus on self-discovery and personal vision is often interpreted as outright self-centeredness or autocratic individualism. In fact, this interpretation of the self as the "radical individualism" that Barzun identifies as having entered into the general lore surrounding romanticism perpetuates a false notion of the personal. In a similar vein, expressivist rhetorics appear to have been infused with this generally held misconception, and are perhaps too unthinkingly thought of as self-centered and "radically" individualistic (Berlin 1988, 492).

The expressivist and romantic notion of self, however, is more complex than these charges assume. A deeper understanding of expressivist heritage dispels the tendency to stereotype expressivists because an ill-conceived myth has clouded our view of current expressivist rhetorics. It is a commonly held misconception that romanticism is primarily subjective to the point of solipsism.

Perception, observation, and reflection led the romantics to a sharpened sense of empathy that allowed them to go beyond solipsism. Coleridge makes it clear in *The Philosophical Lectures* [1818–1819] that the poet should transcend personal interest and any form of radical individualism (Wellek, 162). As poets, indeed as human beings, we should "live in the universal, to know no self but that which is reflected not only from the faces of all around us, our fellow-creatures, but reflected from the flowers, the trees, the beasts, yea from the very surface of the waters and the sands of the desert. . . ." (Wellek, 162).

For Wordsworth, poetry exists primarily to work on human feelings for the purpose of reaching mental and moral happiness. He thought the circumstances of the poet were often a buffer to what others actually suffered in the world; thus, he believes sympathy and empathy both critical. To be empathic requires a self or selves very different from the radically individualistic self that most charge expressivism and romanticism with:

> However exalted a notion we would wish to cherish of the character of a Poet, it is obvious, that while he describes and imitates passions, his employment is in some degree mechanical, compared with the freedom and power of real and substantial action and suffering. So that it will be the wish of the Poet to bring his feelings near to those of the persons whose feelings he describes, nay for short spaces of time, perhaps, to let himself slip into an entire delusion, and even confound and identify his own feelings with theirs. (*Poetical Works* [1815] 1984, 737)

Wordsworth also argued that one of the functions of poetry is to agitate people out of their "savage torpor" and spread "relationship and love." He aspired to give people more feeling, to create not only happy and moral individuals, but a happy and moral society. In Wordsworth's eyes, his job as a poet was to bring all of society together: "the Poet binds together by passion and knowledge the vast empire of human society, as it is spread over the whole earth, and over all time" (*Poetical Works* [1815] 1984, 738). To agitate people to action through language is not to be radically individualistic.

Blake said that the most sublime act is to give up the self for another, and scholars have noted that Keats was sincere, generous, and open-minded, having "extraordinary sympathetic and tolerant understanding of other people" (Bate 1959, 317). Keats' concept of "negative capability" suggests that one way to grasp the complexities of life is by negating our own egos while being imaginatively open-minded, sympathetic, and receptive to differing kinds of experience. Shelley ([1840] 1956), too, believed in an individualism that did not create an unfeeling, isolated, or totally subjective self. In *A Defence of Poetry* he argues for a moral and just society which will rely, in part, on love "or a going out of our own nature, and an identification of ourselves with the beautiful which exists in thought, action, or person not our own. A man, to be greatly good, must imagine intensely and comprehensively; he must put himself in the place of another and of many others; the pains and pleasures of his species must become his own" (Noyes 1956, 1101).

Toward a Social-Expressivist Pedagogy

Within the romantic enterprise, then, rests the undergirding for a rhetorical pedagogy based on the opposite of radical individualism. The subject, the self, is not a single definable entity that stands alone. The work of the romantic, or neo-romantic subject, is not merely for the individual as Berlin (1988) wants to argue. The romantic subject is defined only through the connections to other objects, subjects, and, unless in the throes of a mystical experience, through language.

It still remains however, that those of us who teach first-year college students are painfully aware of just how easy it is for students to get stuck in the subjective, to believe that what they think and feel is more important than what anyone else feels or has to say. I have had students, in response to something we read for class, say that they did not finish the reading because they could not relate to the experiences being relayed in the essay. In my view it is one thing to be a resisting reader, but something quite different to lack the imaginative ability to even attempt connection with differing experiences. When we consider how willing some students are to remain in a totally individualistic position, it is possible, in fact probable, that some expressivist rhetoricians, in their hope to foster uniqueness, personal vision, and voice, have focused on individualism in such a

way as to promote an already predisposed solipsism that does not
result in empathy. Many have not, however. Peter Elbow (1986)
echoes Coleridge's cry for living in the "universal," for instance,
when he argues that an organism cannot grow, the mind cannot grow
toward knowledge, unless we allow ourselves to be "swallowed by
what is different from the self—to merge or expand into what is
different" (97). This sort of merging and expansion is dependent
upon an awareness of culturally bound ideas and selves. Elbow's
doubting and believing game promotes a methodology for learning
based on empathy. It is a concept reminiscent of Keats' negative
capability.[3] "The believing game," says Elbow, "is essentially coop-
erative or collaborative." In fact, it is when we consider passages like
this from expressivist compositionists that we begin to see more
clearly the social aspects of expressivism. "The central event is the
act of affirming or entering into someone's thinking or perceiving. It
tends to imply a pluralistic model of knowledge—namely, that truth
is often complex and that different people often catch different aspects of it; and that we get closer to seeing correctly by entering into
each others' conflicting perceptions or formulations" (289).

Like Keats, Elbow is aware that empathic action often creates a
chaotic or disjointed feeling. Empathic action deconstructs any
sense of a solid, unified self. It brings into sharper focus the ways
in which, as subjects, we are fragmented and non-unified beings. As
Keats argues, it is the ability to sit comfortably with chaos, uncer-
tainty, the fragmentation of self, that is valuable: the value comes in
being "capable of being in uncertainties, mysteries, doubts, without
any irritable reaching after fact and reason" (Keats [1817] 1986,
863).

Donald Murray, though he differs from Elbow in that his pedagogy seems less obviously based in empathy, also tries not to foster
a solipsistic individualism in students. He urges students toward an
empathetic understanding of otherness. In *Write to Learn* (1984),
Murray's text for student writers, he writes:

> Another way to make yourself receive information that may be
> helpful to you as a writer is to practice empathy, the ability to put
> yourself in other people's skins. We can imagine what it might be
> like to be rich if we are poor or poor if we're rich, to be a police-
> man, to be selling or buying. (33)

Along with role-playing, he urges students to make personal
contact with people. Observe and join a child at play, he might suggest. Or interview a poor person to find out what it is like to be
without food and medicine, to hear firsthand about the pangs of
hunger. Just as empathy allows Keats to take part in the existence

of the sparrow that comes before his window, Murray wants his students, through observation, imaginative role-playing, and interviewing, to be able to take part in the existence of the lives of other people. He wants them, through their receptiveness, sympathy, reflection, and ultimately their writing, to discover other worlds, and make connections that make them aware, allowing them the greater possibility for communicating through language with those who are different from them. This discovery of others and of other worlds is, in reality, a discovery of the ways in which the self positions itself within, and is positioned by material conditions. A social-expressivism, building on the lead of scholars like Elbow and Murray, allows for an understanding of self as subject but also for others as subject. In doing so, student "selves" cannot remain radically individualistic, because every time they explore their own selves in relation to others they are working within the realm of social construction. So, as I have argued, the romantic self is not based on an individualism that supersedes either concern for others or concern for the sociopolitical context that surrounds and creates this self. Nor, as Murray and Elbow show us, do current expressivist rhetorics necessarily promote solipsism or negative forms of individualism in this regard. It is important to note, in fact, that the expressivisms of Murray, Elbow, and as we shall see, Berthoff, are already pointing toward a social-expressivism.

The simplification of the romantic philosophies of the self and of the pedagogical theories of expressivist rhetoricians does not stop with issues of empathy and understanding of others. Unfortunately, expressivist theories have perpetuated a sense that audience is unimportant and thus that writing in expressivist terms truly is only for self-expression. This again wrongly indicates that selves, in expressivist doctrine, are asocial and arhetorical.

Historically speaking, it is true that prior to the romantics, poets saw pleasing an audience as the major concern of artistic endeavor, and that part of what is so revolutionary about romantic thought is the importance of individual vision and self-expression. It is a major shift in artistic orientation when the mind in the act of creation and composing becomes a major part of the rhetorical situation, and the role of the audience seems subordinate to this vision. Although this shifting to include the importance of the individual vision can be interpreted as slighting the importance of audience, it certainly does not exclude all concern with audience.

Wordsworth, for instance, usually evaluates his poetry by its effects on the reader. He recognizes that in order to gain the effect that he wants he must revise and perfect technique. There is overwhelming evidence of Wordsworth's laborious and constant revisions of both his theoretical discussions and his verse. Further, where critics traditionally have viewed Wordsworth as a poor theorist, and his argument in the Preface ([1815] 1984) to the *Lyrical Ballads*, as "illogical" the nature of Wordsworth's Preface is in actuality quite rhetorical.

John Nabholtz (1986) sees the Preface as a rhetorical work in which Wordsworth is attempting to build a relationship between himself as writer and his audience as reader. Although Anuradha Dingwaney and Lawrence Needham (1989) take issue with Nabholtz's reading, insisting that Wordsworth was not uniting reader and writer, they nonetheless argue that the Preface is audience-directed and "rhetorical in a specific sense" because it "seeks to clear the way and create a taste for the Ballads by taking to task those 'codes of decision' (and the audience which subscribes to them) standing in the way of a genuine appreciation of the poems; by doing so, it seeks to influence the subsequent reception of the Ballads" (334).

Coleridge, despite his attempts to make his poetry appear as though it came effortlessly and fully forged from the mind, always worked to create a product of careful and conscious organization. Finally, let us not forget that like most poets, the romantics meant for their works to be read and taken seriously by an audience: "Poets do not write for Poets alone" (*Preface* 1815, 739). In fact, the romantics were the first generation of writers to appeal directly to the reading public, not to patrons.

The propensity for expressivist rhetorics to face similar criticisms—that their focus on spontaneity and personal voice slights the importance of audience—seems natural considering how eagerly we have accepted only those parts of romantic doctrine that speak of art solely for purposes of self-pleasure and self-expression and how commonplace ill-conceived generalizations surrounding romanticism have become today. Donald Murray helps to distinguish deserved criticisms from unwarranted criticism that takes its power from stereotypes.

Murray exemplifies an expressivist approach that acknowledges the rhetorical importance of audience as well as encourages a focus on the self. Murray does not allow his own writing, nor that of his students, to remain egocentric or isolated from a wider audience. The writing is for the benefit or betterment of the audience as well as the individual writerly self. Murray pushes his writing, and that of his students, beyond the personal and private to the social. Murray is, after all, a poet, novelist, journalist, and regular columnist for the *Boston Globe*. As a writer, his goal is to reach an audience. He has written innumerable articles on audience and revision: "What

Makes Readers Read," "Write Research to be Read," "Teaching the Other Self: The Writer's First Reader," "Make Meaning Clear: The Logic of Revisions," "The Maker's Eye: Revising Your Own Manuscripts." His texts always contain discussions of this part of the writing process, and he structures his classes in a way which incorporates multiple revisions. His students draft, and they meet in conferences with Murray and then draft again. They try out a variety of leads and conclusions. They rewrite the same paper in a different style or voice. Sometimes they work on one project, continuously revising throughout the semester.

Because Murray (1982) believes that the most accurate definition of writing is "the process of using language to discover meaning in experience and to communicate it" (73), he advocates, like cognitivists and others who consider themselves non-expressivists, moving from what Linda Flower calls "writer-based" prose to "reader-based" prose. "Communication" is the key word, and the end goal, for Murray and his students. If you can order information, he says, "into significant meaning and then communicate it to others [you] will influence the course of events within town or nation, school or university, company or corporation" (Murray 1984, 4). This passage exemplifies Murray's belief in writing for social change. The writing is not just a method of pleasing the self. The awareness, the empathy, the greater understanding of self and others gained by Murray's students is set before the world in an attempt to communicate. Contrary to what critics of Murray's pedagogy might think, this focus on self in his teaching philosophy does not totally eclipse the importance of audience. In fact, it is yet another indicator that there is a social-expressivism that does not fit the current construction of tidy categories.

Peter Elbow (1987) seems an easier target than Donald Murray for the accusation that expressivist rhetorics ignore audience. It is certainly clear that audience is not the central element of Elbow's rhetorical teachings. He acknowledges that there are charges of "audience dismissal" pending against him when he states: "It will be clear that my argument for writing without audience awareness is not meant to undermine the many good reasons for writing with audience awareness some of the time" (50). That Elbow anticipates resistance to his position is not surprising when, a few paragraphs later, he takes the controversial stance that "ignoring audience can lead to better writing—immediately. In effect, writer-based prose can be better than reader-based prose" (53). In part, Elbow's stance here is a rhetorical one, similar to the one taken by Wordsworth in poems like "Tables Turned." Elbow's argument in "Ignoring Audience" is a direct response to other critics' (Hairston, Flower, etc.)

criticisms of writer-based prose. Elbow is deliberately overstating his case for rhetorical effect.

Those of us familiar with Elbow's (1981) work know that he does directly address the issue of audience in his texts. For instance, he writes:

> They [readers] don't have us with them as they read and they lack all those cues they would get from watching our movements and hearing our tone of voice and emphasis. In writing we must get the words on the page so clear that there's no need for audio-visual aids. Thus, readers in their solitariness need more of the very things that writers in their solitariness are most likely to omit. The moral of the story is obvious: pay lots of attention as you write to your audience and its needs. (177)

Elbow is aware that the most "frequent weakness in the writing of beginners . . . is too little attention to the needs of the reader" (178). This is why discussions of audience remain important, even in the expressivist's classroom.

Admittedly, audience is not the initial focus for Elbow, because, like Murray, Elbow believes that a premature emphasis on audience can have a deadly effect on student writing: "some of their worst writing—both jumbled and flat—comes from worrying too much about audience" at an inappropriate time (178). He returns to this argument in the more recent "An Argument for Ignoring Audience": "It is not that writers should never think about their audience. It's a question of when" (51). And when the time is wrong, suggests Elbow, not only is bad writing the result, but the process of making meaning comes to an abrupt halt. Elbow has placed his argument about audience in opposition to that of neo-classical rhetoric:

> Notice that two points of composition theory are in conflict:
> (1) Think about audience as you write (this stemming from the classical rhetorical tradition).
> (2) Use writing for *making new meaning*, not just transmitting old meanings already worked out (this stemming from the new epistemic tradition I associate with Ann Berthoff's classic explorations). (53)

As with the romantics, the onus for expressivist teachers has shifted from audience as the cardinal rhetorical concern, especially at the beginning of a writing task, to personal voice and vision— what the writer is trying to say. Nonetheless, audience remains a part of the rhetorical situation and slighting audience at the beginning of a writing task does not make an arhetorical writing theory of expressivism. Furthermore, a concern with self, voice, and vision does not mean that Elbow, or any of us who honor these elements, is unaware that both visions and selves are socially constructed.

Rather, when I talk about personal visions, for instance, I am talking about discovering what it is I know, what I think, what my perspective is on what ever matter is at hand.

I would certainly grant, however, that students might misunderstand Elbow's teachings unless we apply his theoretical stance with care. The possibility for misconstruing Elbow's perspective on audience is linked to the cultural assumptions surrounding the "myth of the inspired writer" that I discussed earlier. When teachers like Murray and Elbow focus on personal voice and vision, it is easy for students to cling to Bizzell's (1986) notion of "instant text production." As she notes, the result of this notion is a resistance to revision. "After all," students might think "this is my personal vision. I said it in my voice the way I wanted to say it, and it was inspired." From here it is an easy leap for students to resist revision and to deny that an audience should have any impact on their writing. What seems crucial, then, is that we be extremely careful when we apply Elbow's argument for ignoring audience, and that we be sure that the focus on personal vision does not continue to reinforce a misunderstood version of romantic inspiration. Also, we can urge students to examine the ways in which their personal visions are situated within a cultural context.

It is interesting to see how the denigrated theories of the romantics come into play with current rhetorical theories when Elbow (1987) himself writes, "To celebrate writer-based prose is to risk the charge of *romanticism*: just warbling one's woodnotes wild. But my position also contains the austere classic view that we must nevertheless revise with conscious awareness . . ." (55). Elbow seems to wish to dissociate himself from the romantic tradition from which his theories have evolved, perhaps because he resists all labels, or perhaps because he has not considered an interpretation that sees romanticism as already containing the delicate balance between raw material and revision. Romanticism is not advocating "warbling one's woodnotes wild," and it is worth offering another interpretation so that expressivists, and their students and critics, begin to realize that the expressivist heritage offers a version of inspiration that comes only after hard work and much practice. Even "an inspired piece of writing" is usually laboriously revised in light of an awareness of audience. This is true for the romantics, Elbow, Murray, and many professional writers.

Balancing the Focus: Self and World

Scholars, such as Karen Burke LeFevre, James Berlin, and David Kaufer, who align themselves with marxism, social construction, or social-epistemic rhetorics espouse the harshest criticisms against expressivism. They spurn expressivist theories for many reasons, but, once again, primarily because expressivism supposedly focuses on the individual as opposed to the relationship that involves the dialectical interaction among writer, community, and social, political, and economic conditions of existence. While I have addressed some of these concerns there is more to consider. LeFevre (1987) has written that within the romantic tradition "the inspired writer is apart from others and wants to keep it that way" to "prevent himself and his creation from being corrupted by society" (17). Berlin (1988) has claimed that

> expressionistic rhetoric is intended to serve as critique of the ideology of corporate capitalism, proposing in its place an ideology based on radical individualism. In the name of empowering the individual, however, its naiveté about economic, social, and political arrangements can lead to the marginalizing of the individuals who would resist a dehumanizing society, rendering them ineffective through their isolation. (492)

Kaufer (1979) assumes that expressivist rhetorical theories commit only to their "personal point of view" for reasons of "self-development," and that they are not "bound to social action" (185).

While these criticisms are based on a denial of a social-expressivism, it is possible to see how this denial has come about. LeFevre's criticisms, for instance, are at least partially founded on the debased commonplace definitions of romanticism that Jacques Barzun has found so prevalent. Of course, the myth of the inspired and solitary writer, since it is so widely accepted, will continue to do the damage that LeFevre reports until we actively debunk it, as I am doing throughout this work. Berlin's charge against expressivism relies, at least in part, on the misinformed generalizations surrounding romanticism. The misunderstanding, however, also stems from some expressivists themselves, as well as from critics of expressivism. What Berlin presents in his scenario is a clear case of expressivist theory gone awry in its application. That is, I believe Berlin (1988) is correct in his assessment that "expressionistic rhetoric is intended to serve as a critique of the ideology of corporate capitalism," but that, in practice, expressivism can backfire. But it does not have to, and even if in the real world of some classrooms, a sort of "radical individualism" is practiced, there is nothing inherent in a theory of expressivism that creates "ineffective" citizens.

As I have already pointed out, expressivist rhetorics and romanticism evolved in part as a reaction to the establishment and to the sometimes tyrannical social institutions shoring up against political and social change. In the case of contemporary expressivism, individuality becomes important since the individual so easily becomes lost in the face of modern bureaucracy and corporate capitalism. Students often feel lost in the bureaucracy of higher education. Rather than people known and respected as individuals, they become numbers. Their grades are often posted outside office doors where they find themselves through an assigned number. Often times they become a seat and row number in the faceless masses attending large lectures. Many economically underprivileged students and citizens find themselves outside the American mainstream feeling distinctly faceless, voiceless, and personless in a society that gives faces and voices to those in economic power. One way to regain any sense of selfhood in the modern capitalist world is to shift some of the focus to the individual.

It can be difficult in practice, however, to balance the focus on the individual with the complexities of our social contexts. An ethnographic study by Amber Ahlstrom (1991) suggests that teachers trained in a primarily expressivist writing program are unaware of the complexities and the depth of expressivist theory, and thus latch onto what is most accessible about it: a belief in personal voice, a belief in personal vision, and a continual reinforcement of the individual in its opposition to a society that diminishes the individual. Personal voice and vision are crucial to any theory and pedagogy. This is the main reason why I find value in expressivism and why I want to argue so strenuously for social-expressivisms.

The teachers in Ahlstrom's study understand voice, vision, and individualism in the most limited of terms, so that enacting or coming to grips with the social aspects of language, writing, and learning seems difficult for them. Consequently, Berlin's (1988) appraisal has merit: it is possible for "empowered" individuals to change a "dehumanizing society," but, because they can be unaware of the "economic, social, and political arrangements," they might remain marginalized themselves and thus unavailable to precipitate change. Although expressivist theory evolves from a tradition that recognizes the economic, social, and political conditions of existence, the practitioners of expressivism can certainly fail to incorporate this tradition into their pedagogy.

These possibilities for failure are why I find it imperative that we begin articulating social-expressivisms that focus on writing for discovery, development of self and voice, and development of power and authority in our own and our students' writing. We need social-expressivisms that focus on the self in the world and on writing for change. We need social-expressivisms that envision subjects both acting and being acted upon. I find the current versions of social-epistemicism too deterministic. That is, they imply a zero sum scenario in the classroom where students are constructed solely through language and the material conditions of existence. While social-epistemicism does not necessarily intend a zero sum application, the hands-off personal voice and vision approach bolsters this picture of it. I envision a social-expressivist classroom where the best of both expressivism and social-epistemic theories are practiced: students carry out negotiations between themselves and their culture, and must do this first in order to become effective citizens, imaginative thinkers, and savvy rhetorical beings. Learning to enact these negotiations means first developing a sense of one's own values and social constructions and then examining how these interact or do not interact with others' value systems and cultural constructs.

As I have already said, expressivist rhetorics, according to critics like Berlin, do not recognize the material conditions of the writing situation because they focus on self-expression rather than on expression for or toward a democracy. But, as is becoming clear, while this can happen, current expressivists, the romantics, and other post-romantics do not necessarily fit this mold. Berlin (1989) himself sees at least one expressivist ancestor as an exception to this. In his chapter entitled "Emerson and Romantic Rhetoric," Berlin argues that scholars generally see Emerson's rhetorical thought in one of two ways. "The first sees Emerson as a romantic individualist" concerned with the "expression of self" and the second sees Emerson as committed to democracy (43). Berlin reads Emerson in this latter light, believing that Emerson positions the "rhetor at the center of political and social action" (43). Berlin's reading of Emerson also indicates the possibility of a social-expressivism where an expression of self and a commitment to democracy are fused.

Berlin favors the interpretation of Emerson as democratic rhetor because he sees Emerson as having anticipated modern epistemology by "arguing for reality as the product of the interaction of the perceiver and that which is perceived" (43). As I have argued, however, Wordsworth and Coleridge also saw reality as an interaction between the perceiver and the perceived. Thus, in this they anticipated "modern epistemology." Current expressivists such as Murray and Berthoff also affirm this version of reality. When Berlin notes the current expressivist tie to Emerson, however, it is only through what he sees as the misunderstood side of Emerson—that which sees him as individualist and concerned only with self-expression. In contrast to my position, Berlin does not see any expressivists displaying a "modern epistemology."

At the heart of Berlin's vision of Emerson as a romantic rhetorician who makes his rhetoric "central to democratic society" is the fact that Emerson believes "language is action" (55). Berlin is convinced "that those who find in Emerson a rhetoric of self-expression are mistaken, even though this reading may be used in support of modern expressionistic rhetoric. Emerson was a diverse and fecund thinker whose rhetoric, as in poetic, has taken remarkable turns" (55–56).

There are a couple of things worth considering here about Berlin's position. First, I find it limiting to assume, as Berlin does, that a rhetoric of self-expression must necessarily deny language as action or deny a rhetoric central to democratic society. By not allowing both readings of Emerson—one as self-expressivist, one as democratic rhetor—Berlin denies modern expressivism's concern with writing for and in a democratic society. Berlin's tendency to keep things so tightly boxed leaves him with a dichotomy that leads to these either/or propositions and a denial of the existence of a social-expressivism. Self-expression takes place within a social context and self-expression also is language as action. This action may be focused toward the transformation of the individual, but such a transformation also leads to societal transformation. This must be so if individuals are constructed socially. A change in an individual occurs within a social context; thus, both individuals and societies are altered, if only minutely. Transformation of self and society is a part of what is important to other expressivist predecessors, and current expressivists, as well as to Emerson.

Second, I would like to point out that expressivism has a long historical lineage of "diverse and fecund" thinkers like Emerson. Like Emerson, many of them placed language as a tool for action at the center of their attempts to bring about social and democratic change.

Third, I suggest that when it comes to the possibility for a rhetoric to isolate individuals from the "empowerment" necessary to change a "dehumanizing society," expressivist theory is not alone. It is as easy for those who are advocates of a social-epistemic rhetoric as it is for expressivist teachers to unintentionally render students "ineffective through their isolation." Is it not as much of an alienating and isolating experience for a student to be constantly forced to examine herself in terms of a political and economic existence, to hold an opinion that is not yet hers, to be told that her conservative ideas are oppressive and undemocratic?

I am not suggesting that there is something intrinsic to social-epistemic rhetorics that makes them equivalent to raw propagandizing any more than there is something inherent to expressivist rhetorics that guarantees "ineffective" citizens. The potential for misuse is present for teachers who honor social-constructivist and marxist theories for writing instruction, however. Yes, students must take responsibility for their ineffectiveness and the ways in which they oppress others, but the social-epistemic agenda, if not carefully applied, can shut down students rather than empower them. Of course, force-feeding students an ideology, whether it is one we would consider desirable or not, will not necessarily create politically aware students. Indeed, we can create students who isolate themselves in the ways we are fighting against. Often they do so as a protection against what they see as an onslaught of political motivations.

Fourth, Berlin (1988) claims that social-epistemic rhetoric "offers an explicit critique of economic, political, and social arrangements, the counterpart of the implicit critique found in expressionistic rhetoric" (490). He then goes on to imply that expressivist rhetorics lead students to false consciousness where they fall victim to such things as reification (preoccupation with consumerism, for instance), pre-scientific thinking (a belief in such things as luck and a fixed human nature), acceleration (the pace of every day urban life that denies critical reflection), and mystification (responses to the problems of a capitalist society that obscure the real sources of the problems—sexism, racism, etc.) (490–491). Berlin also suggests that what keeps social-epistemicism out of this bind is a social understanding of self, resistance to disempowering social influences, interdisciplinary classroom methods, and the means with which to self-criticize and self-revise social-epistemic positions.

Expressivist theories and pedagogies could enforce false consciousness, but there is nothing that would absolutely make this so. Especially if we rethink expressivism as I am doing here. Nothing restrains an expressivist teacher from asking students to examine who gains from their "personal visions," from their "individualistic stances." Examining racism and sexism is easily enough done in the expressivist classroom. Moreover, critical reflection, what Berlin calls on to defeat acceleration, is a major facet of expressivist theories and practices. The unbinding of social-epistemicism is the unbinding of expressivism: the expressivist classroom can resist disempowering social influences, use interdisciplinary classroom methods, and posit a social understanding of the self. Expressivist rhetoricians certainly can be self-critical and self-revisionary. My point is simply this: contrary to how social-epistemic hard-liners would have us believe, the important things that Berlin outlines here are not solely the province of social-epistemicism as his own discussion of Emerson ultimately points out.

Anti-expressivists are apt to assume that expressivist approaches will be more apt to fail in preparing students for democratic citizenship because of the current version of expressivist history that suggests that expressivist rhetorics bear the weight of past ignorance of the material conditions of existence and the sociopolitical contexts of the individual self. But my version of the tradition from which expressivism arises differs. While expressivists' ancestors, in particular the romantics, might well have helped to perpetuate a vision of themselves as isolated, lonely, and misunderstood by society, and thus even anti-rhetorical, it is shortsighted to believe that the romantics thought isolation was a natural or desirable condition or that an extended application of romantic ideas has to result in a naiveté about political and social issues. A more accurate view of romantic "individualism" reveals that there is nothing inherently naive or undemocratic about the self, nor that the romantic honoring of individuality implies a disparaging of social interaction. In fact the romantic self is not as different from the social-constructivist self as we have been inclined to believe.

Within past romantic versions of the self are the beginnings of what I am calling the self of social-expressivism. If current expressivists are true to their romantic roots, they are returning to a moral vision of the human as a being with powers and rights. As Kathleen Coburn (1984) suggests, Coleridge demanded that we respect the individuality of our friends, and even our opponents. She suggests that in Coleridge's view, "the worst thing one human being can do to another is to deny her or him autonomy, powers, and rights" (34). While the romantics and expressivists might use terminology such as "autonomous," the fight against oppression is nonetheless as important to Coleridge and expressivists as it is for social-epistemic teachers. Coleridge insisted on the need for self-consciousness, in part, because he felt it could help alleviate prejudice. He believed that we could not know others until we had a "consciousness of self," and that until we know ourselves difference would continue to be linked with hatred (32). In part what Coleridge meant by knowing the self is understanding the social and environmental things that shape us. Expressivist teachers like Murray (1989) uphold the romantic tradition on this issue with statements like "respect them [students] as individuals, delight in their difference" (108).

Contrary to popular misunderstandings, the romantics did not deny the social construction of the self; they simply asserted the importance of the individual in a social environment that ignored or suppressed autonomy and individuality in children, women, and all but the elite classes. In fact, as sociologist Dmitri Shalin (1984) argues, it was during the romantic era that the notion of the self as a social product was first established (51). It was painfully apparent to the romantics that social and political contexts and the ideologies of church and government were indeed constructing the citizens of

Britain. Blake's "London" ([1794] 1986, 42) and "The Chimney Sweeper" ([1789, 1794] 1986, 33–34, 39) are two poems that unveil the social construction of the most demoralized and oppressed of England's people. In attempts to rectify what they saw as horrific mistreatment of human beings they not only wrote and argued for change but they wrote and argued for the primacy of human beings, of individuals, in a social and political machine of destruction.

Romantic art directly tried to display the balance between self and culture or world (including, of course, nature) which the artists longed for. David Perkins (1964) points out that "beginning with Wordsworth, it is generally accurate to say that art tends less to distinguish between the outer world of events and the inner world of consciousness" (16)—that it attempts increasingly to display their "interfusion." Thus, it is Wordsworth's understanding that "we can know outward things only as they are reflected and modified in some particular consciousness or 'point of view'; and we can know our inner world only as we are responding to something outside" (16). Wordsworth argues for this repeatedly in the various versions of the "Preface" to the *Lyrical Ballads* (Poetical Works, [1815] 1984). In Wordsworth's arguments we have Berlin's interaction between the perceiver and the perceived that catapults Emerson into modern epistemology. What we have is a dialectical relationship between self and world. Shalin (1984) points out that this dialectic is also present for the romantics between the "structure of self and the structure of society" (55):

> The [Romantic] self is social not only because it reflects the needs of the moment, because it can assume this or that mask depending on the others with whom it interacts; it is social through and through because it has no objective being outside of its interaction with other selves, because it comes into being within a community, rather than merely adjusts to it, as the predecessor of Romanticism tacitly supposed. (51)

The paradox here is that, in refusing the idea of an objective self and embracing that of a subjective one, the self is always changed, created and constantly recreated by the community that self is in. As I have already suggested in my discussion of empathy, the main goal of the self for the romantic was to commune with another self. As Shalin puts it, "to be conscious of oneself," to be "conscious of anything at all, according to the romantics, the individual must become another to oneself, see oneself from without, from the standpoint of the other—a feat one can perform only as a member of society" (51). Shalin's position is the one that informs my vision for social-expressivisms.

In part, the romantic desire to honor individuality is in reaction to Locke's view of the human infant as a blank slate or "tabula rasa." The self that arises from a Lockean model is entirely a social and environmental construct, but is not in interaction with its environment. The romantic self, on the other hand, is shaped by environment but is also self-unfolding. In other words, as Coleridge's plant metaphor implies, the individual is the joint product of an innate seed and the extrinsic or environmental soil, air, and water. The community and the individual are interdependent; they cannot be separated.

My point is that it is false to assume that expressivism, because of its ties to romanticism, is defined by a "radical individualism" that is unaware of how the self is socially shaped. It is, in fact, an awareness of the ways in which we are socially shaped that prompted a special focus on the personal and subjective. And, as Shalin suggests, the romantics were the first to acknowledge the self as a social product; thus our current elaborations on notions of social constructivism are further extensions of a very valuable romantic idea.[4]

Some current expressivist rhetoricians, like their romantic predecessors, also acknowledge the social aspects of the self and of the writing situation forthrightly. Ann Berthoff, for instance, embraces social theories as a part of her expressivist rhetoric. Her ability to clearly incorporate such theories into her rhetoric is probably one reason she is not more often identified as an expressivist. When seen through Derrida's logic of supplementation, however, it is easier to note how much of Berthoff's (1984) expressivist theory supplements her social-epistemicism and how much of her social-epistemicism supplements her expressivism. She often writes from an expressivist's point of view with a social theorist's insight into social influences; in effect, she writes as a social-expressivist:

> Language seen as a means of making meaning has two aspects, the hypostatic and the discursive. By naming the world, we hold images in mind; we remember; we can return to our experience and reflect on it. In reflecting, we can change, we can transform, we can envisage. Language thus becomes the very type of social activity by which we might move towards changing our lives. The hypostatic power of language to fix and stabilize frees us from the prison of the moment. Language recreates us as historical beings. (751)

Berthoff believes in experience, reflection, the imagination, and knowing as the "mind in action." She sees language and thought as not meaningful "outside a social context" and as necessarily established in a "social setting" (749). These ideas identify her as a pioneer of a social-expressivist theory fully attuned to, and willing to embrace, social theories of the self, learning, and writing.

I find Kaufer's argument that neo-romantic rhetorics are not "bound to social action" more suspect then either LeFevre's or Berlin's problems with these rhetorics. Current expressivists and their intellectual ancestors like Emerson, and the earlier British romantics who were so influential to Emerson's romanticism and rhetorical posture, were, in actuality, very aware of political and economic concerns, and they were without doubt dedicated to "social action." The British romantics saw the people of nineteenth century England as indifferent and apathetic. The romantics envisioned a better world, changed through their educational ideas and their writing. They wished to stir the imagination of the masses. They wanted their readers concerned about war, the reform of Parliament, dislocation of rural life, and a starving lower class, so they could improve, as Mill says, "the physical and social condition of mankind." They yearned to be, as Shelley argued they were, the "legislators of the world."

The romantics were actively involved in the movement for social change. Coleridge, for instance, preached "sedition" from both pulpit and pamphlet for many years. Wordsworth went to France twice during the Revolution and, though ultimately disillusioned, was quite taken with political fervor. Young Shelley went to Ireland and printed leaflets of advice for social change, and Byron, who denounced crown policy in his first speech in the House of Lords, died in Greece while trying to help the cause of Greek independence.

The romantics were greatly concerned with, and wrote extensively on, the forces and political ideologies behind the French Revolution, the consequences of the ideologies behind the French Revolution, and the consequences of these ideologies for English society. Blake wrote of the atrocities done to children in poems like "The Chimney Sweeper." He pointed a harsh finger at both the church and the government in poems like "London," while graphically bringing to our attention the squalor and destitution of the city streets. Shelley spent a great deal of time writing and talking earnestly about renovating society, and in "England 1819" he draws an unflattering portrait of George III while revealing the horrid realities of this ineffectual king's rule:

An old, mad, blind, despised and dying king,—
Princes, the dregs of their dull race, who flow
Through public scorn, —mud from a muddy spring,—
Rulers who neither see, nor feel, nor know,

But leech-like to their fainting country cling,
Till they drop, blind in blood, without a blow,—
A people starved and stabbed in the untilled field,—
                    (Noyes [1819] 1956, 107, lines 1–7)

Even Wordsworth is clearly, in Kaufer's terms, "bound to social action." The poet's job, according to Wordsworth, is to shake people out of their "savage torpor" and to bind society together. In poems like "The Ruined Cottage," Wordsworth wants to force readers into questioning a society where the horrors of poverty are abundant. Margaret, the main character of "The Ruined Cottage," suffers the ravages of war and rural poverty. Her husband has left her and two children behind to join the army so that they might receive the bonus money given him for enlisting. Margaret obstinately awaits his return, and, in so doing, she and her humble cottage fall into ruins. By the end of the poem, Margaret's moral decay matches her physical decay. Wordsworth indicates her final devastating fall into despair when the church takes the eldest son and the infant dies of neglect. Wordsworth does not make our task as readers easy in this poem. He does not make a moral judgment for us, but instead unfolds the scene in front of the reader, pushing us into thinking, questioning, and reflecting on the gender, economic, political, and societal structures that are the root cause of Margaret's demise.

As my earlier discussions on audience indicate, Elbow, and especially Murray, are also bound to social action and change. Murray's focus on communication, if we remember, is one that includes "influencing the course of events" within our various social settings. While writing for neo-romantics and expressivists might well lead to "self-development" and might even hinge on "personal point of view," this does not preclude a dedication to social as well as personal transformation through writing. Kaufer's understanding of neo-romantic rhetorics is simply too narrow and thus forces him into inaccurate statements about them.

Political and Social Issues in the Expressivist Classroom

When we consider expressivism and its traditions more fully it becomes clear that neo-romantic rhetorics are not apolitical, and that expressivist teachers themselves can and do strive to problematize social and political concerns as part of the classroom agenda. We can continue to politicize our courses and make the students socially aware through discussions and writing about campus, state, national, and international events, issues concerning class, race, poverty, and bigotry, and how these issues relate to the self. The expressivist tradition as it rises out of romanticism, and the first generation of expressivist teachers and theorists have given us much to build on.

In a sense, I am calling for a new generation of social-expressivists who can reclaim even more of the romantic heritage and put into action what is best about the rich and complex theories of the romantics; of scholars and philosophers such as Mill, Arnold, Emerson, James, and Dewey; and Elbow, Rohman, Murray, and Berthoff. To do so results in a social-expressivism, a rhetorical theory and practice, which remains concerned with our students as whole beings. They are no longer just writing students in need of analytical and academic literacy skills who must leave their emotional selves and value systems, no matter how unpopular, at the classroom door. Practitioners of social-expressivisms understand that selves are not entities able to separate at will from the culture from which they derive; yet they still honor lived experience, discovery, reflection, imagination, and personal voice and vision. A social-expressivism allows for students to come to know who they are, what their beliefs are and why this is so. It views students as subjects in negotiation with language and the material conditions of existence, not merely as objects. They are the shapers and the shaped.

Most of us who teach freshman writing at the University of Mississippi teach from multicultural positions as best we can at a predominantly white, wealthy school. We also understand that the act of writing is a social act and we try to place reading, writing, and classroom activities in relationship to gender, social class, race, and politics. In practice and theory, we find ourselves blending the major components of expressivism (a concern with voice and individual perspectives along with such classroom activities as freewriting, writing for discovery, and reflective writing) with the most important elements of social-epistemicism, in order to teach from this position I am calling social-expressivism. It is not always an easy or comfortable approach to take at a school as homogeneous as the University of Mississippi.

When we allow these students to explore self and feelings and tell personal stories, we hear things that many teachers feel should never be tolerated in the classroom. Justin, for instance, a student of one of our teaching assistants, spoke freely about his racism in nasty ways. In his journals he calls blacks "a certain breed" and sees himself as a "proud Caucasian" and of "superior race" (Sewell 4). He believes that whites are more "prosperous" because of this superiority and that although "Japs" are successful they are also "very short, slanty-eyed and carry funny accents" (4). Sewell's gut reaction, like many of ours, I would hazard to guess, was to want to keep these racist attitudes silent and to deem them inappropriate, while at the same time trying to prove to the student that his beliefs were foisted upon him by the dominant ideology that constructed him. If we silence them, however, our students at Mississippi tend to react to our demands for examination of their socially constructed selves by pulling back into themselves, against the onslaught of "yet another bleeding-heart liberal" teacher. They play the game, in other words, nodding their heads at the right time and saying what they know we, as teachers, want to hear. They often leave the classroom neither having changed, nor having any more desire than before to strive for the "democratic ideal" as Berlin terms it. To allow for "self-expression" to continue in the classroom, however, at least puts the cards on the table.

What I am getting at here, is that self-expression leads students to feel as though they have a voice. This is important, because, without this voice, students are unwilling to begin the first part of the negotiation that I find so important: understanding what their beliefs are and where they come from in terms of their own experiences, so that they can see how their value systems might differ from others'. Ideally, the classroom would have plenty of student perspectives that are different from the dominant culture's. The reality at Mississippi, however, is that this rarely happens. We consider ourselves lucky to have the occasional Black, Asian, or lower socioeconomic student in the classroom. Our differing perspectives usually come from the teacher and the various texts (not just written texts) we bring into the classroom. But if we allow the students to examine first their own feelings, beliefs, and the ways in which their experiences have brought them to these, they are then able to at least begin the process of negotiating difference and seeing how they relate to and in the larger social world. Crucial to the success of this enterprise is not only self-expression and coming to voice, but the critical self-reflection that expressivist practices demand.

The social-expressivism that I am arguing for here probably seems much more politicized than the expressivism that we have come to associate with people like Murray and Elbow. However, expressivism is currently more political than we have recognized. For instance, the expressivist teacher who views herself as an authority but not as the absolute repository of knowledge is the buttress for a democratic and non-oppressive classroom environment. Expressivists assume that the act of writing, and the things that go into it—observation, discovery, vision, reflection—will lead to knowing. Thus, the teacher's job is not to parcel out what she knows, but rather to help students create knowledge. An expressivist pedagogy, and a social-expressivist one even more so, will push students toward a social awareness from within their subjective stances, not from externalized social analyses. When students take responsibility for social awareness from within their own subjectivities, it means more to them. They are less likely to resist and sandbag against what my freshmen often call the "railings" of "militant liberals" and "political correctness"—the constant demand by superiors to recognize and act "correctly" regarding externalized social analyses. By allowing students their own authority, expressivist pedagogies can begin to dismantle the hierarchy of the traditional classroom.

In this regard, expressivists share an important tenet with the liberatory pedagogy of Paulo Freire. Like Freire, expressivist pedagogues offer "a revolutionary model" because they provide "a method which does not depend on knowledge that has been 'deposited' (in Freire's best-known metaphor of education as banking)" (Berthoff 1990, 364). Ann Berthoff, for instance, has become Freire's ardent proponent. She recognizes that Freire's "pedagogy of knowing" is the pedagogy she cultivates as an expressivist. Of course, Berthoff differs from Murray and Elbow in that she does not hesitate to make politics a central part of her educational philosophy. Murray is adamant about not making politics the center of his pedagogy, because he in no way wants to force a political agenda on his students. Yet, as a student of Murray's, I never knew him to discourage or reject highly political analysis and subject matter.

The issue of student and teacher authority is not easily settled, but expressivists are not naive about the difficulties that arise when teachers attempt to shift traditional patterns of power within the classroom. Donald Murray prefers to stay out of the discussions on "liberatory pedagogy." Elbow, though he disagrees with Ann Berthoff's wholehearted acceptance of Freire, enters freely into the political fracas. In "The Pedagogy of the Bamboozled," for instance, Peter Elbow (1986) argues (and agrees with Freire) that in order to create a "truly liberatory" classroom "the *teacher* must work as a collaborating ally of the student, not as a supervisor" [original emphasis] (87). But this is difficult to achieve within the institution, and Elbow insists that it only "seems" as though we have a genuine collaboration with students:

> There is a crucial contradiction in the role of almost every institutional teacher that prevents our being genuine allies of the student: we are both credit-giver and teacher. As credit-giver we are the hurdle the student has to get over; as teacher we are the person who helps the student get over the hurdles. It is very common for

teachers to imply that they are more truly allies of the student than this contradiction permits. This is a source of bamboozlement for students, especially in their relations with experimental, liberal, open teachers who profess to be entirely "on the student's side." (88)

Elbow's analysis here is clearly that of a social-expressivist. He recognizes and articulates the socially constructed positions that both students and teachers are forced into. Since we cannot truly give up all authority, what we can do, according to Elbow, is to be forthright with our authority. When we choose the readings for our students, we should do so as an authority; when we give a grade, we should do so as an authority. As Elbow argues, "An honest exercise of authority, even if it is hated, would not bamboozle" (91). Unmasking our authority is itself a step toward dismantling the traditional hierarchy—a hierarchy that, in part, claims its power by hiding the extent to which it owns the reins of control.

The expressivist emphasis on personal voice and vision also helps to establish a pedagogy of equality. But this is not just a given for the social-expressivist. As Elbow's qualms about equality in *Embracing Contraries* suggest, notions of what constitutes equality must continually be problematized and reproblematized as both Elbow and Berthoff continue to do. In nurturing individual uniqueness, vision, and voice, expressivists are creating a climate in which all students have the opportunity to be heard. Those who remain silent or oppressed in other courses, or in their daily lives, are more likely to enter into the empowering act of naming their own experiences, when they know that their voices and experiences are not only encouraged but heard. Also, the fostering of each voice leads to a chorus of perspectives.

We must be wary, however, of letting the focus on individual vision and voice isolate our students from the social aspects of writing and selfhood. Even though I believe expressivist, or what Patricia Bizzell calls "personal-style" pedagogies, are valuable and more socially oriented than critics have recognized, there are pitfalls that we must watch out for. Bizzell (1986) reminds us, for example, that it is necessary to bear in mind how

> One's speaking, reading, and writing are always shaped by one's social and cultural background and by the political relations this background creates with audiences of similar or very different background. This shaping is as much a matter of what the writer knows as of what she does. (55)

If we are not aware of the social, political, and economic conditions that bind us, our success will be limited and we may, in fact, oppress the very individuals we are attempting to liberate. I am not, however, suggesting that we should back away from personal introspection and the kinds of writing that elicit personal reflection. As Kurt Spellmeyer (1989) argues, the sorts of personal essays that expressivists often ask their students to write are probably the last opportunity our college students have to "discover the relationship of mutual implication, a relationship fundamental to all writing, between the self and the cultural heritage within which selfhood has meaning" (269).

While I do believe that the cultivation of personal voice and personal perspective should not be compromised, at the same time, I do not believe that any opinion, especially those that are bigoted or fascist, should be unconditionally tolerated. To believe that expressivist rhetorics actually provide a catalyst for bigoted thinking is a simplification of the expressivist stance. Unfortunately, this accusation has arisen in discussion with colleagues more than once. Donald Murray realizes that diversity, in its fullest sense, cannot become a reality if any opinion, no matter how atrocious, is cut off and not given the chance to be heard. Even though Murray is generally thought of as apolitical, his perspective on diversity is as radically political as, and perhaps more political than, some social-epistemic perspectives.

Although the bigot in an expressivist classroom has the chance to speak, he or she will hopefully face hard-line resistance. Elbow's point in "Methodological Doubting and Believing" is valid, however. The student will not grow—there is no hope for a change in perspective—if the teacher and classmates do not play the "believing game" before the "doubting game." More often than not, if the student holding the bigoted belief is not afforded this initial hearing, he or she will retreat, sandbagging his or her opinion against the flood of criticism and holding onto a bigoted conviction in defiance. Doubting remains important, but, if what Elbow calls a "bargain and an exchange of temporary or conditional assent" ("Doubting") is reached, then the student is more willing to examine his belief critically. And it is in unexamined convictions that the greatest danger lies. The expressivist acceptance of personal vision is an attempt to protect diversity, but it is not an acceptance of bigoted thought. Rather, expressivists like Murray and Elbow realize that the unacceptable opinion needs to be voiced, and heard, to be examined. If it is not examined, there is no hope for change. And, if we move more fully into a social-expressivist position, the examination of self within the world is immanent, just as with other social rhetorical theories.

Expressivist classrooms also encourage group and collaborative work, and the recent surge of research and scholarship on student collaboration has increased the opportunity for successful results. Group work provides a built-in forum for differing perspectives to be heard, tried out, revised, and sometimes rejected. Since many expressivist pedagogies rely on group work, student interaction, and discussion rather than lecture, plenty of opportunities are created for conversation and dialogue to take place. Further, the expressivist emphasis on empathy helps assure that a diverse classroom will become a reality. Diversity can thrive where a multiplicity of voices is truly heard, and where students and teachers lean into those voices in order to empathize with and understand, though not *unthinkingly* accept, a plethora of divergent perspectives. It is in the expressivist classrooms of Donald Murray and Peter Elbow during the 1960s and 70s that collaborative group work first made its mark in the composition classroom.

We might argue, then, that expressivist theories were a breeding ground for collaborative learning theories. In fact, as Daniel J. Royer (1991) points out, the basic features of the social-epistemic classroom as defined by Knoblauch and Brannon contain many facets already a part of expressivist rhetorics: "student-centered activity as opposed to teacher directives; the assumption that writing is a natural competence rather than an acquired skill; the assumption that writing needs to be facilitated rather than directed; and the insistence that the development of meaning should always take precedence over static form" (287–288). While a fuller understanding of the social nature of writing has changed the face of collaborative work in our classrooms, we should not diminish its beginnings in the expressivist movement.

Like expressivism, social-epistemicism arises from a mixture of philosophical positions and traditions; and yet, clearly expressivism has been a valuable starting ground for social theories. The expressivist approach to classroom pedagogy is, then, broadly political in nature—even though it does not necessarily have politics as a subject, and even though we are inclined to forget and thus unintentionally ignore or misuse what is already there. It strives for a democratic classroom, equality, and true diversity. It pushes hard against pedagogies that strive for the assimilation of those who are different. By consciously working from a foundation of empathy and personal voice and vision, it offers the chance for students to become critical rather than "ineffective" or uncritical citizens. In the end, expressivist rhetorics and pedagogies are capable of creating a democratic classroom, and, if we allow for the emergence of a social-expressivism within the field, the probabilities of a democratic pedagogy and rhetorical situation grow even stronger.

There is much about romanticism and expressivism that has been misunderstood by scholars in composition studies and the culture as a whole. These misunderstandings have led to perspectives that assume romanticism and expressivist rhetorics promote a dangerous form of radical individualism. In reality, however, the expressivist heritage is much more balanced and complex than expressivists know and anti-expressivist critics have been willing to admit. In its embracing of emotion and the particular individual, for instance, expressivism's goal is to accept humankind as it really is—diverse. The romantic vision itself arose out of a great political and social need for change and reconstruction. As Jacques Barzun (1961) insightfully argues:

> The vast horizons opened up by war and social upheaval gave romanticism its scope: it was inclusive, impatient of barriers, and eager for diversity. It . . . respected the individual as a source . . . Accordingly, its political philosophy was an attempt to reconcile personal freedom with the inescapable need of collective action. (137)

If we understand expressivism's traditions as well as expressivism itself, and reevaluate our conceptions and interpretations of them, perhaps we will find aspects of this tradition worth keeping alive as we continue to explore the rhetorical theories of the present and the future. If expressivists can reclaim the rich heritage from which they evolve, new possibilities for social-expressivist rhetorics will arise, and we will be better able to define expressivism in useful terms.

Notes

1. Wordsworth, in *The Prelude*, actually calls the reader's attention to the fact that he has shortchanged explaining the importance of books in both his childhood and in later years: "Thus far a scanty record is deduced\ Of what I owed to books in early life; \Their later influence yet remains untold;" (Book V, 606–608).

2. What Russell does in this article is label Lounsbury and Campbell romantics because of their desire to abolish writing courses since writing cannot be taught and good writing only happens to those few who are inspired.

3. Keats, of course, argued that Coleridge, though he wanted to be, was incapable of really living "in the universal" or practicing "negative capability" because Coleridge was not able to "remain content with half knowledge."

4. Shalin's article, "The Romantic Antecedents of Meadian Social Psychology," chronicles the growth of George Herbert Mead's stance on social psychology emerging out of romantic philosophy.

Chapter Six

Women in the Writing Classroom: Feminism, Romanticism, and Social-expressivist Rhetorics

To my dismay, more than one feminist colleague has suggested that an astute feminist would not wish to align herself with expressivism. I wish to argue the contrary: an astute feminist can find much of value in what I call social-expressivism. I have been, as woman student and woman professional, drawn to the ways in which expressivist pedagogies and theories have empowered me and my women students. Having now examined an expressivist tradition and a definition of social-expressivism which parallel my personal experience and knowledge, I understand more fully how expressivist theories have rectified and can continue to rectify gender inequalities within a patriarchal system. In this chapter, I explore how social-expressivism and feminism can work together in the writing classroom by turning not only to others' scholarly insights, but to my personal history as a woman student and professional within the academy as well.

Problems with the Romantic and Expressivist Legacy

Scholars have begun to recognize that the university is an alienating place for many women (Aisenberg and Harrington, Meisenhelder, Chiseri-Strater, Gannett, Goulston). As a teacher, I have noted that the poses the academy demands are generally harder for my women students to strike than for my male students. As a woman trying to "speak" as a professional, I have noted that my women colleagues and I have a more difficult time speaking in the academy, whether it be in a scholarly article or in a faculty meeting. The academy privileges forms of discourse and styles of speaking that are largely androcentric. Many women are socialized to speak and write in alternative discourse styles—to converse through connection and consensus and to incorporate emotive processes into our discourses. We are often less comfortable with the rational argumentation privileged by the academy. After all, for centuries we were excluded from the public domain as speakers and writers.

And, in some ways, we still are. Even though many women now hold public office, actively participate in the work force, and attend school and institutions of higher learning, we do so in unequal proportions to the number of men in these positions. In part, women remain less actively a part of the public domain because we are still the primary caretakers in families and in relationships. Society still normatively relegates us to that private realm. Even though we now have expanding access to the public domain, our energies and time are still often split between the two. This might well be part of the reason that even though women make up the majority in the field of composition, they still publish less frequently than men.[1] We should not dismiss the complexities that result in this discrepancy—including the fact that most publishing houses are run by men, publishing decisions are most often made by men, most of our journals are edited by men, and most external evaluators and reviewers are men.

There are other reasons, too, that women find themselves uncomfortable with the rational argumentation privileged by the academy. It is hierarchical and linear, and rarely allows for a more circular form of argumentation or more "personal" kinds of writing. Even though women may now be trained and socialized into the preferred discourse of the academy and thus able to speak in this style if we so choose, when we do choose other discourse styles we produce work that the traditional masculine academy has identified as inferior.

Wendy Goulston (1987) explains the "maleness" of the academy and its relationship to women's styles in this way:

> Writing, as it has been traditionally required in college, can be understood to be a "male" establishment form, in as much as the aims and modes of scientific, informative, exploratory and persuasive discourse, even until recently, literary discourse, have been defined and developed by men heading intellectual institutions and by predominantly male writers whose ideas the professors

have valued. College writing trained and still does train students to use their minds in time-hallowed ways. For female students, this still, I suspect, means straining to attain a style, voice, and role that is hard to integrate with sexual and domestic success. (21–22)

As I will show shortly, Goulston describes my dilemma quite accurately.

Feminist discussions of romanticism and expressivism have been slow in coming. This is especially so in the case of expressivist composition theory. As Elizabeth Flynn (1991) has recently reminded us, there is a noticeable absence of feminist critique of composition as a whole (137). A collection of essays edited by Cynthia L. Caywood and Gillian R. Overing (1987), is the one major contribution to the conjoining of feminist perspectives and composition. In this text they do suggest some interplay between expressivist theories, or what the authors call "revisionist" writing pedagogies, and feminism. Other scholars will sometimes mention the compatibility of expressivist and feminist teaching styles, but they do not make a critique of expressivism their major concern.

Feminist studies of literary romanticism have also been slow to appear. Ann K. Mellor (1988) points out, for instance, that the romantic canon has lagged behind all others in any reformulation in light of feminist perspectives. This fact is a reflection of just how resoundingly male the romantic tradition has been. Currently this "lag" in the canon, as Mellor calls it, is twofold: feminine voices from the romantic age have been slow to enter the literary canon; and the canon of scholarship, if I might call it that, has been slow to see the influence of feminist scholarship on romanticism. Virtually hundreds of writers, many of them women, from the late 1700s to the mid-1800s continue to be marginalized or ignored as possible members of that group we have come to call romantics. Prior to the early 1980s and the contribution of feminist scholarship by such writers as Margaret Homans, Anne Mellor, Susan Wolfson, Mary Jacobus, and Susan Levin, the English romantic canon consisted primarily of six males: Blake, Wordsworth, Coleridge, Shelley, Byron, and Keats. As my own work here illustrates, the tradition from which expressivist rhetorics arise is, in large part, identified as male. Some feminists would question my desire to turn to such a male tradition in search of a workable feminist pedagogy (indeed, I questioned this). My position here is one of a pluralist. Just because a tradition is all male does not mean there are no useful aspects of it for feminist perusal and classroom practice. We can take what is useful from the expressivist tradition and leave what is damaging. We can redefine, reenvision, and reimagine new forms of expressivism. This does not mean that we excuse the patriarchal and sexist aspects of romanticism and neo-romantic rhetorics. Nor does it change the fact that my work in this book falls short as a feminist enterprise, precisely because I do not include the numbers of women that I might.

In an essay on romantic pedagogy and gender, Mary Jacobus (1989) baldly asks: "to what extent does installing oneself in this tradition also mean constituting oneself as looking like Wordsworth, or Bloom, or Hartman—i.e., masculine?" (238). This question is well worth asking. The time has come to examine from a feminist perspective the implications and consequences of this male tradition for expressivist theories and pedagogies. A feminist critique will certainly raise provocative philosophical questions for a rhetoric and theory of education based on such a thoroughly male tradition. Mellor (1988) suggests that the canonization of only six of the writers from the romantic age has "legitimized the continued repression of women" (8). Notably these six writers did not canonize themselves— male literary historians of a later date have done so. We still might ask, though, whether a rhetorical pedagogy primarily grounded in the philosophies of two of these six romantics might not also continue the repression that Mellor notes. After all, there is a long history of denial of education for women, and the romantics did not all work to ensure women's access to a full education. Although Percy Shelley argued for full and equal educational opportunities for women, Coleridge, a major figure in my history of expressivist theories, makes clear that his argument for a schooling that would nurture the "truly educated mind" was solely for men. Women were to be educated differently and for other purposes than that of the cultivation of the imaginative and reflective mind. Coleridge held this view even though he argues that the imaginative mind cannot reach its full potential unless it is feminine as well as masculine, unless it is an androgynous mind. This, of course, raises the philosophical question for feminists as to whether the romantics wanted to grant the feminine power at all, or whether they really wanted to absorb the feminine into the masculine.

As Jacobus reminds us, a Wordsworthian education was not meant for William's sister Dorothy. While she enjoyed the same free range and interaction with nature that he did, she was limited by her "obedience to the decorum of her sex and age, and her maidenly condition" (DeQuincey in Jacobus 253). Dorothy may well have interacted with nature, but, as Margaret Homans (1980) argues, her relationship to it is very different—she is equated with nature by the male poets and is thus left without the poetic "I" with which to inscribe herself upon nature as her brother does.

Also, as I noted earlier, Ian Hunter (1988) has pointed out that the romantic tradition, as it relates to the teaching of literature at any rate, is riddled with problems—problems that I see as germane to feminist concerns. Arnold's program for "high culture" was surely sexist and classist. This reminds us that expressivism's romantic heritage was originally meant to foster the encompassing intellect for those living the noble life—for a special class of men. Feminists should be wary of any pedagogical or theoretical approach that promotes or systematizes Arnold's romantic version of mass education, as it stems from this notion of high culture.

As I have argued, however, the romantic "literary" pedagogy Hunter speaks of is not enacted in most expressivist theories and pedagogies. Expressivists have not formed an elite class of students for a particular caste. I find this accusation more easily made against proponents of academic literacies because "mastery" of academic language is training students to be members of the academic elite.

To my mind, of more immediate concern than Hunter's critique of romantic ideology as it relates to literary pedagogy is James Catano's argument that the expressivist rhetorics of William Coles, Peter Elbow, and Ken Macrorie are masculine because they rely on a male self-formulation. It is worth considering whether Catano has put his finger on one of the more interesting and problematic aspects of expressivist genealogy. As Jacobus argues about Wordsworth's original romantic pedagogy, the masculine self actualizes itself at the expense of the feminine, in part because the masculine poet inscribes himself on nature, who is woman (see also Homans). According to Catano, this self-formulation of current expressivists describes learning to write in language that is combative and aggressive, and sees learning to write as a form of mastery. Masculine aggression is apparent in Coles and Elbow, and this aggression excludes women and is even "anti-feminine," according to Catano ("The Rhetoric of Masculinity" 1990, 433). Peter Elbow's language in *Writing with Power* demonstrates what Catano (1990) identifies as aggressive male language: "Having rejected 'subjective bullshit' in the first text (141), Elbow follows up in the second with a variety of aggressive descriptions and metaphors of writing: "the experience of battle conditions with live ammunition" (33); 'my decision . . . to force the world to listen to me' (122); 'wielding the knife and seeing blood on the floor' (123); and 'the power of the words to hit readers in the gut' (369)" (429).

This "masculinist" use of language is widespread, and the works of other writing theorists are also saturated with a language of aggression and combat. Susan Meisenhelder (1985), for instance, has noted that "examining modern conceptions of rhetoric and the handbooks on writing we teach shows us that we often teach an adversarial model of discourse" (186). Meisenhelder suggests that when we teach writing based on discourse models built on metaphors of war and violence such as "attacking" and "defending" points of view, and when we talk of using words as weapons and as acts of aggression, we are "promoting a patriarchal mode that encourages students to internalize a rhetorical stance of dominance . . ." (186). This has negative consequences for some women students because it reinforces a way of acting and writing in the world, which, in its combativeness, is uncomfortable for them, and it works to keep women oppressed by a male hierarchy.

That expressivists' discourse models also harbor language that is exclusionary and even "anti-feminine," as Catano suggests, is an issue that should concern expressivist rhetoricians as well as feminists. We should make concerted efforts to remove these metaphorical constructs and to replace them with language that welcomes and invites, rather than excludes, women. Perhaps we can make better use of nurturing and connecting metaphors and help bring forward the expressivist focus on empathy and discovery. Peter Elbow, for instance, has a pedagogy that so clearly rests on empathy that it seems strange to find these aggressive metaphors, and I suspect that there are fewer of them than more accommodating metaphors. Yet it does seem urgent that he reconstruct his language in passages like those quoted by Catano.

To alleviate the patriarchal rhetoric that Catano has perceptively pointed out in expressivist pedagogies will take critical self-reflection; and to incorporate feminist theoretical and pedagogical perspectives into expressivist stances will help with this self-reflective project: we can examine and change troublesome metaphors so that they are not anti-feminine or anti-woman; we can include a feminist rhetoric which models a mode of composing founded on metaphors of collaboration and caring, rather than on metaphors of "war" and "rape" (193). We can recognize and problematize the fact that the powerful autonomous self of the Western world is normatively that of the "self-made" man and not the "self-made" woman or the socially constructed woman.

As Carol Gilligan (1988) suggests, there is an alternative construction to that of the autonomous self—"self is known in the experience of connection" (7). We can take our cue from feminists and change the expressivist rhetoric of the self to a plurality of selves. Likewise, we can be explicit about the fact that "sincere" or "authentic" voice is not confined to a notion of a particular, universal, or monolithic voice. Rather, as I have come to do, we can reconceive of voice as bell hooks (1989) does in *Talking Back* attending all-black segregated schools with black teachers meant that I had come to understand black poets as being capable of speaking in many voices, that the Dunbar of a poem written in dialect was no more or less authentic than the Dunbar writing a sonnet. Yet it was listening to black musicians like Duke Ellington, Louis Armstrong, and later John Coltrane that impressed upon our consciousness a sense of versatility—they played all kinds of music, had multiple voices. So it was with poetry. The black poet, as exemplified by Gwendolyn Brooks and later Amiri Baraka, had many voices—with no single voice being identified as more or less authentic. The insistence on finding one voice, one definitive style of writing and reading one's poetry, fit all too neatly with a static notion of self and identity that was pervasive in university settings. (11)

In sum, we can publicly articulate feminist-expressivist and social-expressivist theories in contrast to traditional masculine and anti-social theories.

The Romantic Legacy and Women's Ways of Knowing

I do not want to unthoughtfully dismiss the problems with expressivism, or its historical precursor, romanticism. But the philosophies of expressivism's forebears, the male poets, are not completely antithetical to feminist perspectives. The feminist educational philosopher Jane Roland Martin (1985) calls for a rethinking of education that will enable emotion and feeling to become as much a part of the educational process as analysis, critical thinking, and self-sufficiency (192–193). This was the basis for Wordsworth and Coleridge's educational plan.

Martin also asks for an educational system that honors, and melds together, both "reproductive societal processes" that have traditionally been seen as the feeling and emotional realm of the female, and the analytical realm of knowledge-making which is seen as the "productive societal processes" usually ascribed to the world of the male (197). Martin recalls a 1977 address by Adrienne Rich to women college students in which she asked the students to claim an active education that would connect with their experiences as women, rather than to passively receive one that privileges the male experience. Rich, writes Martin, "was saying that in becoming mere receptacles for a university learning that excludes their experience and thought, women's lives can be damaged beyond repair" (2). As I have been arguing throughout, the romantic philosophies allow for a version of an ideal education that promotes what Rich and Martin argue for: an active rather than passive education, and a wedding of the emotional and analytical, or the productive and reproductive processes.

Although William Wordsworth has been accused of relegating nature to the realm of the feminine in order to assert his masculine poetic identity over the natural world (Homans 1980), he is just as likely to assert a more feminine consciousness. As the feminist critic Susan Wolfson (1988) argues, "just as typically, and with a full range of investigation, this poet may represent male consciousness as passive, itself inscribed by voices of the 'other'" (147). She quotes *The Prelude* [1850]:

'the changeful earth . . . on my mind has stamped
The faces of the moving year' (Prelude I. 586–588); the 'common
face of Nature spake to me . . . impressed
Collateral objects and appearances,
Albeit lifeless then, and doomed to sleep
Until maturer seasons call them forth
To impregnate and to elevate the mind.' (I. 615–24) (147)

In these lines, argues Wolfson (1988), "the self is not just passive but feminine, and imaged, implicitly, with the potential of female (re)productivity" (147). In effect, Wordsworth's lines here depict his male consciousness in a state that is not asserting its identity against the natural world. Rather, as Wolfson suggests, his male consciousness is being "inscribed by voices of the 'other'." The result, as Wordsworth implies, is an "impregnation" of the mind and the distinctly female ability to give birth, to (re)produce. Wordsworth's description of the philosophical mind is androgynous.

Coleridge, too, strove for a consciousness that was as much feminine as masculine. As I have already pointed out, he believed that the imaginative and "truly educated" mind must be androgynous, must combine the feminine and the masculine. Indeed, by using the figure of the androgyne as a central metaphor throughout his philosophical discussions, Coleridge was able to suggest a union between the masculine and the feminine consciousness, thereby creating a mind that is potentially (re)productive.

The male poets were certainly not always successful in their attempts to nurture a feminine consciousness along with their male consciousness. This failure prompts some feminist critics to argue that the romantics' attempts to incorporate the feminine did irreparable damage to the women of their community (Homans, Richardson). It is also clear that both Wordsworth and Coleridge viewed the feminine in a stereotypical manner. An examination of their writings, for instance, shows that they associate the feminine part of the androgynous mind with passivity rather than activity. Coleridge's model of the androgynous mind breaks down into typical opposites—the masculine as light, life, mind, and reason and the feminine as darkness, death, body, and passion. Coleridge and Wordsworth's acceptance of the feminine as crucial to the education of the encompassing intellect, then, is premised on diminishing views of the feminine.

Feminists should be leery of terms like "male" and "female" or "masculine" and "feminine" when referring to the mind or consciousness. It is but a simple step from there to essentializing masculinity and femininity. When the creative mind is viewed as masculine, feminine, androgynous, or in any way gendered, it is because centuries of male writers have constructed these metaphors. My ambition is not to argue for these essentializing metaphors, but for the intent, no matter how badly represented, that Wordsworth and Coleridge had in trying to deconstruct the image of the creative mind as solely masculine. They did work toward cultivating a "feminine" consciousness during a historical time in which the feminine was categorically and stereotypically seen as inferior.

At the same time that Wordsworth and Coleridge were working from this stereotypical perspective of the feminine, they were also attempting to work against it, for embedded in Wordsworth's quest for the philosophic mind and Coleridge's belief that the creative mind is androgynous is a philosophy that honors the connection of feeling and emotion, analysis and critical thinking, and the productive and reproductive processes necessary to create an education that truly accommodates women as well as men. If we are willing to join with feminists in diffusing the stereotypical views of the feminine and masculine and in deconstructing the belief that the attributes of masculine and feminine must be separate, perhaps current expressivists can succeed where their romantic forebears failed.

Mary Field Belenky, Blythe McVicker Clinchy, Nancy Rule Goldberger, and Jill Mattuck Tarule's (1986) study of women's intellectual development also suggests that aspects of romantic and expressivist educational philosophy are beneficial for women. They chronicle the psychological development of women as they move from positions of "silence" to positions of "constructed knowing," from powerless to empowered selves capable of not only receiving knowledge, but of making knowledge. Their study suggests that the development of voice and self is crucial to the development of women's minds; they also find that, for the most part, the process of education has traditionally not allowed for the psychological and intellectual growth of women because it has separated the affective from the analytical, and lived experience from academic experience.

Likewise, although she differs with Belenky et al. on other points, Jane Roland Martin (1987) finds that the educational journey is primarily one that is damaging because it splits reason from emotion. Interestingly enough, the suggestions Belenky et al. (1986) make for creating an educational system that would foster the development of women echo many of those made by the romantics for the cultivation of the "philosophical" or "truly educated" mind:

> We have argued in this book that educators can help women develop their own authentic voices if they emphasize connection over separation, understanding and acceptance over assessment, and collaboration over debate; if they accord respect to and allow time for the knowledge that emerges from firsthand experience; if instead of imposing their own expectations and arbitrary requirements, they encourage students to evolve their own patterns of work based on the problems they are pursuing. These lessons we have learned in listening to women's voices. (229)

The romantics advocated growth of the self, discovery of voice, "connection," "understanding," "experience," and although we don't usually perceive of the romantics as "collaborative," in practice they formed writing communities, shared their work, and even collaborated on the writing of their poetry. Wordsworth and Coleridge, for instance, not only collaborated to compile the *Lyrical Ballads,* but often made additions, sometimes adding full stanzas, to each other's poems. They used each other's poetical ideas and conversations with each other as ways of overcoming writing blocks or as means of "inspiration."

Moreover, the epistemological stages in women's development identified by Belenky et al.—"silence," "received knowledge," "subjective knowledge," "procedural knowledge," and "constructed knowledge"—are similar to the developmental path described by the poets in the growth of the creative, knowledge-making intellect.[2] In the stage of silence, for instance, women seem to be "'deaf and dumb' and are unaware of the power of words for transmitting knowledge" (36). "Silent" women are cut off from their experience, they are unable to connect with the world around them, they are unable to connect with language. They are voiceless and without self.

> Even though each of the women had the gifts of intelligence and of all their senses, they were unaware of the potential of such gifts. While no one was actually "deaf and dumb," this metaphor suggests their experience more accurately than does "gaining a

voice." They felt "deaf" because they assumed they could not learn from the words of others, "dumb" because they felt so voice-less (24).

Because they are cut off from the practice or privilege of "making sense" of the world around them, do not "perceive" as the romantics would say, cannot connect with experience, these women are missing a crucial link in the discovery of self, which leads to "finding a voice" and making meaning through language.

Belenky et al. also suggest that the silence these women suffer is culturally imposed. In its most extreme form, this imposition comes through such tragic and drastic forces as emotional, physical, and sexual abuse. If, however, women can shed this cultural imposition and the consequent "deafness and dumbness," if they can learn to connect with experiences in some way, they move toward a means of knowing that is analogous to Wordsworth's wise passiveness. During a time of "received knowledge," women begin to observe, perceive, and experience. They "learn by listening" (36). As it is for Wordsworth, this position is important to women because, although passive, it is a time of experiencing and discovering through observation, and this experiencing becomes important in creating knowledge through language.

Having found ways to move from silence to the ability to "receive," the women in the study by Belenky et al. were able to begin the important job of constructing self-knowledge through language. This necessarily comes from a position of subjectivity, just as it did for the romantic poets. What becomes important is the individual's lived experience or vision, and, at this juncture, the "subjective knower" starts to see the world in terms of self. She finds her own experience worthwhile, perhaps for the first time in her life. She is in a position to identify, to understand, and to begin speaking of her experience as it relates to her "self." This initial stage of experiential recognition—or perhaps what we could call ego building—is so all consuming that self-experience overrides an awareness of how experience might connect with the world. In a quotation from a young woman who was a "subjective" knower, the authors of *Women's Ways of Knowing* capture the difficulty women have connecting with the experiences of others, when they finally learn to trust their own experience. This woman could find little sense in the experience revealed in the lectures of her male professor and the discussions on the classical texts they were reading, because it seemed irrelevant to her own experience: "A college senior was highly critical of a male professor: 'I never knew what the man was talking about. It was the way he spoke or the words he used or just the way he put words together that was hard for me to understand. You can't learn from teachers and books like you can from experience'" (74).

This discrepancy in experiences may not be solely a gendered issue. Both my men and women students at the earlier stages of their academic careers seem to struggle with this matter of irrelevancy. I do think, however, that this gap between self-experience and academic experience and knowledge is more poignant for women. In the case of the college senior quoted above, her experience did not match her sense of the academic world, and, at this point, she was able to trust little else but her own words and experience. In part, this happened because reading, writing, and "correct" academic response is masculine identified. It is a powerful moment in a woman's life to realize, finally, that her experiences are important; and perhaps it is even more powerful to finally be able to articulate her experiences and yet realize these experiences are not fully empowering in terms of academic survival. In effect, Belenky et al.'s (1986) "subjective knower" is so centered within her own experience and words that she finds it difficult to relate her experience to anyone else's. She seems hesitant to reflect on the disparity between her own experience and that revealed in the texts she is reading or that the professor is trying to convey. She remains stuck as a "subjective knower" because she has not, as the romantics knew was crucial, "abandoned both subjectivism and absolutism in some areas [of her life] . . . in favor of reasoned reflection" (88).

According to Belenky et al., reflection is of utmost importance to women's intellectual development, just as it is to the growth of Wordsworth's philosophical mind and Coleridge's educated mind. For Coleridge, and for current compositionists like Berthoff and Elbow, reflection leads to mental growth, which eventually leads to a "distinct consciousness," which is, in effect, a mind capable of making meaning. Likewise, the ability to be reflective is the catalyst that moves women into an epistemological position that the authors of *Women's Ways of Knowing* call "procedural knowledge." Within this stage are two modes of knowing: "connected" and "separate" knowing. Separate knowers seem to be the less productive of the two. When separate knowers work on a writing task, for instance, they "write well," but often "feel the papers they write are pointless. They have no connection to the papers they write for teachers and they [the papers] are empty of their own feelings, ideas, and voice" (188). "Connected" knowing, on the other hand, is not disconnected from the self and world as separate knowing is. It is the "epistemological orientation that is toward relationship" (101). It is the balanced position between subjectivity and objectivity that the romantics strove to find and that many expressivists are beginning to locate in their pedagogical and theoretical approaches. Connected knowing seems to bear much in common with expressivist and romantic philosophies. In fact, the authors suggest that Coleridge is a connected knower (113). The ties are not limited to Coleridge, however. They are evident in expressivist thought. Belenky et al. (1986) write: "Connected knowers develop procedures for gaining access to other people's knowledge. At the heart of these procedures is the capacity for empathy. Since knowledge comes from experience, the only way they can hope to understand another person's ideas is to try to share the experience that has led the person to form the idea" (113).

This quotation seems to describe the expressivist and romantic desire to connect with others. It is reminiscent of Keats' negative capability: the ultimate ability to negate one's own ego in order to identify and connect with an other. It is certainly reflective of Wordsworth's entire project as a poet: "to bring his feelings near to those of the persons whose feelings he describes" ([1815] 1984, 737). But it is also describing the heart of expressivist pedagogy as enacted by Elbow and Murray.

Unlike "separate knowers," women who are connected knowers are not only able to write well in the conventional sense, but they are also able to do so with voice, feeling, and critical thought. Separate knowers are examples of what the romantic poets and their nineteenth-century and current followers find to be the result of a misguided education of analysis, severed from the emotive and experiential. Separate knowers are capable of parroting back information they have received, but as Belenky et al. (1986) note, they are incomplete and uninvested in the making of knowledge: "For women . . . who are separate knowers, thinking and feeling are split asunder; they feel fraudulent and deadened to their inner experiences and inner selves" (135).

If women are able to cultivate experience, feeling, voice, self, and reflection, they can become connected knowers, and connected knowers are able to move into the fifth epistemological position identified in *Women's Ways of Knowing*, that of "constructed knowledge." This is most like William Wordsworth's mature mind, the philosophical mind. Constructed knowers have the abilities of the encompassing intellect. They blend reason and emotion, subjective and objective. They are able to create knowledge, because they have incorporated those things the expressivists find crucial to a viable educational process, "reflection," "experience," "empathy," "self-consciousness," and "personal voice":

These women [constructed knowers] were all articulate and reflective people. They noticed what was going on with others and cared
about the lives of people about them. They were intensely self-con-
scious, in the best sense of the word—aware of their own thought,
their judgments, their moods and desires. . . . Each was ambitious
and fighting to find her own voice—her own way of expressing what
she knew and cared about. Each wanted her voice and actions to
make a difference to other people and the world. (133)

Belenky et al. refer to and quote Peter Elbow extensively in their
study. They cite him as a writing teacher who fosters a learning climate in which women can excel. Both his focus on development of
voice, and the privileging of "believing" over "doubting" allow
women to take part more fully in their own education, because they
are able to work from a center of assent rather than dissent and
debate.

Peter Elbow's pedagogy relies on connection and empathy, two
qualities critical to women's emotional and intellectual growth.
Small groups provide Elbow's students with the environment necessary for connections among people to take place. His "sharing"
groups, where students learn to share their writing and listen
closely to each other, are helpful for women who are both searching for their own voice and learning to "hear." These groups stress
active listening. They give students a chance to say what they know
without facing, in the beginning of the search for voice, negative
criticism and harsh response. As Belenky et al. point out, many
"silent" women do not survive the academy, because they are not
themselves secure with language. For many of these women, language is a weapon that has been used against them to ensure their
continued silence in the face of male dominance and abuse.

I suspect that many, feminists and non-feminists alike, will be
uneasy with my seemingly uncritical acceptance of the data presented in *Women's Ways of Knowing*. Some significant criticisms
have, after all, been made about the book and what it presents. The
most vital concern is that the authors' position on women throughout the work could be construed as essentialism. They do call these
"women's ways of knowing," implying a biological difference from
men's ways, even if they also claim that these women's ways are
happening in a sexist society programmed by patriarchy. Essentialism is a volatile subject for feminists, as well it should be. The cod-
ifying of difference as biological has allowed the patriarchy to maintain a power hierarchy that sees women, blacks, and others who are
different from the "normative" white male as inferior for centuries.
To suggest that women "know" differently from men is to open the
door, again, for women to be perceived as intellectually inferior.

There are no easy solutions to the problems raised by the possibilities of essentialism. It remains an ongoing and provocative tension among feminists of many camps. American feminists like Elaine Showalter and French feminists like Helene Cixous and Julia Kristeva have also been called essentialist. In the case of *Women's Ways of Knowing,* I find none of this insurmountable. In fact, to dismiss the findings of the research done by Belenky et al. on these grounds is to force the work into a biological trap in which it does not fit, and perhaps more importantly, obscure what is valuable about it.[3]

The following excerpt from an interview with Mary Belenky makes the authors' position on the question of essentialism clear:

> Q: The research into women's cognitive, intellectual and ethical development that Gilligan and your collective are doing is exciting. But doesn't it have the potential to reinforce gender stereotypes and essentialist definitions of femininity? Can't research into gender differences ultimately reinforce cultural myths about gender, including gender hierarchy?
>
> A: Of course, that's a real danger, and I don't know what to do about it. There's also a real danger in *not* trying to give voice to this whole range of human experience that has not been articulated and is not an integral part of the culture—you give away the whole ball game. Men continue to set the standard and perpetuate a world where individualism and competition take precedence over relationships and connections. They create a world where competition is practically the only game in town, and collaboration and cooperation are not cultivated. That seems more dangerous, and I don't know how to get around it. Of course, many people consider the four of us "essentialists"—that is, they classify us with those who see sex differences as immutably rooted in biology. What we are really doing, though, is describing characteristics that women and men have developed in the context of a sexist and aggressive society, a society in which public and private spheres of living have been drastically segregated. (Ashton-Jones and Thomas 1990, 284)

As Belenky points out, they are describing the ways in which the self is shaped by social context, not biology. Their work is "steeped in the very deepest roots of constructivism" (291). In the introduction to their book, the authors are also careful to acknowledge that men may well fit these patterns, but, since previous work by scholars like William Perry look solely at men, they wanted to look only, and carefully, at women.

Admittedly, my openness to their work is in large part because what they present in their research so thoroughly fits my own experience. My epistemological development and entrance into academic life seem directly related to culturally and patriarchally constructed experiences. And those educational and life experiences that the authors identified as beneficial for the women in their study were beneficial for me, including experience with romantic educational philosophies and expressivist rhetorical theories and pedagogies that might benefit women students enormously.

Unlearning Silence: A Personal Journey

My experiences as a woman, in and out of the academy, drive my exploration of the valuable aspects of expressivism. I want in particular to acknowledge the ways in which the theories and practices of expressivists, especially those of Elbow and Murray, empowered me to survive and finally to come to voice in the academy.

When I entered college, I found myself in a foreign setting unable to negotiate the language barriers. Part of my difficulty in entering into the academic discourse of college was not necessarily gender specific. My grammar school and secondary educations did not prepare me, or other students, for the complex language use that the academy demands of us. My reading and writing experiences were very limited. In elementary school I did some creative writing, but writing became almost nonexistent in the later years of my schooling. Writing was soon replaced by workbook drills on vocabulary, punctuation, and grammar.

What was gender specific throughout all of the years of my schooling, however, was the recurrence of subtle messages that reading, writing, speaking, math, and science were more important for boys than for me, since I would be getting married and staying home, while the boys would be going on to college and out into the working world. While in high school, I did do more reading and writing, and even received some support for the idea of going to college. However, other girls and I were never encouraged to join the debate team or to write for the school paper in the same way the boys were.

My decision to enter graduate school opened up even more sexist pressure, which shaped my ability to enter into academic discourse and debate with any confidence. Some of the messages about women's place were subtle, some were not so subtle. My father could not understand why I would want to go to graduate school, since I could teach with a B.A. and women were teachers, not professors. More than one male professor actually suggested that graduate school for me would be a waste of everybody's time, since I would never finish. Either I was, by virtue of being woman, not graduate material, or I would drop out to have children. My story is not an isolated one. Academic women often talk with each other about the ways in which they were discouraged from academic reading and writing or even from academic pursuits in general.

My problems were, and still are, exacerbated by a history of childhood sexual and physical abuse. As researchers such as Carol Barringer (1992) and Belenky, Clincher, Goldberger, and Tarule (1986) point out, coming to voice in the academy is difficult enough for women, but it becomes even more difficult when we have been silenced in other areas of our lives.

Barringer (1992) argues that the silencing of abuse victims is parallel to or emblematic of the silencing of women in general (4–5). The silencing is multi-layered. For the abuse victim, it might take the form of physical threat not to tell and/or a lack of words to name the violating experience. In some cases, these traumatic experiences are so deeply suppressed that a literal amnesia takes place. Neither language nor memory remains. In more general situations, the silencing takes place in our cultural perception that women should speak less than men, it happens because men interrupt women in conversation and debate, and it happens when male students are consistently called on more often than female students (Gannett 1992, 66–80).

This silencing is not something abstract. It is a tangible and physical reality, and one that I and many women have struggled with both in and out of the academy. What expressivist pedagogies have done for me is to help me come to voice—or rather to voices—in my writing and speaking. Before I could begin the difficult task of negotiating the androcentric domain of academic discourse and argument, I first had to come to voice by re-constructing myself—in part by writing myself through the pain, the silence, the anger, and the fear.[4]

In my case, the language used by the males in my life was meant to silence me. If I spoke back to my father, I was told to keep silent, and if I didn't, the language command was followed by a physical command. In the composition course I took in college—a course founded on Elbow's expressivist theories—I began writing back to the abusers in my life. But even before I could find my voice to speak to them directly in my writing, or face to face, I had to write these things in veiled forms to my grandmother (my father's mother), who knew of the sexual abuse inflicted upon me, and in turn blamed me, inflicting yet more abuse and silencing upon me. The following is an excerpt from a personal essay I wrote in this class:

> I cried out from the shock and my skin prickled as it turned red hot—the water was scalding. Grandmother said it had to be this

way to wash away all the dirt. I didn't know Grandmother very well. She didn't come to live with us until I was six or seven. Even when she died, many years later, I didn't know her well. But it was me she wanted to be with her at the end, after the cancer had eaten away what little there was of her. She was small and very sick. I guess that's why I kept going back at the end—her smallness and her sickness—and my need to purge the guilt.

She could no longer stay at home and Father had to move her into the nursing home. She didn't fight it at all. That's when I knew she was never coming home again. It was there, in that other place, that I went to visit her. I hated being there. The smell of death was so overpowering that I found myself just wishing she would die so I could leave that room and never come back.

But she didn't die right then and I kept going back. I touched death every day. The nurses couldn't touch her—"They hurt me" she would say. "You are the only one strong enough and gentle enough." But I didn't want to be strong and gentle. She made me angry and I hated her. She made the little blind lady that shared the room cry. "You filthy thing. You've made a mess again. You are dirty and disgusting," she would yell as the blind lady curled up in a ball, trembling on her bed. I want to hit Grandmother, not help her and be gentle with her. Why had she chosen me in death? I carried the guilt of dirt and filth with me—it seemed odd that she of all people should forget this.

The familiar words echoed throughout the years as I stood in that little room amongst the smells of cancerous death. You see, those same words had become my grandmother's ritual during my childhood. I felt again the heat of humiliation and guilt just as it was then—the too hot bath closing around me. "You are dirty and must be cleansed. Filthy. Disgusting. Dirty." She scrubbed between my legs until I was raw and would cry out. Sometimes my skin would bleed. The she would smile and stop. I was cleansed.

The quality of this piece of writing, by academic standards, is not what is important here. Had I not been given the place to voice these things in language at that point in my college career, had I not been afforded this kind of self-expression, I would not have continued school. I would have remained silenced and voiceless in all ways—including academic ways. Until the writing of this piece, I had been unable to write more than a paragraph or two of struggling prose. When all else failed I would fall back on the formulaic writing of the five-paragraph theme.

Neither my writing group nor my teacher suggested that this essay was academically incorrect or inappropriate. Rather, they helped me recognize that a voice had been born. Finding this voice was the start to finding the many kinds of voices and identities I needed to survive in the academy. The work that the academy accepts as worthwhile requires the striking of particular kinds of poses, selves, and voices. If women professionals are to have the kinds of academic selves that generate publication, action, respect, and, finally, tenure within the university, we, as women, must somehow learn to compose different voices from those our culture at large has designated as acceptable or typical for us. Likewise, if our women students are to find success within the university, they must learn a myriad of voices. In other words, academic selves need suitable academic voices. Or, alternatively, academic writing and language must become more multiple, if not completely redefined.

The kind of group work Elbow and Murray advocate provided at least two important educative needs for me. First, a place to practice using language and finding a voice. And second, an environment in which negative criticism is deferred until the writer has enough sense of self(ves) and voice(s), to alleviate the feeling that language is necessarily a weapon meant to silence. Not all women, of course, have suffered the extreme silencing that I have, but as I pointed out, women in our culture are silenced in various and subtle ways. The piece on my grandmother was not the only essay I wrote that arose from my own cultural experiences. My teacher and writing group members did not demand that the rest of my writing for the course take the form of objective critical essays and other more typically academic discourses. While I did write some clearcut academic pieces, I more often wrote essays that fused the personal and the more objective, that explored the tensions between my cultural experiences and the academy, and that brought awareness of my struggle to write within the academy.

Feminists have recognized that the private language used by women in journals can be an important step toward learning how to speak in the public language of the academy (Gannet 1992). Here, for example, are some personal journal entries that were important for me to write before I could get to work on a large academic project—my dissertation.

> 12/8/89 Almost 10:00 and I've not started anything. I hate it when my life gets like this. How can I find time to get that elusive academic voice when I spend my energy putting away dishes, picking up the kitchen, vacuuming the rug? Why do I think this is my responsibility? Why can't my job just be sitting down and writing academic prose? Enough of this self-indulgence. Write.

> 3/7/90 I was leveled after last Monday's writing group. They gave me great feed back—stuff I know I needed to hear. It allowed me to turn Chapter 2 into my own. Their biggest criticism was that there was no me. NO SHERRIE VOICE. I've always tried to please

the fathers, my academic fathers too. But I learned at such a young
age that silence is what the fathers really want of women (and little girls). Now, for these academic fathers I'm suddenly supposed
to have a certain kind of voice—it has to look and sound a certain
way. It's not a way of speaking I'm comfortable with. I'll keep trying but I know my voice has been subsumed by all those critics I'm
reading.

This writing reveals that I understand my problem as one of
lack of voice, a struggle within academic discourse, and a tension
between the role I was trying to play as a Ph.D. candidate and society's defined roles for women. At that moment, I had no answers for
my problem. Moreover, I ended the journal entry of 12/8/89 by
admonishing myself for self-indulgence for even contemplating the
struggles, itself a patriarchal response to my own dilemma. In the
second entry, I have made an implicit connection between the literal silence imposed by my abusers, and the silence imposed by the
patriarchal academic institution I was writing within.

Although I was not fully cognizant of the connections between
an abusive home life and what I then was feeling as an abusive
institution, this personal journaling about voice was essential for
me. Without it, I felt paralyzed—unable to sit down to work at the
academic project at hand. Expressivist teachers like Murray and
Elbow nurture experience but also encourage students to come to
terms with past experiences by working with these experiences
through language—putting them into words. Journaling and freewriting are pedagogical techniques that invite women into the
realm of discourse. It is worth remembering, however, that as Flynn
(1991) argues, freewriting and finding voice, while perhaps empowering to a degree, will remain limited in their empowerment until
there is a "change in the social order, a shift in the balance of
power" (149).

Linking Feminism and Expressivism

I do not mean, from my own experience, to generalize that all
women benefit from expressivist pedagogies, nor do I mean to suggest that expressivism, romanticism and feminism are perfect counterparts or even necessarily easy allies. There is, however, much
about expressivism that accommodates feminist theory and pedagogy, and it would, I think, behoove compositionists to consider
expressivist rhetorics in light of recent feminist contributions to
both literary and composition studies. If, for example, expressivist

theories and pedagogies are already empowering for women in various ways, then a conscious revision of expressivism that includes feminist perspectives would be invaluable for creating a theory of composition that strives for gender equality.

Meisenhelder (1985), for example, also finds the journal invaluable for women students and feminist teachers:

> In this way [through journal writing] we aim to launch students—often especially women students—on a private search for self-identity and meaning in their own lives. This is an important development for several reasons. Besides the value in helping students develop awareness, teaching such a form of writing has been an important step in transforming notions about discourse and language. This kind of writing allows students to experience the power of important feminist ideas about language—especially the value of the particular, the concrete, and the emotional. From journal writing students learn that language doesn't have to be distanced, logical, objective, and abstract in the traditional model of rational thought for it to convey meaning. (184)

Peter Elbow's freewriting is also a way in which students can learn that language that is emotional and "non-logical" has value. In fact, freewriting and prewriting of all kinds is an especially inviting form of discourse for women. As Wendy Goulston (1987) reminds us, "Prewriting is, after all, what women have been doing for centuries in letters and journals and conversations with each other, 'freewriting,' 'brainstorming,' meditating, overflowing with uncensored feelings and ideas" (25).

When we use these familiar and "expressive" modes as a foundation for academic prose, says Goulston, "women can draw on their own thinking and feeling to develop the rhetorical strategies that best suit their styles, their arguments, their values" (25). As I suggested in Chapter One, the fact that expressivism values the autobiographical, the intimate and subjective voice that has been codified as "feminine" in our culture, may well be one reason that expressivism is continually denigrated. This may be especially important when we consider that many in the field are trying to raise the status of composition within the academy. The androcentric orientation of the academy still finds these more "feminine" modes of being, writing, and teaching inferior.

Prewriting, freewriting, journal keeping, exercises of observation and reflection are the kinds of activities that can help move our women students from the position of silence where they are without self, voice, and power, to a discursive position where they can break through "dumbness and deafness." By learning to experience, perceive, and listen they can move to the position of "received knowledge." Activities such as prewriting and freewriting can allow our women students, as well as men students, to make their personal experience part of their learning process. As Peter Elbow suggests, they can write about their feelings and what is important to them. Elbow believes that freewriting can help in the development of voice, and voice is a crucial part of women's emotional and intellectual growth, according to feminist researchers.

Also, the expressivist focus on reflection, empathy, and voice can provide the vital means of moving through "subjective knowing" to "connected knowing," and eventually to the stage of "constructed knowledge." When teachers like Donald Murray create a learning environment that focuses on discovery of both self and others, women students can learn to become connected knowers through empathy and an understanding of how the self interacts with, and is shaped by, the world. Moreover, through practice such as Ann Berthoff's students gain while writing in double-entry notebooks where they rethink, question, study, and reflect on their own observations and experiences, our students receive the chance to move beyond subjective knowing to connected knowing. Since expressivist rhetorics, both in original and modern forms, foster an encompassing intellect in our students through pedagogies that blend the emotive and analytical, the subjective and the objective, discovery of self and discovery of others, they offer a theory and practice that can help women reach their potential as "constructed knowers."

The ties between expressivism and feminism may be stronger than we as compositionists have previously considered. Some feminist researchers have noted a correlation between feminist theories and expressivist theories. Cynthia Caywood and Gillian Overing (1987), for instance, suggest that "revisionist" writing theories are a critique of a patriarchal system just as are feminist theories:

> In assembling it and reviewing these two bodies of research, we have discovered a consistent pattern, one characterized by the recurrent intersection of several major premises at the heart of both bodies of research. The most important of these are: the relation between revisionist critiques of traditional writing theory and the feminist critique of masculinist, patriarchal ways of being; and the correlation between the revisionists' restructuring of pedagogy and revaluing of the student and feminists' restructuring of cultural models and revaluing of the experience of women.
>
> The familiar revisionists view of writing as process, which challenges the classical view of writing as product, offers a paradigmatic dialectic appropriate to feminist discourse. (xii)

Both feminist theories and revisionist writing theories question authority: feminist theory, that of the patriarchy, and revisionist theory, that of the product.

While Caywood and Overing do not specify expressivist theory as the "revisionist" theory they argue for, the focus on the "private" and "individual" voice, personal experience, and process over product, which they identify as aspects of "revisionist" theory, clearly belongs to the realm of expressivism. It seems to me that expressivist rhetorics are linked to feminist theory in their critique of oppressive hierarchies, as in earlier decades, when romantic ideas and philosophies arose in people like Mill, Emerson, and Dewey, and in Berthoff, Murray, Rohman, and Elbow as reactions to oppressive establishments and traditional schooling curricula. As Caywood and Overing argue, expressivist theory (what they call "revisionist" theory) and feminist theory are kindred in their opposition to an established hierarchy: "the process model, in so far as it facilitates and legitimizes the fullest expression of the individual voice, is compatible with the feminist revisioning of hierarchy, if not essential to it" (xiv).

Flynn (1991) posits that expressivism has reversed the traditional hierarchies of discourse (147). Writing of Britton, she argues that, in essence, he and his colleagues are "privileging female ways of thinking over male modes, creating a place for intimacy and nurturance in otherwise product-oriented educational institutions. They are protecting the feminine—mothering—and fending off the dominance of the father" (147). But, as Flynn also suggests, expressivism may be feminine, yet it is not necessarily feminist. To become feminist, expressivism must consciously concern itself with gender issues.

While I have initiated a feminist response to romantic teaching philosophies and expressivist rhetorics, this response has been only to an all male tradition except for Ann Berthoff. I do not wish to ignore that romantic educational theories are historically male-centered, nor as Hunter points out, exclusive of certain classes. As Jane Roland Martin (1982) notes, women have been excluded throughout the history of education, both as objects of educational thought and as subjects (135).[5] Another way, then, that we can bring feminist perspectives to bear on expressivism and enrich its tradition, is to expand the realm of expressivist rhetorics by widening the male romantic tradition to include the women who contributed so significantly to the movement. This widening can take place on several levels. It can include both women who were contemporary with the romantics and it can include women as writers, readers, and learners in today's academy. While I have not undertaken this project here, I believe there needs to be further scholarship on the ways in which a feminist tradition can add to social-expressivisms. As compositionists, we can join our colleagues in literary studies to explore what Mary Wollstonecraft, Mary Shelley, Felicia Hemans, Emily Bronte, Dorothy Wordsworth, and others can add to our tradition. We can examine, as many feminist composition scholars like Cheryl Glenn, Lisa Ede, Andrea Lunsford, and C. Jan Swearingen are beginning to do, what the lost voices have to contribute to contemporary composition and rhetorical theories.

Many will be surprised to find that Wollstonecraft anticipated current social theories by arguing that women are social constructions, shaped by our environment and the type of education we receive (Martin 1987, 77), and that the writings of Dorothy Wordsworth offer a "female version" of the romantic self that takes into account "the complexities surrounding a woman's psychological development" (Levin 1987, 5). Further, feminist literary scholars have already begun to show that Dorothy Wordsworth's vision of the self forthrightly expands "individual subjectivity to visionary community" (Wolfson 1988, 145), offering further reason for not dismissing expressivist rhetorics on charges of radical individualism.

Although we are inclined to see "collaboration" and writing "communities" as primarily social-epistemic orientations, feminists themselves are reminding us that romantic writers very consciously formed discourse communities through which they enabled their art and writing. Levin (1987) reminds us, for instance, that the Wordsworth circle at Grasmere was a "community of language; and it was finally a community of writing, a mutuality of writing energies in which each shared in his or her own way."[6] The work of such writers as Dorothy Wordsworth and Mary Shelley gives us an alternative to the myth of the lonely writer. Their works show the community in action and collaboration, a community of men and women alike.

By continuing to explore expressivist rhetorics from a feminist perspective, we can not only widen the tradition from which they arise, but we can continue to illuminate what is valuable about them. Although romantic educational philosophies and expressivist rhetorics do provide a favorable educational climate for women by integrating reason and emotion, thought and action, and self and experience, it is not satisfactory to merely make note of this. As Jane Roland Martin (1982) argues, changing the educational realm in any valuable way will require an understanding that

> the exclusion of both women and the reproductive processes of
> society from the educational realm by philosophy of education is

a consequence of the structure of the discipline and not simply due to an oversight which is easily corrected. Thus, philosophical inquiry into the nature of those processes or into the education of women cannot simply be grafted onto the philosophy of education as presently constituted. (148)

Thus, it is only in continuing to revise and redefine an understanding of our theories and pedagogies, the academy at large, and education in general through feminist perspectives that we can create a theory for composition that truly strives for an education of equality.

Notes

1. See Sue Ellen Holbrook's 1989 essay.

2. I am grateful to Thomas Newkirk for noticing that Wordsworth was a "connected knower." Newkirk's insight led me to explore more fully the parallels between women's ways of coming to the act of knowing and that of the poets.

3. Joy S. Ritchie has a very interesting article regarding these issues entitled "Confronting the 'Essential' Problem: Reconnecting Feminist Theory and Pedagogy," *Journal of Advanced Composition*, Fall 1990: 249–273.

4. I do not mean to imply here that academic discourse is somehow the "better" form of discourse. What I do mean to be explicit about, however, is that expressivist theories and pedagogies, including the import they place on expressive discourse, allow for alternative discourses that, although different, are as valuable and worthy as academic discourse.

5. Martin points out that Rousseau's educational plan for Sophie, which was drastically different from Emile's, is rarely mentioned throughout the history of educational thought and philosophy.

6. Other romantic communities included Byron and the Shelley household, the Hedge Club, and the Transcendental Club in America. All of these groups included writing women members. (See Levin 1987)

Chapter Seven

A Note on Expressivist Rhetorics and Culturally Diverse Classrooms: "The Weight of Too Much Liberty"

Traditional academic form would require that, in this final chapter, I begin to tighten down and tie up loose ends. In a more expressivist fashion, however, I am going to resist this dictum of academic style and end with tentativeness, with questions, and with loose ends. Rather than a tidy argument about expressivism and multicultural classrooms, I offer my thinking in progress on these issues.

As is clear by now, I am not recommending an uncritical acceptance of the entire program of romanticist or expressivist theories. The lashings expressivist theories have been receiving from proponents of social-constructivist rhetorics will hopefully push expressivists to examine closely our assumptions, theories, and pedagogies and move us to articulate the social aspects of expressivism. If we are not willing to reflect on, question, and critique with rigor the underpinning philosophies of expressivism, we will not only fail to draw on a valuable tradition as advantageously as we might, but we will be blind to its problems and pitfalls as well. I believe, for example, that expressivists have not reflected enough on multicultural issues, and on the special situations of minority and non-native students. There is a great deal for expressivists to learn from our ethnic students and non-native speakers, and from our colleagues in linguistics and English as a Second Language. James Paul Gee and Shirley Brice Heath, for example, have shown us that ethnic and minority students come to our classes with discourse conventions that are culturally, socially, and historically formed; and students themselves have pointed to differences between what writing teachers ask for and what they traditionally do as writers in their own culture. It is important, in light of what these students and scholars can tell us about cultural issues, to examine closely whether expressivist theories and pedagogies are helpful to students of varying cultural backgrounds.

Minority Students and the Academic Forms

Fan Shen, a Chinese graduate student at Marquette University who has underscored the cultural determination of writing structures, noted the distinctly different forms that the writing of his native Chinese and that of the Western world take.[1] He claims, for instance, that although it is often the expected form in the American academy, the topic sentence format is not "natural" for Chinese writers:[2]

> A Chinese writer often clears the surrounding bushes before attacking the real target . . . before touching one's main thesis, one should first state the "conditions" of composition: how, why, and when the piece is being composed. (1989, 463)

According to Fan Shen, this "bush-clearing pattern" has been accepted as the norm in China for over two thousand years (463). He notes that "clearing the bushes" began with Kong Fuzi (Confucius) who says that "one first needs to call things by their proper names" (463). Fan explains that this requires stating how, why, and when the essay is being composed before one states the major thesis: "like the peeling of an onion: layer after layer is removed until the reader finally arrives at the central point, the core" (463). In time, this technique became formalized and the "Ba Gu" or "eight-legged" essay became the norm.

Most Chinese students, according to Fan, follow a certain pattern in the writing of narrative essays as well. A recent Chinese textbook for writing, he tells us, lists six necessary "steps for writing a narrative essay, steps to be taken in this order: time, place, character, event, cause, and consequence" (463). I often try to get my students to shake up the order of things in a narrative essay. It is apparent by what Fan points out that the request to shift place and time or consequence and cause might be especially difficult for a Chinese student, because of the long history of Chinese writing that demands a particular order.

My own limited experience with Japanese women suggests that they are culturally shaped in ways that make argument, as usually defined in American terms, an almost impossible task for them. Most of these women appear to work within a language of conformity and obedience, and they seem to have an unwavering respect for age and authority. To these students, for whom polite negotiation and accommodation are the norm of social interaction, the confrontational American approach to argument is threatening and silencing. When asked to write an argumentative paper, the Japanese women in my classes have been unable to do so in "conventional" American style. Their papers take a completely different form, a form that is usually a summation of ideas but that contains no personal disagreement with any of the ideas presented. Since Japanese society is a culture where bringing shame on oneself or on another is to be avoided at all costs, to disagree is a dishonor not only to the student, but to the person she is disagreeing with. Thus, argumentative papers by these students tend to present various perspectives without critical or negative comment.

It stands to reason, then, that if this is the "natural" (culturally determined) form the writings of at least some of our Asian students will take, we either have to accept it as is or work with the students so they may become conversant in the American traditions as well. I imagine that many would object to the first. The academy's preference for stringent, western academic style is generally quite unforgiving. While some individual instructors might give non-native writers more latitude, it remains quite clear that foreign students are expected to "master" our academic discourse conventions. This expectation requires pushing against "two thousand years" of cultural tradition in the case of Chinese students and resocializing a way of being in the world for many Japanese women. Not all non-native students will come to us with such drastically different forms as Chinese and Japanese students do, but we can be sure that differences will be abundant. The more the structural forms of our students differ from what we are familiar with, the easier the forms may be to address. If the differences are subtle, it may prove more difficult to ferret them out in order to address the various structures. If we choose to help these students learn the American forms, expressivists will need to address the "varieties of structures" (Mitchell 1990) in a forthright manner.

Some ESL experts argue that expressivist rhetorics are not helpful, and are perhaps even harmful, when it comes to writing instruction and the minority student or non-native speaker. Candace Mitchell, for instance, a multicultural literacy specialist, suggests that the expressivist assumption that writing will "naturally" find form can be less than helpful. She argues that what "Berthoff and others of the expressive school" do not address is the "issue of the varieties of structures and ways of coherently ordering reality through texts that exist across cultures" (13). Mitchell seems to suggest that there is something inherent in expressivist theories that keeps us from addressing the different traditions and culturally bound written forms of our minority and non-native students:

> The message is, again, that as long as we provide opportunities to engage in the "process," form will emerge naturally. No explicit statement as to what constitutes good form is needed as the assumption is that students will come to uncover the implicit expectations of the academy. Somehow out of the search for the subsequent finding of meaning will emerge a coherent form. Form-finding and form-creating may be natural abilities.
>
> Coherence may in fact emerge in the act of writing. The point remains, however, that the form to emerge may not be the form anticipated by the academy. (13)

Although I find nothing inherent in expressivism as a theory that would make Mitchell's charges inevitable, she does raise issues that expressivists should explore. In practice, does our acceptance of organic form privilege forms "natural" to American students while excluding the "natural" forms that arise from the cultural heritage of our ethnic minority students? (When I use the term "natural" in quotes it is with full recognition that what is "natural" for our students is culturally determined.) If so, are we unintentionally placing these students at a disadvantage? To minimize the risk of this possibility, we can make efforts to recognize and understand the various structures that will "naturally" arise when students of differing cultural backgrounds write. And it seems that expressivists are in a good position to do so since it is less likely that we would demand an ethnic minority student to write, at least initially, in a structure privileged by the Western world if we truly allow "organic form" to emerge. In other words, expressivists are apt to have created the opportunity to consider and understand the various cultural structures by fostering an environment that forgoes extrinsic structure for what comes about "naturally."

Mitchell also argues that the "organic" form the student writer comes to may not be "anticipated" or accepted by the academy, and she hints that the expressivist emphasis on organic form excludes the teaching of these anticipated academic conventions and structures. She further implies that for expressivists "academic" form is the only "good" and right form: "[expressivists provide] no explicit statement as to what constitutes good form . . . as the assumption is that students will come to uncover the implicit expectations of the academy" (13). These are troublesome issues indeed.

Composition scholars like Bizzell and Bartholomae have joined Mitchell in taking expressivists to task for not specifying and making explicit the discourse conventions of the academy. They agree with Mitchell that the "natural" forms students produce do not always take the forms expected and privileged by the academy. David Bartholomae believes that unless we teach the academic discourse conventions to all of our students, and especially our underprepared students, they will remain outside academic conversations and will thus remain marginalized and perhaps even be winnowed out of the academy as failures.

But most expressivist teachers recognize the potential discrepancy between academic conventions and the forms that students come to. The expressivist emphasis on voice, sincerity, reflection, and organic form is often an attempt to counteract the academy's forms and conventions. The expressivist stance is a conscious stand against the barrage of empty, lifeless prose that often mirrors our students' lack of critical thought or investment in a subject, and which often comes neatly packaged in one or another of the academic prose forms.

Admittedly, the primary goal of an expressivist rhetoric is to foster the growth of the whole being, the imagination—ultimately the encompassing intellect—rather than to teach specific forms. However, the expressivist goal of educating the encompassing intellect through a pedagogy that honors student voices, lived experience, and the emotional capacities does not preclude introducing students to the forms and conventions of the academy. Mike Rose's success with underprepared students, for instance, relies heavily on incorporating his students' lived experience and interests into his pedagogy. Rose (1985) is aware, as are expressivists, that a model for teaching writing "must honor the cognitive and emotional," and he is aware, as are social-expressivist and social-epistemic theorists, that these cannot be separated from the "situational" dimensions of language (357).

Rose, then, like the romantics, and like Mill, Dewey, Murray, Elbow, and Berthoff, knows that the cognitive and the affective should not be split asunder. He also shares with expressivists the perspective that writing is a "means of defining the self and defining reality . . . and is an activity that develops over one's lifetime" (348). When it comes to academic discourse, however, he joins Mitchell, Bartholomae, and Bizzell in the argument that to deny students explicit practice within the discourse conventions of the academy is to perpetuate the potential for failure. He argues that our students ought to be required to enter into "a complete, active, struggling engagement with the facts and principles of a discipline, an encounter with the discipline's texts and the incorporation of them into one's own work, the framing of one's knowledge within myriad conventions that help define a discipline . . ." (359).

To require of students this engagement with a discipline is a tall order, and it certainly would require the cooperation of the university as a whole. Some expressivists, moreover, might argue that it is not the composition teacher's job to teach students to write for a discipline, but rather to teach students to write for a more general knowledge and for the world at large.

Expressivists can learn from teachers like Rose how to prepare students to be successful within the discourse requirements of the academy while still preserving the focus on lived experience, self, and voice. Rose, it seems, has begun the synthesis of cognitive, expressivist, and social theories that Faigley (1986) has called for (537). Ultimately, expressivists need not ignore academic discourse conventions, for even if academic forms are only some of many to choose from, they do have their place. This is not to say, however, that expressivists will not continue to differ from many of their critics in that academic forms remain of secondary importance to the more important goal of educating the whole being and the encompassing intellect.

More problematic, however, than whether the teaching of academic forms is of primary or secondary importance, is Mitchell's implication that academic forms are anything but good. I am regularly dismayed by the formal correctness of our students' writing when it matches what the academy asks for, say an "objective" essay that argues a point through a particular linear structure and that contains a clear thesis statement at the end of the first paragraph. What is often distressing about this "correctness" is that it more often than not lacks, on the student's part, any critical thought, insight, or even personal involvement with the content of the writing. The crux of expressivist theory lies in personal vision (not necessarily denying the ways in which this vision is socially shaped) and engagement, and in deep, reflective thought. Therefore, it is not surprising that expressivists question whether we should teach academic forms that often seem lifeless—forms that students are capable of producing, but that are not necessarily going to promote learning or the making of knowledge.

Questions surrounding academic forms become even more muddy in light of some liberatory pedagogies and social-epistemic rhetorics that accuse the academy of replicating non-critical, "corporate-minded" students who leave the ivy halls and enter mainstream America (e.g., Berlin, Ohmann). The problem, according to scholars like Ohmann (1976), is that these "corporate-minded," non-thinking students become citizens who perpetuate the most destructive and oppressive facets of the "military industrial complex" that fuels America. Writing instructors have come to realize that students can produce forms the academy requires without necessarily engaging on any personal level with what they are writing, or without engaging in critical thought. Thus, it has become the opinion of many in the field of composition that those academic forms that are more concerned with particular stylistic or discourse conventions than with any making of new knowledge might actually contribute to this replication of non-critical students. It was expressivists during the 1960s, for example, who precipitated the movement away from academic form. Patricia Bizzell (1986) describes the anti-academic prose movement this way:

> the academy itself began to seem discredited, in the eyes of many students and teachers, by political developments in the nation at large. . . the academy was reluctant to incorporate new methods of responding to these developments . . . . this reluctance was seen as enforcing discriminatory social sorting, with white middle-class men being educated for positions of power and all others being disenfranchised. Academic expository prose, the mastery of which was a prerequisite for traditional academic work, was implicated in the indictment of the academy as an institution of political oppression . . . By fostering students' own styles, instead of forcing conformity to an oppressive institutional standard, writing teachers could feel they were making their own contribution to reform of oppressive academic and political institutions. (52–53)

Having seen little change in the academy as a whole over the intervening years, some expressivists continue to wonder whether our emphasis ought to be on traditional academic expository prose, especially in introductory writing courses. Feminist scholarship that argues that academic forms are oppressive, especially for women, because they privilege a white male discourse, has helped bolster expressivists' resistance to academic conventions. Further, if there is a correlation between the "mastery" of academic forms and oppressed American citizens, it seems insidious to turn our ethnic minority students, students who might well work to correct what is most negative about our society, into the same passive and non-critical writers and thinkers as are many of our non-minority students.

Granted, many students outside the dominant culture might well be eager to enter into what many of us find negative about mainstream American ideology and participate in what they see as the rewards. Expressivist theory and pedagogy, however, and its stand against empty form, can still play a vital role in engendering the necessary critical capacities in all students, majority and minority. Because of the focus on diversity, expressivist approaches to the teaching of writing might be especially useful in promoting the differing perspectives minority students already hold. In other words, expressivist pedagogy can offer the opportunity for identity within diversity to flourish, and this can enable our ethnic and minority students to both participate in, and also criticize, mainstream American culture, including the academy.

It is, of course, unfair to assume, as Mitchell seems to, that no expressivists ever talk about what constitutes "good" or "academic" form. Some may not, but it is not an emphasis on "natural" form that precludes this, nor is it expressivist rhetoric as a whole. The expressivist stance is simply that pre-determining form can be inhibitive and limiting. Writing that grows into form will find its own coherence, and it does not necessarily have to conform to traditional conventions of academic discourse. Joseph Harris (1989) argues against the notion that "our students should necessarily be working towards the mastery of some particular, well-defined sort of discourse. It seems that they might better be encouraged toward a kind of polyphony—an awareness of and pleasure in the various competing discourses that make up their own" (17).

If we are not careful with the instructional trend toward pedagogies that focus primarily on making students conversant in academic discourses, our students can end up like Richard Rodriguez—fully fluent in the public language of the academy but exorcised of the private language of their cultural discourse and community. There is, of course, a debate raging over whether the loss of an ethnic cultural background is debilitating or even whether replacing one's culture with another constitutes a loss at all. Rodriguez (1982) suggests that the loss of his familial culture and his assimilation into the majority culture was not a bad thing, and was even necessary. What seems to me, however, to be the better option is the one Harris offers: students can become members of a number of discourse communities "whose beliefs and practices conflict as well as align" (18).

Perhaps, then, we should not push our students toward the leaving of one community, so that they might replace it with another. The better solution might lie in creating a classroom where they can reorient themselves in connection to several discourses, or what Harris calls a "polyphony." "Our goals as teachers," argues Harris, "need not be to initiate our students into the values and practices of some new community, but to offer them the chance to reflect critically on those discourses—of home, school, work, the media, and the like—to which they already belong" (19). Social-expressivist theory would seem to supply what is necessary for students to take a critical look at these various discourses. The expressivist focus on reflection, for instance, especially if we apply Coleridge's summation of reflectiveness, which requires critical examination not only of the self, but of what is read and written, might easily initiate the opportunity to "reflect critically" as Harris requests. Moreover, the emphasis on organic form allows for the "polyphony" or multiple discourses to arise in the first place.

This is not to deny that expressivists should address "variety of structures" with our students—non-native, minority, majority, and native alike. If we ignore these structures, the consequences may be greater for our minority students, and, as Mike Rose has argued, for those underprivileged students on the "boundary." One of the insights I have gained from colleagues in ESL is that many foreign students are overwhelmed by the expressivist tendency not to offer some formal structure. Initially this lack of explicit form is too great a liberty and students are left confused and unable to write at all. Perhaps, then, we should reevaluate our position: we can still let the form emerge "naturally," _if_ we ensure that our multicultural students are able to overcome confusion in order to begin composing at all; we can also make sure our students know the various forms from which they can choose.

In fact, if we look back to the romantics once again, we can see that the romantic emphasis on organic form does not deny the usefulness of formal structure. Here is William Wordsworth ([1807] 1984) on the value of form:

> Nuns fret not at their Convent's narrow room;
> And Hermits are contented with their Cells;
> And students with their pensive Citadels:
> Maids at the Wheel, the Weaver at his Loom,
> Sit blithe and happy; Bees that soar for bloom,
> High as the highest Peak of Furness Fells,
> Will murmer by the hour in Foxglove bells:
> In truth, the prison, unto which we doom
> Ourselves, no prison is: and hence to me,
> In sundry moods, 'twas pastime to be bound
> Within the Sonnet's scanty plot of ground:
> Pleased if some Souls (for such their needs must be)
> Who have felt the weight of too much liberty,
> Should find short solace there, as I have found. (199)

Through the tightly structured form of the sonnet, Wordsworth not only illustrates the value of form, but suggests that it is not always confining. Structure, then, can be liberating, and our prison of academic forms may not always be a prison for our students, especially for those who have "felt the weight of too much liberty."

Expressivists, then, face these questions: Do we need to make explicit, perhaps especially for minority and ethnic students, how the form that their writing takes differs from what the academy asks for? Are we inclined to accept the "natural" forms of our American students over those of our non-native and minority students? Are we promoting forms that privilege a certain race, gender, and class? Do we wish to teach academic forms at all? Finally, what are the consequences of the ways in which we answer these questions for our ethnic and minority students?

In order to find answers we need to enter into conversation with our associates in ESL, and we must not stop examining and reflecting on our goals and assumptions. If, for example, our agenda is to subvert the expectations of the academy in an attempt to change its literacy conventions rather than continuing to accept them, we must ask whether we are harming or sacrificing students by not giving them every opportunity to empower themselves within the codes of convention upheld by the academy. We must determine whether we are explicit enough about varieties of form, including academic form, so that our students of all cultural orientations will be able to manipulate form and discourse conventions well enough as readers and writers to survive and flourish in the university and in the public world for which it prepares us. In other words, we must answer for ourselves, as well as for our critics, how the emphasis on organic form can lead to student empowerment through choice and flexibility rather than to a naïveté about, or unthinking acceptance of, academic forms. Let's rise to the charges leveled by Mitchell and others, and, as social-expressivists, consider the "varieties of structures" and the ways in which forms that "naturally" arise are determined socially, culturally, and historically.

The Culturally Determined Self

A particular cultural concern, for instance, which needs reflection and investigation in this regard is the nature of the self or "I." Since the growth of the self is such an important aspect of expressivist rhetorics, it is necessary to consider that the self will be very different for our students depending on their cultural heritage. The "I" of the middle-class white student will differ greatly from that of a student whose culture has taught her to suppress the "I" for the good of the collective. Remember that Catano, for instance, in his article,

"The Rhetoric of Masculinity," argues that the self of male rhetoricians like Peter Elbow and William Coles is that of America's "self-made" man, the hero of the Protestant work ethic or the ideal corporate entrepreneur. We must examine the cultural "I" we privilege as rigorously for our cross-cultural students as feminists have for women. We must be aware that the singular, autonomous "I" that Elbow and Coles are comfortable with for themselves is one that values individuality, whereas the "I" of our students might not.

In fact, the self is not even a concern in many non-Western cultures. Xio Ming Li, a former graduate student colleague and a friend with whom I have talked extensively on these issues, suggests that a focus on self is a problem unless we explain what the "self" is. Li questions the validity of "self-expression" because it can, in Western culture, presuppose an autonomous self. For her, self exists only in relationship to others. Since, as Xio Ming Li suggests, many cultures do not have as much of a stake in what is "personal" as we do here in the United States, Asian students will often have difficulties writing a personal essay at all, and they will be more confused than liberated by an expressivist emphasis on self discovery and personal voice. Perhaps reading and discussing, with these students, concepts of the self that arise in American writings like Thoreau's *Walden*, Whitman's *Song of Myself*, and Maya Angelou's *I Know Why the Caged Bird Sing*s would help. Nonetheless, the concept of self raises important questions if we wish to retain the self as an important element in expressivist rhetorics. Is our goal to have our non-native and minority students learn to take on the more American "I" of the majority of our students? Is it to allow the students to retain their own culture's concept of self while also being able to understand and employ American selves? How can we best aid this transformation?

Since the "I" or self is culturally formed, and since the "I" plays such an integral part in expressivist theory and pedagogy, expressivists would do well by their students to consider whether social-expressivist theories of the self can successfully cross cultural boundaries. Fan Shen (1989) suggests that they can, but that in order to help Chinese writers, it would be "helpful if he or she [the teacher] pointed out the different cultural/ideological connotations of the word I, the connotations that exist in a group-centered culture and an individual-centered culture" (466). Are we willing to do as Fan Shen asks? And if not, are we willing to consider that the result might be expressivist rhetorical pedagogies that are less than helpful, perhaps even harmful, as our critics like Candace Mitchell suggest?

Expressivism in the Multicultural Classroom:
A Supportive Environment

Terry Dean's essay, "Multicultural Classrooms, Monocultural Teachers" suggests that expressivist classrooms are beneficial for ethnic minorities in some ways. Dean (1989) points out that ESL students, no matter how educated, often stumble into difficulties with errors and pronunciation which become what she calls "writing blocks":

> It is not unusual for ESL errors to persist in the writing or the pronunciation of highly educated people (doctors, lawyers, engineers, professors) because, consciously or unconsciously, those speech patterns are part of the person's identity and culture . . . Language-oriented topics are one way to allow students to explore this kind of writing block. Assignments that require students to analyze their attitude towards writing, their writing processes, and the role that writing plays in their lives can make these conflicts explicit. (30)

Expressivism's orientation toward "process" predisposes it to be useful in solving the problem Dean has identified here. Moreover, some expressivists make it common practice for students to write reflective papers about their writing processes, about ways in which these processes may have changed, and in which learning about these processes have changed or not changed them as writers and people (see Elbow and Belanoff 1989).

Dean (1989) notes that response groups, a mainstay of many expressivist pedagogies, can also assist the teacher of a multicultural classroom: "peer response groups encourage active learning and help students link home and university cultures" (31). Working in peer groups can help students to function in more than one discourse community at a time. Dean argues that group work is valuable for providing "a supportive environment for exploring culturally sensitive issues that students might hesitate to bring up in class discussion or with the teacher" (32). Joan Wauters (1988) suggests that a non-confrontational approach is especially valuable in the multicultural classroom. She points out that in some cultures a "direct verbal criticism implies 'loss of face'" (159). Wauters' argument in this essay is for pairs of students to work on editing in a non-abrasive way, rather than for students to work in peer response groups that can sometimes lose their supportive tone in the fervor of criticism. However, it appears that Elbow's non-confrontational sharing groups might also achieve worthwhile results, since participants follow a hard and fast rule which allows no nasty or non-constructive confrontation or harshly spoken criticism. Yet, we must not just assume that this nurturing environment is helpful in all regards. An article in the *Boston Sunday Globe* (June 10, 1990), for instance, points to the negative aspects: "the nurturing and cultural reinforcement in bilingual classrooms often unravel when the students move on to regular programs. . . ." The possibility exists, then, that the nurturing aspects of expressivist pedagogies set students up for a way of learning that does not exist elsewhere in the university.

There are many questions that arise when we consider expressivist rhetorics and the cross-cultural classroom. But, as Peter Elbow (1981) says, in the search for knowledge we must "fight the itch for closure" (177), and thus I have offered few, if any, direct answers here. My discussion merely brushes the snow from the top of the multicultural crevasse. We need further investigation into the ways in which our theories and pedagogies are helpful or shortsighted in multicultural classrooms. We need to listen to the experiences of non-native writers like Fan Shen, and we need to turn to our colleagues in second language acquisition, cross-cultural literacy, sociolinguistics, and anthropology for information and guidance. Expressivism needs to continually consider and reconsider itself in light of cultural issues. Expressivists can draw more on the social aspects of our theories and pedagogies, adapting to them and perhaps embracing many of them since, clearly, even "organic" form is not "natural" in the sense that form is, in important ways, culturally determined. Finally, we must not dogmatically hold onto cherished assumptions and theories, assuming that if they work for American students they will work for all students. We can and must begin to reconsider social-expressivist pedagogy as it relates to students from various cultures.

Notes

1. Throughout this section "form" is a term that shifts meaning. At times I use it to mean types of discourse defined by a topic (as in the discourse of science or the discourse of literary studies), at other times, the way the subject is constituted, and at times, sentence or speech patterns or methods of exposition. There is a problem, I believe, in coming up with any clear definition of what I mean by "form" because the word has multiple and conflicting uses in the rhetoric of our discipline.

2. I am not willing to grant that the topic sentence is necessarily "natural" for the Western tradition either.

Conclusion

A common complaint among educators in general, and teachers of writing in particular, is that many of our students are passive and indifferent. They seem not to care about the problems of the modern age. They seem to ignore the urgent environmental dilemmas that have become an undeniable part of their inheritance; they often appear untroubled by moral issues such as abortion, the arms race, capital punishment, sexism, and racism, believing that if they are not immediately and directly affected by these concerns, then these pressing issues need not—even *should* not—be addressed.

In response to this legacy, we have witnessed calls for "new" approaches to teacher education, critical pedagogies, and literacy. Paulo Freire, for instance, argues for a "pedagogy of the oppressed" in which literacy becomes the means for oppressed peoples to take action against dictatorial leadership. Maxine Greene argues for a dialectic leading to an "education of freedom" achieved through imagination and resistance to forces that limit, determine, and oppress. Henry Giroux and Peter McLaren strive for a "democratic" schooling that values student experience and student voice. James Berlin, speaking for many in the field of composition who have turned toward social theories for composition, calls for a "social-epistemic" rhetoric that educates students to become conscious of economic, material, social, and political concerns and strive for a more ideal democracy. What these various perspectives have in common is that each is informed by a perceived need to find a pedagogy that reduces the passivity and indifference of students and offers them an active role in their own intellectual growth.

What I have argued here is that, inasmuch as these scholars call for an approach that places individual students as participants in their own education rather than as mere "observers" or "beneficiaries," these scholars may turn to, and rely on, many of the tenets of the educational philosophies of the British romantics and their intellectual offspring—expressivists. Romantic educational philosophies offer expressivists a teaching approach that denounces oppression and that educates students to become democratically conscious. Wordsworth and Coleridge articulated a theory of education and the intellect which is built on active and participatory education. These ideas have been passed down to us not only

163

through their own writings, but through those of other educators such as Mill, Arnold, Emerson, and Dewey.

When we examine the romantic tradition from which expressivist rhetorics arise and the assumptions under which expressivists themselves operate, it becomes clear that there is much to value. Expressivists like Elbow, Murray, and Berthoff have actually set the stage for social-expressivisms. Social-expressivist rhetorics honor writing as discovery, development of self and voice, and the importance of the individual, but, at the same time, social-expressivisms do not ignore the fact that selves are socially constructed. Expressivist rhetorics also lend much to feminist theories and pedagogies, in working against patriarchal hierarchies by privileging the feminine. Although not all expressivists have been consciously feminist, expressivist rhetorics can easily and consciously embrace feminist principles. Expressivist rhetorics, like the original romantic movement in England, are not anti-intellectual nor even lacking in intellectual rigor. An expressivist pedagogy need not exclude challenging reading and writing, both in depth and breadth. Rigorous study and a wealth of knowledge gathered from various doctrines and disciplines are valued parts of what Wordsworth has called the "philosophical mind." So, too, is imaginative activity, which, by combining both analytical and imaginative study for our students, can result in a synthesizing intellect. The important elements of expressivist theory, in effect, are the driving force behind some of the newer and more radical approaches to teaching—write-to-learn pedagogies, for instance.

A fuller understanding of romanticism and expressivism shows that these traditions do not require our students to be geniuses or "inspired" (in the generally misunderstood sense of the "inspired writer") in order to communicate and write well enough to make changes in their world. So, as teachers we need not fear that composition cannot be taught, or that our students cannot learn to be good writers. As teachers of writing, we can cultivate both analytical and imaginative ability in our students; we can model what Coleridge has called reflection and a "mind self-consciously aware of its own imaginative potential." From this position of subjectivity, students can begin to become personally invested as critical and "effective" democratic citizens.

The charge that expressivist rhetorics have a tendency to create isolated and self-centered students who do not write to communicate with an audience beyond themselves might be true some of the time. This short-sighted application of expressivist theory, however, is not inherited from the British romantic poets, as has often been assumed, nor is it an inherent flaw in expressivism. To believe so is to believe in a false conception of those poets, current expressivists, and their work. To the contrary, the poets and current compositionists like Murray, Elbow, and Berthoff have given us a model of open-mindedness and empathy. We can capitalize on this by choosing teaching models that urge students to practice empathy. We can create the opportunity for contact with ethnic students and others who differ in some way from the majority in our classes. We can introduce reading and writing assignments that bring students in touch with other ways of living, thereby setting various ways of seeing against each other, enabling them to "recognize the political and moral implications of competing models of understanding" (Paul Armstrong, "Pluralistic Literacy," 31). Through seeking new experiences, and understanding and awareness of others, our students are able to take part in the existence of the lives of other people. Through their receptiveness, empathy, and ultimate self-discovery, they gain knowledge and the ability to imagine and reason about ways in which to work with those who are different. And they begin to understand how they themselves are products of their culture.

If we work from a more fully articulated social-expressivism than we have in the past, we will make a concerted effort to make sure our students recognize the material conditions of their existence, so that they might move beyond isolated and solipsistic selves into the social world. As social-expressivist rhetoricians, we can continue to embrace social theories while retaining what is most valuable about expressivist doctrine. We can nurture the process of discovering meaning in experience and communicating it. We can make sure that our students know that personal experience is information that can be shared as public information, and that communicating it can influence "the course of events within town or nation, school or university, company or corporation" (Murray 1984, 4). The awareness, the empathy, the greater understanding of self and others that students can gain through a rhetoric based on the philosophy of social-expressivism need not be kept within the individual, and it need not undercut an awareness of social and political realities. Nor need it deny that the self is socially as well as individually defined. Even Kinneavy (1971), who has argued so energetically against expressivist and romantic theories must finally admit this:

> expressive discourse is, in a very important sense psychologically prior to all the other uses of language. It is the expressive component which gives all discourse a personal significance to the speaker or listener. Indeed, the expressive component of discourse is what involves a man [or woman] with the world and his [her]

fellows to give him his [her] unique brand of humanity ... A democracy which ignores expression has forgotten its own roots. (396)

A personal definition of self aids, and is indeed necessary in, the development of an awareness of one's socially defined interactions with others.

What I am finally arguing is that a social-expressivist rhetoric and pedagogy, as it arises out of romanticism, can be visionary and full of possibility, urging students to see and understand themselves and others. A pedagogy that works from a basis of empathy and diversity is vital if we are to teach students how to interact and communicate in the challenging, changing, and complex world they will live and work in. For too long we have focused our concern primarily on preparing students to be productive members of the labor force, whether inside or outside the academy.

In a time when human beings are destroying their own environment, facing starvation, drought, world-wide epidemics, and the possibility of nuclear destruction, we must prepare students for more than competency in reading, writing, and arithmetic. They need more than the technical knowledge to discover a cure for AIDS; they need also the vision to understand the importance and significance of their work outside the laboratory walls. They must be encouraged to imagine a better world, and not dismiss the idea as "unrealistic" or "utopian." They must learn to empathize and communicate. As teachers we must aid them in doing this, by ensuring them at least the potential for reaching the full use of their intellectual powers. A better world may become a reality through social-expressivist rhetorics and teaching philosophies that celebrate self-discovery, personal experience and the experience of others, empathy and awareness, and the imagination as well as reason.

Bibliography

Abrams, M.H. 1953. *The Mirror and the Lamp: Romantic Theory and the Critical Tradition.* New York: Oxford Univ. Press.

———. 1974. "English Romanticism: The Spirit of the Age." In *Romanticism: Points of View*, 2d ed., edited by Robert F. Gleckner and Gerald E. Enscoe. Detroit, MI: Wayne State Univ. Press.

———. 1989. "The Strangeness of Wordsworth." Rev. of *William Wordsworth: A Life* by Stephen Gill. *New York Review of Books* 21 (December): 45–50.

Ahlstrom, Amber. 1991. Reflects, actions: theory and practice in teaching writing, Ph.D. diss., Univ. New Hampshire.

Aisenberg, Nadya and Mona Harrington. 1988. *Women of Academe: Outsiders in The Sacred Grove.* Amherst, MA: Univ. of Massachusetts Press.

Alexander, Edward, ed. 1967. *John Stuart Mill's Literary Essays.* New York: Bobs-Merrill.

Annas, Pamela J. 1987. "Silences: Feminist Language Research and the Teaching of Writing." In *Teaching Writing: Pedagogy, Gender, and Equity*, edited by Cynthia L. Caywood and Gillian R. Overing. Albany: State Univ. of New York Press.

Armstrong, Isobel. 1982. *Language as Living Form in Nineteenth-Century Poetry.* Totowa, NJ: Barnes and Noble.

Armstrong, Paul. 1988. Pluralistic Literacy. *Profession* 88, Modern Language Association of America: 29-32.

Arnold, Matthew. 1962. *Democratic Education.* Ed. R. H. Super. Ann Arbor: Univ. of Michigan Press.

———. 1964. *Schools and Universities on the Continent.* Ed. R. H. Super. Ann Arbor: Univ. of Michigan Press.

———. 1969. "From Reports on Elementary Schools." In *Matthew Arnold and the Education of the New Order*, edited by Peter Smith and Geoffrey Summerfield. Cambridge: Cambridge Univ. Press.

Ashton-Jones, Evelyn and Dene Kay Thomas. 1990. "Composition, Collaboration, and Women's Ways of Knowing: A Conversation with Mary Belenky." *Journal of Advanced Composition* (Fall): 275–292.

Babenroth, Charles A. 1922. *English Childhood.* New York: Columbia.

Barringer, Carol. 1992. "The Survivor's Voice: Breaking the Incest Taboo." *National Women's Studies Association Journal* (Spring): 4–22.

Bartholomae, David. 1988. "Inventing the University." In *Perspectives on Literacy*, edited by Eugene R. Kintgen, Barry M. Kroll, and Mike Rose. Carbondale, IL: Southern Illinois Univ. Press.

Barzun, Jacques. 1961. *Classic, Romantic, and Modern*. Chicago, IL: Chicago University Press.

Bate, Walter J., G. B. Harrison et al., eds. 1959. *Major British Writers*. Vol. 2. New York: Harcourt.

Belanoff, Pat and Peter Elbow. 1989. *A Community of Writers: A Workshop Course in Writing*. New York: Random House.

Belenky, Mary Field, et al. 1986. *Women's Ways of Knowing: The Development of Self, Voice, and Mind*. New York: Basic Books.

Berlin, James, A. 1984. *Writing Instruction in Nineteenth-Century American Colleges*. Carbondale, IL: Southern Illinois Univ. Press.

———. 1987. *Rhetoric and Reality: Writing Instruction in American Colleges, 1900-1985*. Carbondale, IL: Southern Illinois Univ. Press.

———. 1988. "Rhetoric and Ideology in the Writing Class." *College English* (September): 477–491.

Berthoff, Ann E. 1990. "Paulo Freire's Liberation Pedagogy." *Language Arts* (April): 362–378.

———. 1984. *Reclaiming the Imagination: Philosophical Perspectives for Writers and Teachers of Writing*. Portsmouth, NH: Boynton/Cook.

———. 1981. *The Making of Meaning: Metaphors, Models, and Maxims for Writing Teachers*. Portsmouth, NH: Boynton/Cook.

Bizzell, Patricia. 1986. "Composing Processes: An Overview." In *The Teaching of Writing: Eighty-fifth Yearbook of the National Society for the Study of Education*, edited by Anthony R. Petrosky and David Bartholomae, 49-70. Chicago, IL: National Society for the Study of Education.

Blake, William. 1986. "The Chimney Sweeper." In *The Norton Anthology of English Literature*, 5th ed., edited by M. H. Abrams, et al. Vol. 2. New York: W.W. Norton and Company.

———. 1986. "London" In *The Norton Anthology of English Literature*, 5th ed., edited by M. H. Abrams, et al. Vol. 2. New York: W. W. Norton and Company.

Bogdan, Deanne. 1992. *Re-Educating the Imagination: Toward a Poetics, Politics, and Pedagogy of Literary Engagement*. Portsmouth, NH: Boynton/Cook.

Booth, Wayne C. 1974. *Modern Dogma and the Rhetoric of Assent*. Notre Dame, IN: Notre Dame Univ. Press.

Brannon, Lil. 1993. "M[other]: Lives on the Outside." *Written Communication* (July): 457–465.

Britton, James. 1970. *Language and Learning*. Coral Gables, FL: Univ. of Miami Press.

———. 1982. "Writing to Learn and Learning to Write." In *Prospect and*

Retrospect: Selected Essays of James Britton, edited by Gordon M. Pradl. Portsmouth, NH: Boynton/Cook: 94–111.

Carmichael, Leonard. 1956. Introduction to *The Child and Curriculum and The School and Society* by John Dewey. Chicago, IL: Univ. of Chicago Press.

Catano, James V. 1990. "The Rhetoric of Masculinity: Origins, Institutions, and the Myth of the Self-Made Man." *College English* (April): 421–436.

Caywood, Cynthia L., and Gillian R. Overing, eds. 1987. *Teaching Writing: Pedagogy, Gender, and Equity.* Albany: State Univ. of New York Press.

Chandler, James K. 1984. *Wordsworth's Second Nature: A Study of the Poetry and Politics.* Chicago, IL: Chicago Univ. Press.

Chiseri-Strater, Elizabeth. 1991. *Academic Literacies: The Public and Private Discourse of College Students.* Portsmouth, NH: Heinemann.

Christensen, Francis. 1984. "A Generative Rhetoric of the Sentence." In *Rhetoric and Composition: A Sourcebook for Teachers and Writers.* 110-118. Ed. Richard L. Graves. Portsmouth, NH: Boynton/Cook Publishers, Inc.

Coburn, Kathleen. 1977. *Experience into Thought.* Toronto: University of Toronto Press.

————. 1974. *The Self Conscious Imagination.* London: Oxford Univ. Press.

Coburn, Kathleen, ed. 1979. *Inquiring Spirit: A New Presentation of Coleridge from his Published and Unpublished Prose Writings.* rev. Toronto: Univ. of Toronto Press.

Coleridge, Samuel Taylor. 1987a. "To Thomas Poole: October 9th, 1797." In *Selected Letters,* edited by H. J. Jackson. New York: Oxford Univ. Press.

————. 1987b. "To Thomas Poole: October 16th, 1797." In *Selected Letters,* edited by H. J. Jackson. New York: Oxford Univ. Press.

————. 1987c. "To Thomas Poole: Monday Night, 23 March 1801." In *Selected Letters,* edited by H. J. Jackson. New York: Oxford Univ. Press.

————. 1985a [1798]. "Frost at Midnight." In *The Oxford Authors,* edited by H. J. Jackson. New York: Oxford Univ. Press.

————. 1985b. *The Oxford Authors.* Ed. H. J. Jackson. New York: Oxford Univ. Press.

————. [1817] 1983. *Biographia Literaria.* Ed. James Engell and W. Jackson Bate. Princeton: Princeton Univ. Press.

————. [1813] 1969-71a. *Collected Works of Samuel Taylor Coleridge.* 15 vols. Princeton: Princeton Univ. Press.

————. [1813] 1969-71b. "New System of Education." In *Collected Works of Samuel Taylor Coleridge.* 15 vols. Princeton: Princeton Univ. Press.

————. 1956-71c. *Collected Letters of Samuel Taylor Coleridge.* 6 vols. Ed. Earl Leslie Griggs. Oxford: Clarendon.

————. [1798] 1912. "Kubla Kahn." In *Coleridge Poetical Works*, edited by Ernest Hartley Coleridge. Oxford: Oxford Univ. Press.

————. 1895. *The Letters of Samuel Taylor Coleridge.* 2 vols. Ed. Ernest Hartley Coleridge. Boston: Houghton Mifflin.

————. [1825] 1884. *Aids to Reflection and The Confessions of an Inquiring Spirit.* London: George Bell and Sons.

————. 1835. *Specimens of the Table Talk of the Late Samuel Taylor Coleridge.* New York: Harper & Brothers.

Coles, William, Jr. 1967. The Teaching of Writing as Writing. *College English* (29): 111–116.

Coveny, Peter. 1967. *The Image of Childhood: The Individual and Society: A Study in the Theme in English Literature.* Baltimore, MD: Penguin.

Dean, Terry. 1989. Multicultural Classrooms, Monocultural Teachers. *College Composition and Communication* (February): 23–37.

Derrida, Jacques. 1976. *Of Grammatology.* Trans. by Gayatri Chakravorty Spivak. Baltimore: John Hopkins Univ. Press.

Dewey, John. 1987. *Art as Experience: The Later Works 1925–1953.* Vol. 10. Ed. Jo Ann Boydston. Carbondale: Southern Illinois Univ. Press.

————. [1940] 1969. *Education Today.* Foreword by Joseph Ratner. Westport, CT: Greenwood Press.

————. 1967. *Psychology. The Early Works 1882–1898.* Vol. 2. Ed. Jo Ann Boydston. Carbondale: Southern Illinois Univ. Press.

————. 1964. *John Dewey on Education: Selected Writings.* Ed. Reginald D. Archambault. New York: Random House.

————. [1902] 1956a. "The School and Society." In *The Child and the Curriculum and The School and Society.* Chicago, IL: The Univ. of Chicago Press.

————. 1956b. "The Child and the Curriculum" In *The Child and the Curriculum and the School and Society.* Chicago, IL: The Univ. of Chicago Press.

Dickens, Charles. [1854] 1987. *Hard Times.* Reprint. New York: Penguin Classics.

Dingwaney, Anuradha, and Lawrence Needham. 1989. "(Un)Creating Taste: Wordsworth's Platonic Defense in the Preface to *Lyrical Ballads.*" *Rhetoric Society Quarterly* (Fall): 333–346.

Elbow, Peter. 1987. "Closing My Eyes as I Speak: An Argument for Ignoring Audience." *College English* (January): 50–69.

————. 1986. *Embracing Contraries: Explorations in Learning and Teaching.* New York: Oxford Univ. Press.

————. 1981. *Writing With Power.* New York: Oxford Univ. Press.

————. 1973. *Writing Without Teachers.* New York: Oxford Univ. Press.

Emig, Janet. 1983. *The Web of Meaning: Essays on Writing, Teaching, and Thinking.* Ed. Dixie Goswami and Maureen Butler. Portsmouth, NH: Boynton/Cook.

Faigley, Lester. 1989. "Judging Writing, Judging Selves." *College Composition and Communication.* (December): 395–412.

————. 1986. "Competing Theories of Process: A Critique and a Proposal." *College English* (October): 527–532.

Fan, Shen. 1989. "The Classroom and the Wider Culture: Identity as a Key to Learning English Composition." *College Composition and Communication.* (December): 459–466.

Fishman, Stephen, and Lucille Parkinson McCarthy. 1992. "Is Expressivism Dead?: Reconsidering Its Romantic Roots and Its Relation to Social-Constructionism." *College English* (October): 647–661.

Flower, Linda. 1981. *Problem Solving Strategies for Writers.* New York: Harcourt Brace Jovanovich.

Flynn, Elizabeth. 1991. "Composition Studies from a Feminist Perspective." In *The Politics of Writing Instruction: Postsecondary*, edited by Richard Bullock and John Trimbur. General ed., Charles Schuster. Portsmouth, NH: Boynton/Cook.

Fotheringham, James. 1899. *Wordsworth's "Prelude" as a Study of Education.* N.p.,n.d.

Fox-Genovese. 1991. *Feminism Without Illusions: A Critique of Individualism.* Chapel Hill, NC: Univ. of North Carolina Press.

Freedman, Aviva, and Ian Pringle, eds. 1980. *Reinventing the Rhetorical Tradition.* Conway, Arkansas: L&S Books.

Freire, Paulo. 1982. *Pedagogy of the Oppressed.* Trans. Myra Bergman Ramos. New York: Continuum.

Fulwiler, Toby. 1991. "The Quiet and Insistent Revolution: Writing Across the Curriculum." In *The Politics of Writing Instruction: Postsecondary*, edited by Richard Bullock and John Trimbur. Portsmouth, NH: Boynton/Cook: 179–187.

Gage, John. 1986. "Why Write?" In *The Teaching of Writing: Eighty-fifth Yearbook of the National Society for the Study of Education*, edited by Anthony R. Petrosky and David Bartholomae, 8–29. Chicago, IL: National Society for the Study of Education.

Gannett, Cinthia. 1992. *Gender and the Journal: Diaries and Academic Discourse.* Albany: SUNY Press.

Gere, Ann Ruggles. 1986. "Teaching Writing: The Major Theories." In *The Teaching of Writing: Eighty-fifth Yearbook of the National Society for the Study of Education*, edited by Anthony R. Petrosky and David Bartholomae. Chicago, IL: National Society for the Study of Education.

Gill, Stephen. 1989. *William Wordsworth: A Life.* Oxford: Clarendon.

Gilligan, Carol, Janie Victoria Ward, Jill McLean Taylor, eds., with Betty Bardige. 1988. *Mapping the Moral Domain*. Cambridge: Harvard Univ. Press.

Giroux, Henry A. 1983. *Theory and Resistance in Education*. South Hadley, MA: Bergin.

Giroux, Henry, and Peter McLaren. 1986. Teacher Education and the Politics of Engagement: The Case for Democratic Schooling. *Harvard Educational Review* (August): 213–238.

Gottfried, Leon. 1963. *Matthew Arnold and the Romantics*. Lincoln, NE: Univ. of Nebraska Press.

Goulston, Wendy. 1987. "Women Writing." In *Teaching Writing: Pedagogy, Gender, and Equity*, edited by Cynthia L. Caywood and Gillian R. Overing, 19-29. Albany, NY: SUNY Press.

Graves, Richard L., ed. 1976. *Rhetoric and Composition: A Sourcebook for Teachers*. New Jersey: Hayden.

Greene, Maxine. 1988. *The Dialectic of Freedom*. New York: Teachers College Press.

———. 1986. "In Search of a Critical Pedagogy." *Harvard Educational Review* 56 (November): 427–441.

Hairston, Maxine. 1986. "Different Products, Different Processes: A Theory About Writing." *College Composition and Communication* (December): 442–452.

Harris, Joseph. 1989. "The Idea of Community in the Study of Writing." *College Composition and Communication* (February).

Herndon, James. 1968. *The Way It Spozed to Be*. New York: Simon and Schuster.

Holbrook, Sue Ellen. 1989. Women's Work: The Feminizing of Composition. Paper presented at the Conference on College Composition and Communication, (March), St. Louis, Missouri.

Homans, Margaret. 1980. *Women Writers and Poetic Identity: Dorothy Wordsworth, Emily Brontë, and Emily Dickinson*. Princeton: Princeton Univ. Press.

hooks, bell. 1989. *Talking Back: Thinking Feminist Thinking Black*. Boston: South End Press.

Hunter, Ian. 1988. *Culture and Government: The Emergence of Literary Education*. London: Macmillan.

Jacobus, Mary. 1989. "Behold the Parent Hen." In *Romanticism, Writing, and Sexual Difference: Essays on the Prelude*. Oxford: Clarendon Press.

Kaufer, David S. 1979. Point of View in Rhetorical Situations: Classical and Romantic Contrasts and Contemporary Implications. *The Quarterly Journal of Speech* 65: 171–186.

Keats, John. [1817] 1986. "To George and Thomas Keats: December 1817." In *The Norton Anthology of Literature*. 5th ed., edited by M. H. Abrams, et al. Vol. 2. New York: W. W. Norton and Company.

Kinneavy, James. 1971. *A Theory of Discourse.* New York: Prentice Hall.

Knoblauch, C. H., and Lil Brannon. 1984. *Rhetorical Traditions and the Teaching of Writing.* Portsmouth, NH: Boynton/Cook.

Kohl, Herbert. 1967. *36 Children.* New York: New American.

Kozol, Jonathan. 1967. *Death at an Early Age.* New York: Continuum.

LeFevre, Karen Burke. 1987. *Invention as A Social Act.* Carbondale, IL: Southern Illinois Univ. Press.

Levin, Susan M. 1987. *Dorothy Wordsworth and Romanticism.* New Brunswick: Rutgers State Univ. Press.

Link, Arthur S., and Richard L. McCormick. 1983. *Progressivism.* Arlington Heights, IL: Harlan Davidson.

Martin, Jane Roland. 1987. "Becoming Educated: A Journey of Alienation or Integration?" *Journal of Education.* (October): 204–213.

———. 1985. *Reclaiming a Conversation: The Ideal of the Educated Woman.* New Haven: Yale Univ. Press.

———. 1982. Excluding Women from the Educational Realm. *Harvard Educational Review.* (May): 133–148.

Meisenhelder, Susan. 1985. Redefining 'Powerful' Writing: Toward a Feminist Theory of Composition. *Journal of Thought.* A Special Topic Edition on Feminist Education. Ed. Barbara Hillyer Davis. (Fall): 184–195.

Mellor, Anne K., ed. 1988. *Romanticism and Feminism.* Bloomington, IN: Indiana Univ. Press.

Mill, John Stuart. [1863] 1969. *Autobiography.* Ed. Jack Stillinger. Boston, MA: Houghton Mifflin.

———. [1834] 1967. "On Genius." *Literary Essays.* Ed. Edward Alexander. New York: Bobs-Merill.

Mitchell, Candace. 1990. Ideology and practice: the acquisition of academic literacy in a university ESL writing class. Ph.D. diss., Boston Univ., January.

Moorman, Mary. 1957. *William Wordsworth: The Early Years 1770–1803.* Oxford: Clarendon.

Morris, R.J. 1990. *Class, Sect, and Party, the Making of the British Middle Class: Leeds 1820–1850.* New York: Manchester Univ. Press.

Murray, Donald M. 1989. *Expecting the Unexpected: Teaching Myself and Others to Read and Write.* Portsmouth, NH: Heinemann.

———. 1989. "Reading for Surprise." In *Expecting the Unexpected: Teaching Myself and Others to Read and Write.* Portsmouth, NH: Heinemann.

———. 1986. *Read to Write.* New York: Holt.

———. 1984. *Write to Learn.* New York: Holt.

———. 1982. *Learning by Teaching: Selected Articles on Writing and Teaching.* Portsmouth, NH: Boynton/Cook.

————. 1969. "Finding Your Own Voice: Teaching Composition in an Age of Dissent." *College Composition and Communication* (May).

Nabholtz, John R. 1986. *"My Reader My Fellow-Labourer": A Study of English Romantic Prose.* Columbia: Univ. of Missouri Press.

————. 1980. "Romantic Prose and Classical Rhetoric." *Wordsworth Circle* (Spring): 119–126.

Neal, Maureen. 1993. "Social Constructionism and Expressionism: Contradictions and Connections." *Freshman English News* (Spring): 42–49.

North, Stephen, M. 1987. *The Making of Knowledge in Composition: Portrait of an Emerging Field.* Portsmouth, NH: Boynton/Cook.

Noyes, Russell, ed. 1956. *English Romantic Poetry and Prose.* New York: Oxford Univ. Press.

Ohmann, Richard. 1976. *English in America: A Radical View of the Profession.* New York: Oxford Univ. Press.

Peacock, Thomas Love. 1971. "The Four Ages of Poetry." In *Critical Theory Since Plato,* edited by Hazard Adams. New York: Harcourt.

Perkins, David. 1964. *Wordsworth and the Poetry of Sincerity.* Cambridge, MA: Harvard Univ. Press.

Phinney, A. W. 1987. Wordsworth's Winander Boy and Romantic Theories of Language. *Wordsworth Circle* (Spring): 66–72.

Prickett, Stephen. 1970. *Coleridge and Wordsworth: The Poetry of Growth.* Cambridge: Cambridge Univ. Press.

Ramsey, Jonathon. Wordsworth and the Childhood of Language. *Criticism* 18: 243–255.

Richardson, Alan. 1988. "Romanticism and the Colonization of the Feminine." Romanticism and Feminism, edited by Anne K. Mellor. Bloomington, IN: Indiana Univ. Press.

Ritchie, Joy. S. 1990. "Confronting the 'Essential' Problem: Reconnecting Feminist Theory and Pedagogy." *Journal of Advanced Composition* 10 (Fall): 249-274.

Rodriguez, Richard. 1983. *Hunger of Memory: The Education of Richard Rodriguez.* New York: Bantam Press.

Rohman, D. Gordon. 1965. Prewriting: The Stage of Discovery in the Writing Process. *College Composition and Communication* (May): 106–112.

————. 1990. "Prewriting: an Idea Evolving." Paper presented at the Conference on College Composition and Communication, Chicago, IL, March 22–24.

Romano, Tom 1987. *Clearing the Way: Working with Teenage Writers.* Portsmouth, NH: Heinemann.

Rose, Mike. 1985. The Language of Exclusion: Writing Instruction at the University. *College English* (April): 341–359.

————. 1989. *Lives on the Boundary: The Struggles and Achievements of*

America's Underprepared. New York: Free Press.

Royer, Daniel J. 1991. New Challenges to Epistemic Rhetoric. *Rhetoric Review* 9: 282–297.

Ruoff, Gene. 1972. Wordsworth on Language: Toward a Radical Poetics for English Romanticism. *Wordsworth Circle* (Fall): 204–211.

Russell, David R. 1988. Romantics on Writing: Liberal Culture and the Abolition of Composition Courses. *Rhetoric Review* (Spring): 132–148.

Schneider, Benn Ross, Jr. 1957. *Wordsworth's Cambridge Education.* London: Cambridge Univ. Press.

Sewell, Lauren. 1992. Talking about Difference in the Segregated Classroom. Paper presented at the International Rhetoric Society, March, Hammond, LA.

Shalin, Dmitri N. 1984. "The Romantic Antecedents of Meadian Social Psychology." *Symbolic Interaction* 7: 43–65.

Shelley, Percy Bysshe. 1956. "A Defence of Poetry." In *English Romantic Poetry and Prose*, edited by Russell Noyes. New. York: Oxford Univ. Press.

———. 1977. "A Defence of Poetry." In *Norton Critical Edition of Shelley's Poetry and Prose*, edited by Donald H. Reiman and Sharon B. Powers, 478-508. New York: W. W. Norton and Company.

Spellmeyer, Kurt. 1989. "A Common Ground: The Essay in the Academy." *College English* 51 (March): 262-276.

Stillinger, Jack, ed. 1969. "Mill's Autobiography: Imagination and the Growth of a Philosophic Mind." In *John Stuart Mill's Autobiography*. Boston: Houghton Mifflin Company.

Sullivan, Patricia A. 1992. "Feminism and Methodology in Composition Studies." In *Methods and Methodology: A Sourcebook for Composition Researchers*, edited by Gesa Kirsch and Patricia A. Sullivan. Carbondale, IL: Southern Illinois Univ. Press.

Thompson, T. W. 1970. *Wordsworth's Hawkshead.* London: Oxford Univ. Press.

Van Til, William. 1960. "Is Progressive Education Obsolete?" In *American Education Today*, edited by Paul Woodring and John Scanlon. New York: McGraw.

Waldo, Mark L. 1985. "Romantic Rhetoric for the Modern Student: The Psycho-rhetorical Approach of Wordsworth and Coleridge." *Rhetoric Review* (September): 64–79.

———. 1982. The Rhetoric of Wordsworth and Coleridge: Its Place in Current Composition Theory. Ph.D. diss., Michigan State Univ.

Walker, J., and C.W. Munn. 1982. *British Economic and Social History 1700–1982.* 4th ed. Norwich: MacDonald and Evans.

Walsh, William. 1958. *The Use of the Imagination: Educational Thought and the Literary Mind.* London: Chatto.

Wardle, David. 1976. *English Popular Education: 1780–1975.* 2nd ed. Cambridge: Cambridge Univ. Press.

Watson, J. R. 1982. *Wordsworth's Vital Soul: The Sacred and Profane in Wordsworth's Poetry.* Atlantic Highlands, NJ: Humanities Press.

Wauters, Joan. 1988. Non-Confrontational Critiquing Pairs: An Alternative to Verbal Peer Response Groups. *The Writing Instructor* 7 (Spring/ Summer): 156–166.

Wellek, Rene. 1955. *A History of Modern Criticism: 1750-1950: The Romantic Age.* Vol. 2. New Haven, CT: Yale Univ. Press.

Williams, Raymond. 1973. *The Country and the City.* New York: Oxford Univ. Press.

Willinsky, John M. 1987. "The Seldom-Spoken Roots of the Curriculum: Romanticism and the New Literacy." *Curriculum Inquiry* 17(3): 267–291.

Winterowd, Ross. 1992. I. A. Richards and romantic composition. Paper presented at the Conference on College Composition and Communication. March 19-21, Cincinnati, Ohio.

Wlecke, Albert O. 1990. Prewriting and Romanticism. Paper presented at the Conference on College Composition and Communication, Chicago, IL, March 22–24.

Wolfson, Susan. 1988. "Individual in Community: Dorothy Wordsworth in Conversation with William." *Romanticism and Feminism*, edited by Anne K. Mellor. Bloomington, IN: Indiana Univ. Press.

Wordsworth, William. [1850] 1954. "Book III of *The Prelude*." In *The Prelude: Selected Poems and Sonnets.* New York: Holt Rinehart and Winston, Inc.

———. [1850] 1954. "Book V of *The Prelude*." In *The Prelude: Selected Poems and Sonnets.* New York: Holt, Rinehart and Winston, Inc.

———. [1850] 1954. "The Prelude." In *The Prelude: Selected Poems and Sonnets.* New York: Holt, Rinehart and Winston, Inc.

———. [1850] 1954. *The Prelude: Selected Poems and Sonnets.* New York: Holt, Rinehart and Winston, Inc.

———. [1850] 1954. "The Tables Turned." In *The Prelude: Selected Poems and Sonnets.* New York: Holt, Rinehart and Winston, Inc.

———. [1807] 1984. "Nuns Fret Not." In Wordsworth's *Poetical Works*, edited by Thomas Hutchinson and Ernst De Selincourt. New York: Oxford Univ. Press.

———. [1815] 1984. "Ode: Intimations of Immortality from Recollection of Early Childhood." In Wordsworth's *Poetical Works*, edited by Thomas Hutchinson and Ernst De Selincourt. New York: Oxford Univ. Press.

———. [1815] 1984. "Preface" to the edition of 1815 of the *Lyrical Ballads.* In Wordsworth's *Poetical Works*, edited by Thomas Hutchinson and Ernst De Selincourt. New York: Oxford Univ. Press.

———. [1815] 1984. "Preface to the Edition of 1815." In Wordsworth's *Poetical Works*, edited by Thomas Hutchinson and Ernst De Selincourt. New York: Oxford Univ. Press.

———. [1815] 1984. "A Slumber did My Spirit Seal." In Wordsworth's *Poetical Works*, edited by Thomas Hutchinson and Ernst De Selincourt. New York: Oxford Univ. Press.

———. [1815] 1984. "Three Years She Grew." In Wordworth's *Poetical Works,* edited by Thomas Hutchinson and Ernst De Selincourt. New York: Oxford Univ. Press.

Young, Art. 1983. The value and function of poetic writing. Paper presented at the Conference on College Composition and Communication, March, Detroit, Michigan.

Young, Richard. 1978. "Paradigms and Problems: Needed Research in Rhetorical Invention." In *Research and Composing*, edited by Charles Cooper and Lee Odell. Urbana, IL: NCTE.

———. 1980. "Arts, Crafts, Gifts, and Knacks: Some Disharmonies in the New Rhetoric." In *Reinventing the Rhetoric Tradition*, edited by Aviva Freedman and Ian Pringle, 53–60. Conway, AK: L & S Books.

Index

Abrams, M.H., 2, 40, 89
Abuse, silencing victims of, 141–142
Active imagination, 39–40
Aggression, in expressivist discourse, 129–130
Ahlstrom, Amber, 109
Aids to Reflection (Coleridge), 50, 68, 77, 86, 92
Analogy, use of, 48
Androgynous mind, 39–40, 132–133
Angelou, Maya, 160
"Argument for Ignoring Audience, An" (Elbow), 106
Arnold, Matthew
    educational philosophies of, 31–35
    fostering active participation from students, activities for, 42–45
    influenced by romantic thought, 29, 31–34
    observation of educational systems by, 32–33, 34
    sexist and classist programs, 129
    societal conditions, response to, 28
Audience, expressivist view of, 104–107
Autobiography (Mill), 29–30, 31, 69, 72

Barringer, Carol, 141
Bartholomae, David, 5, 154
Barzun, Jacques, 6, 99, 108, 123
Behaviorist rhetorics, 3
Belenky, Mary Field, 133–137, 139, 141
Bell, Andrew, 24–25
Berlin, James
    expressivism's view of "self," criticism of, 107, 108, 109, 110–112
    nineteenth century rhetorics, views of, 2–3
    pedagogical theories, problems with mixing, 11
    social theories of rhetoric, preference for, 3–5, 163
    twentieth-century writing instruc-

tion, views of, 3, 4–5, 101
Berthoff, Ann, 53, 78
    categorizing, 14
    chaos, use of, 87–88
    on discovery, perception, reflection and experience, 85–88
    double-entry notebook as tool for composition, 86–87, 98, 146
    educational change supported by, 17, 23, 57–58
    imagination, views on, 38–39, 45, 93
    politics as part of educational philosophy, 120
    as social-expressivism pioneer, 116
    social theories embraced by, 115–116
    theory of the imagination, 86–87
Binary system making, 11–12
Biographia Literaria (Coleridge), 29, 40, 41, 65, 66–67, 74, 88, 94
Bizzell, Patricia, 5
    "myth of the inspired writer," 93, 95, 107
    personal-style pedagogies, 121
Blake, William, 17, 101, 114, 116, 127
Booth, Wayne, 22
Boston Globe, 104
Boston Sunday Globe, 162
Bowman, Thomas, 59
Boyer, James, Reverend, 64, 65
Brannon, Lil, 20
Britton, James, 51–52, 53, 78
Bronte, Emily, 148
Bruffee, Kenneth, 5
"Bush-clearing pattern," 151
Byron, George Gordon, 17, 116
    member of English romantic canon, 127

Catano, James, 129, 159–160
Categorizing
    binary nature of, 11–14
    moving beyond, 14–16
Caywood, Cynthia, 13, 127, 146–147

179